THE SEVENTEENTH-CENTURY STAGE

PATTERNS OF LITERARY CRITICISM

General Editors

MARSHALL MCLUHAN

R. J. SCHOECK

ERNEST SIRLUCK

THE SEVENTEENTH-CENTURY STAGE

A Collection of Critical Essays

Edited and with an Introduction by
GERALD EADES BENTLEY

University of Toronto Press
Toronto

Library of Congress Catalog Card Number: 68-26759

The University of Chicago Press, Chicago 60637
The University of Chicago Press, Ltd., London W.C. 1
The University of Toronto Press, Toronto 5, Canada

CONTENTS

vii   INTRODUCTION

I CONTEMPORARY DISCUSSIONS

3   I. THOMAS DEKKER: *The Gull's Hornbook* (1609)

10   II. THOMAS HEYWOOD: *An Apology for Actors* (1612)

23   III. BEN JONSON: Induction to *Bartholomew Fair* (1614)

28   IV. ANONYMOUS [RICHARD BROME?] Præludium for Thomas Goffe's *The Careless Shepherdess* (c. 1638)

II ACTORS AND ACTING

41   V. JOHN RUSSELL BROWN: On the Acting of Shakespeare's Plays (1953)

55   VI. MURIEL C. BRADBROOK: The Status Seekers: Society and the Common Player in the Reign of Elizabeth I (1961)

70   VII. MICHAEL JAMIESON: Shakespeare's Celibate Stage (1964)

94   VIII. MARVIN ROSENBERG: Elizabethan Actors: Men or Marionettes? (1954)

110   IX. WILLIAM A. RINGLER, JR.: The Number of Actors in Shakespeare's Early Plays (1967)

III THEATERS AND PRODUCTION

137   X.   F. P. WILSON: Ralph Crane, Scrivener to the King's Players (1926)

156   XI.   LOUIS B. WRIGHT: Stage Duelling in the Elizabethan Theater (1927)

170   XII.   CHARLES J. SISSON: Introduction to *Believe as you List* (1927)

196   XIII.   RICHARD HOSLEY: The Discovery-Space in Shakespeare's Globe (1959)

215   XIV.   WILLIAM A. ARMSTRONG: The Audience of the Elizabethan Private Theaters (1959)

235   XV.   J. W. SAUNDERS: Staging at the Globe, 1599–1613 (1960)

267   BIBLIOGRAPHY

269   INDEX

INTRODUCTION

The essays in this collection concern the characteristics of actors and acting, of theaters and theater productions in London during the reigns of Elizabeth I, James I, and Charles I. Such subjects differ basically from those of the other volumes in the series in that they cannot be treated in the same way as Shakespeare's Tragedies, or Russian Literature and Modern English Fiction, or American Drama and Its Critics; for each of those subjects most of the essential documents are extant, and the critics do not need to concern themselves primarily as to whether Henry James ever read Turgenev or whether Shakespeare wrote Hamlet—however much they may disagree as to why he wrote it or what it means.

For the essays in this volume, on the other hand, most of the essential documents are lost or never existed. What we need are photographs and scale drawings and detailed descriptions of the interior and exterior of the Globe, the Theatre, the Red Bull, the Fortune, the Swan, the Blackfriars, the Phoenix, and the Salisbury Court—not to be too greedy. With these documents in hand, the writers in this volume could have made use of detailed discussions by Edward Alleyn and William Heminges and Christopher Beeston, Richard Gunnell and Richard Heton and William Davenant, as to how they customarily exploited the stage facilities and the audience accommodations shown in the photographs of their theaters.

Such a hoard of playhouse materials would tell us only a little about acting styles or casting methods or about the relations of the dramatists to the acting companies and the productions of their plays. Therefore it would be desirable to have a few score long detailed descriptions of performances written by representative members of the audience—preferably including several French and Italian visitors who made extended comparisons of their London theatrical experiences with their Parisian or Venetian ones. This material would supplement the detailed theater diaries of Shakespeare, Marlowe, Heywood, Webster, and Shirley about their dealings with actors and managers and their modifications of their manuscripts to suit theatrical conditions.

With such a treasury of photographs, drawings, and manuscripts conveniently housed in one theater library, all the modern articles assembled in this collection would have been transformed.

Alas, none of this desirable material exists, except for a second-hand drawing, a couple of plans, two vignettes, an incomplete contract or two, and a few meager descriptions, generally of the wrong kind of production at the wrong place. In its absence, the character of essays devoted to late sixteenth- and early seventeenth-century actors and acting, theaters and productions must be very different from critical essays about the plays of Shakespeare and his contemporaries; not evaluation or interpretation, but the establishment of facts once very well known to hundreds of King James's subjects must be the goal of each of the modern essays in this collection.

The need for such background facts about theaters and actors before the Civil Wars has long been apparent to those interpreters of Elizabethan drama (a minority) who have appreciated the fact that they were writing about plays, and not about closet drama or about narrative with impersonation and dialogue, and the attempts to supply such basic facts have been numerous. One of the first was made by the anonymous author [James Wright?] of *Historia Histrionica, An Historical Account of the English-Stage, Shewing the Ancient Use, Improvement, and Perfection, of Dramatick Representations, in This Nation. In a Dialogue of Plays and Players* . . . London, 1699. The treatise is in the form of a dialogue between Truman, an "Honest old cavalier," and his interlocutor, Lovewit. Though the author devotes two-thirds of his space to medieval and early sixteenth-century drama, he tells a good deal—from memory, he says—about actors, roles, and theaters in the reign of Charles I. In spite of the fact that the book was published sixty to eighty years after most of the events and conditions described, very few of Truman's memories can be challenged by any facts unearthed in the last two and one-half centuries, and most of them have been verified.[1]

[1] The parts of *Historia Histrionica* referring to the pre-Civil War theater are reprinted in *The Jacobean and Caroline Stage*, 2: 691–96. A little of

For a century and a half after the appearance of *Historia Histrionica* most of the statements made about the enterprise of presenting plays in the late sixteenth and early seventeenth centuries were made in connection with comments on the life and works of Shakespeare; most of them were made without evidence, most of them were vague, and a good part of them were wrong. The attention to the Shakespearean stage and the character of the remarks made about it during the eighteenth century follow the general line—and often the specific words and phrases—of Shakespeare's first serious editor, Nicholas Rowe, who published with his nine-volume edition of the plays in 1709 a forty-page introduction. About a dozen of these pages are devoted to the life of the poet, and less than half a page to his position in the theater:

> It is at this Time, and upon this Accident, [deerstealing] that he is said to have made his first Acquaintance in the Playhouse. He was receiv'd into the Company then in being, at first in a very mean Rank; But his admirable Wit, and the natural Turn of it to the Stage soon distinguish'd him, if not as an extraordinary Actor, yet as an excellent Writer. His Name is Printed, as the Custom was in those Times, amongst those of the other Players, before some old Plays, but without any particular Account of what sort of Parts he us'd to play; and tho' I have inquir'd, I could never meet with any further Account of him in this way, than that the top of his Performance was that of the Ghost in his own *Hamlet*.

Most of Rowe's eighteenth-century successors followed his lead in the context and character of their remarks on the professional setting of the Elizabethan drama—Pope, Theobald, Hanmer, Warburton, Johnson, Steevens, Capell. Occasionally there are minor additions, mostly in the form of legendary anecdotes, and now and then there are irresponsible inventions of theatrical facts for purposes of textual emendation. Perhaps the most entertaining of these is Alexander Pope's magnificent howler in his attempt to reconstruct the text of *Henry V* in the passage so memorably emended by his rival Lewis Theobald. The corrupt

---

the information in *Historia Histrionica* had been anticipated by Richard Flecknoe in his "A Short Discourse of the English Stage" published with his *Love's Kingdom* in 1664, but Flecknoe had few specific facts to go with his many errors, both factual and critical.

folio rendition of the lines in Dame Quickly's account of the death of Falstaff (2:3) reads

> for his Nose was as sharpe as a Pen, and a
> Table of greene fields.

Pope annotated the passage by supplying a little invented theatrical history to go with his instant analytical bibliography:

> his nose was as sharp as a pen, and a table of green fields. *These words* and a table of green fields *are not to be found in the old editions of* 1600 *and* 1608. *This nonsense got into all the following editions by a pleasant mistake of the Stage-editors, who printed from the common piecemeal—written Parts in the Play-house. A Table was here directed to be brought in, (it being a scene in a tavern where they drink at parting) and this direction crept into the text from the margin.* Greenfield *was the name of the Property man in that time who furnish'd implements &c for the actors. A* Table *of* Greenfield's (1723 edition, 3:422 n.)

Few other eighteenth- and early nineteenth-century editors had Pope's sauvity when they needed theatrical facts for their interpretations or emendations, but his ignorance of theater manuscripts and of customary backstage procedures is not unusual.

Wholly unlike his predecessors is Edmond Malone, the real founder of English theater studies, whose collections of theater evidence and whose judicious interpretations of it in the 1780's and 1790's can still put to shame most nineteenth- and twentieth-century scholars in the field. The bulk of Malone's findings were included in "An Historical Account of the Rise and Progress of the English Stage, and of the Economy and Usages of our Ancient Theatres," part two of volume one of his *Plays and Poems of William Shakespeare* published in 1790. The work is now frequently used in the slightly expanded edition published in volume three of Boswell's Malone in 1821. Most of the essential documents we now use in this field were known to Malone, indeed a high proportion of them were discovered by him, and some—notably the manuscript of Sir Henry Herbert's Office Book—have long been lost, so that we must depend mostly on Malone's transcriptions. Malone's honesty, accuracy, and industry were unrivaled in the English studies of his own time, and they have seldom been equaled since. He was not always right, but he had an admirable ability to stay within his evidence, and a rare reluctance to announce his private preferences as established facts.

Following Malone there was much more general interest in the professional setting for the drama of Shakespeare and his contemporaries. In 1831 John Payne Collier set out a good deal of material in his *Annals of the Stage* which filled all volume one and a quarter of volume two of his three-volume *History of English Dramatic Poetry to the Time of Shakespeare and Annals of the Stage to the Restoration*. Collier was almost as assiduous as Malone in collecting documents, but he was far less judicious, and even before his appointment as librarian for the great collection of the Duke of Devonshire and his familiar entertainment in the Ellesmere collections, he had begun his long career as supplementer and forger of old manuscripts and inventor of old poems. One of the more amusing of Collier's compositions which, he says, "I copy from a contemporary [1617] MS.," appears in the *Annals* of 1831, "A Ballade in praise of London Prentices, and what they did at the Cock-pitt Playhouse in Drury Lane." Collier's notes on his own poem, including one confessing his inability to interpret, are very pleasant. The exposure of such forgeries has tended to make theater historians forget what a large number of genuine records Collier first transcribed.

In the last fifteen or twenty years of the century the Reverend Frederick Gard Fleay printed a good deal about the plays and the theatrical contexts of Shakespeare and his contemporaries. Fleay did not invent, like Collier, but he caused nearly as much confusion by his incorrigible speculation, especially in the two volumes of his *Biographical Chronicle of the English Drama, 1559–1642*, published in 1891. Apparently it was his high resolve that no play should remain anonymous, no collaboration undivided; fortunately he was less ambitious about actors and theaters.

It was the custom of these eighteenth- and nineteenth-century scholars to consider theaters and actors only in connection with surveys of English dramatic development, generally from the Middle Ages to the Restoration. At the end of the nineteenth century and through the first half of the twentieth, more concentrated studies became common, studies of groups of acting companies, of physical conditions in the playhouses, and occasionally of individual theaters.

In the nineties attempts to get at the customary Elizabethan and Stuart methods of staging a play and analyses of the facilities available in the theaters began to appear, many of them in the *Shakespeare Jahrbuch*. Gaedertz, Genée, Kilian, Koepel, Keller, Brodmeier, William Archer, C. W. Wallace and T. S. Graves are among the more frequent contributors of such studies. Most of them were led into their investigations by an eagerness to discover and elucidate the influence of his theater on the compositions of Shakespeare; consequently the Globe theater was the one most often mentioned. The essential fallacy of all these Victorian and of many of the twentieth-century studies, a fallacy which is by no means extinct, is the assumption that the Elizabethan playhouse was the harbinger of nineteenth-century theaters, that the absence of scenery and the fluidity of performance were primitive stages in the progression through the theaters of Davenant and Killigrew to those of Ibsen and Irving. The Germans and their followers were constantly striving to provide for localizing of the action. The results were inventions like the inner stage, the structural principle of the alternation of inner and outer stage scenes, and permanent and practicable windows and doors in the tiring-house facade. These men did not see that the Elizabethan principles of dramatic illusion were medieval and not those which developed in England after the commercial stage began to be regularly ornamented with painted scenes.

Similarly (though less disastrously) fallacious was the tacit assumption—almost never stated—that all Elizabethan and Jacobean theaters were alike, and therefore that contemporary statements about performances or allusive lines of dialogue in the text of any play in any theater before 1642 could properly be applied to an elucidation of the staging Shakespeare had in mind for the production of his plays at the Globe. Corresponding to these false assumptions was the usual inverted method of research: most of these investigators apparently began with a conclusion about features of the theater or the principles of staging and then ransacked the English plays published before 1642 to find evidence for their cherished conclusions. All these fallacious assumptions or methods may be observed not only in most of the Elizabethan theater scholarship during the century following the death of Malone, but also in the two most widely read current books on Shakespeare's Globe.

Somewhat more sophisticated are the methods of W. J. Lawrence, who published seven or eight collections of short studies of theatrical matters between 1902 and 1937. His basic interests were actors and theaters, and he thus escaped some of the bias which had led most of his predecessors to overvalue evidence which they thought bore on performances of Shakespeare's plays and to slight or wholly ignore theatrical evidence which did not. Lawrence was a friendly and enthusiastic man, but he was notably lacking in judicial qualities; he had read widely in dramatic literature, but his natural exuberance made conclusion-jumping a favorite sport, if not a habitual means of locomotion.

A student of the Elizabethan theater who began to publish his findings at about the same time as W. J. Lawrence was George Fulmer Reynolds, whose first serious contribution appeared in a long two-part article in *Modern Philology* in 1905 and who continued to publish theater studies for nearly fifty years. Reynolds' perception of the basically different Elizabethan conception of dramatic illusion, his understanding of the variety of Elizabethan and Jacobean theaters, his scrupulousness in following his evidence, and his objectivity in announcing the fact when his laboriously collected evidence could not be added up to a sound conclusion make him an investigator to be imitated. Unfortunately his most extended study, *The Staging of Elizabethan Plays at the Red Bull Theater, 1605–1625*, concerns a playhouse whose repertory, when uncertain attributions have been eliminated, is too small to allow many clear conclusions. But some of the observations Reynolds makes in his Introduction are as pertinent today as they were in 1940:

> This book is a study of the basic details and principles of Elizabethan staging. Most students are probably of the opinion that we are already pretty well informed about these matters. One book and article after another accepts without question the same general ideas of the stage, and each new model and pictured reconstruction closely resembles its predecessor except perhaps in minor details. This might mean that we had already advanced in knowledge if it were not that this unanim-

ity is in contradiction in some details to probability and in others to evidence on which we can feel most certain. . . .

Thus present widely held theories are less well founded than they appear to be, and do not warrant the dogmatic assurance of some recent descriptions of the Elizabethan stage, nor even a tentative acceptance of everything as fairly accepted and established. . . .

Here I need only note that it [Reynolds' evidence] shows a necessity for a different attitude toward the evidence at our disposal, a more careful skepticism, and a stricter discrimination. Specifically, we have accepted the stage directions as literally true and accurate statements of theatrical fact, when they are demonstrably often as imaginative as the dialogue itself; we have, it appears from this evidence, been even more naïve in drawing information from allusions in the dialogue to settings and properties with as much assurance as we might if they were occurring in a modern realistic play. I myself have sometimes erred in this way and am the more anxious to admit it now. There have also been too many generalizations from a few instances; too many uncontrolled suppositions of what might have been, without any ascertained facts of Elizabethan procedure to support them; too many theories advanced by scholars versed only in books and not acquainted with even amateur dramatic production. In short, many of our present conclusions rest on unsound foundations which demand re-examination.

The pieces selected for the present collection fall into three groups: documents of the early seventeenth century; modern discussions of actors and acting in the period; modern discussions of theaters and productions mostly in the reigns of James I and Charles I. The four passages from contemporary books and plays are the longest and most informative written by men who worked in the London playhouses of the time. They are more helpful than the remarks of Gosson and Prynne, whose strong antipathy makes one doubt the representative character or the accuracy of what they say, e.g., Prynne's remarks in *Histriomastix*, 1633, "the most of our present English *Actors* (as I am credibly informed) being professed Papists" (*Historiomastix*, 1633, p. 142).

Three of the four passages are largely or wholly devoted to conditions or events in the public theaters. Thomas Dekker's experience before the printing of *The Gull's Hornbook* was almost wholly a public theater experience, and he makes it clear that he is imagining his action in one of the public theaters of the Bankside. Heywood is likewise a public theater dramatist, not known to have written anything for a private theater before the year he published his *Apology*, and in that year an active member of Queen Anne's company, which had been playing for the last seven years at the Red Bull with Thomas Heywood as one of its leaders. The actions and episodes he describes are public theater or university theater ones (except for a sneer at the satiric plays of some boy companies) and the actors he names or who write verses to him are public theater actors.

Unlike Dekker and Heywood, Ben Jonson was by temperament and usually by practice a private theater dramatist, but the passage reprinted here is taken from a play written specifically for performance at a public theater, the Hope on the Bankside, and the allusions in the Induction make the locale unusually specific. One might even suspect—because of his preference for private theaters and because of his experience in the composition (during the eleven years before October 31, 1614) of sixteen masques and entertainments for audiences much more like private theater patrons than like public theater audiences—that in this special composition for the Hope theater Jonson was more intent on the distinctive character of a public theater and its audience than were Dekker and Heywood, for whom public theaters were the normal outlet. In any case, Jonson's Induction for the opening performance of *Bartholomew Fair* at the Hope on 31 October 1614 is one of the most theatrically allusive passages in Jacobean literature.

The only one of these four early seventeenth-century compositions which refers to a private theater and its customs is the Præludium written for a performance of *The Careless Shepherdess*. Here the reference to the Salisbury Court theater, its audience, and its actors about the year 1638 is as explicit as Jonson's to the Hope. Since the setting of the Præludium is explicit, "The Scene. Salisbury Court," it is obvious that when the author speaks of soundings, of admission prices, of the money box, of the prompter, of sitting on the stage, of the lattice window, of the pit, he must allude to specific objects and customs at the Salisbury Court and not, as in so many playhouse allusions, to an uncertain theater or to theaters in general.

The second and third sections of the book are made up of modern articles concerned with actors and acting in the English Renaissance theater or with its theaters and production methods. These articles have been selected to represent not only the more distinguished contributions to their subjects but to represent, so far as possible, a variety of interpretations of the evidence. They are all included here with the permission of their authors and of their publishers.

One article, Professor Ringler's "The Number of Actors in Shakespeare's Early Plays," is printed here for the first time.

I

CONTEMPORARY DISCUSSIONS

I

THOMAS DEKKER

The Gull's Hornbook

The Hornbook is one of the most frequently cited satiric pamphlets of the reign of James I, particularly the central chapters on the conduct of a gallant in Paul's walks, in an ordinary, in a playhouse, and in a tavern. It is not always noted that in his references to playhouses in this book Dekker evidently has in mind the public theaters and not the private ones. His experience before the appearance of this pamphlet was almost wholly a public theater one: of the fifty or more plays he is known to have written before this year, nearly all can be assigned to public theater companies, and only two were for a private theater troupe. Moreover, Dekker makes it clear that in chapter 6, "How a Gallant should behave himself in a Play-house," he is imagining his action in one of the public theaters of the Bankside, for the preceding chapter "in an ordinary" concludes:

> . . . the guests are all vp, the guilt rapiers ready to be hangd, the French Lacquey, the Irish Footeboy, shrugging at the doores with their masters hobby-horses, to ride to the new play: thats the Randeuous: thither they are gallopt in post, let vs take a paire of Oares, and now lustily after them.

The pair of oars would transport the author and friend across the Thames, that is to the Bankside, where there were never any private theaters, but in 1609 three public ones.

*   *   *

To all Guls in generall, wealth and Libertie.

Whom can I choose (my most worthie *Mecan-asses*) to be Patrons to this labour of mine fitter thē your selues? your hands

From *The Guls Horne-booke:* . . . By T. Deckar. . . . London . . . 1609.

are euer open, your purses neuer shut. So that you stand not in the *Common Rancke* of *Dry-fisted Patrons*, (who giue nothing) for you giue all. Schollers therefore are as much beholden to you, as Vintners, Players and Puncks are. Those three trades gaine by you more then Vsurers do by thirty in the hundred: You spend the wines of the one, you make suppers for the other, and change your Gold into White-money with the third. . . .

Proœmium

. . . I coniure you (as you come of the right *Goose-caps*) staine not your house; but when at a new play you take vp the tweluepenny roome next the stage, (because the Lords & you may seeme to be haile fellow wel met) there draw forth this booke, read alowd, laugh alowd, and play the *Antickes*, that all the garlike mouthd stinkards may cry out, *Away with the Foole:* . . .

CHAP. IIII

How a Gallant should behaue himselfe in Powles-walkes.

. . . Your *Mediterranean* Ile, is then the onely gallery, wherein the pictures of all your true fashionate and complementall *Guls* are and ought to be hung vp: into that gallery carry your neat body, but take heede you pick out such an houre, when the maine Shoale of Ilanders are swimming vp and downe: and first obserue your doores of entrance, and your *Exit*, not much vnlike the plaiers at the *Theaters*, keeping your *Decorums* euen in phantasticality. As for example: if you proue to be a *Northerne* Gentleman I would wish you to passe through the North doore more often (especially) than any of the other: and so according to your countries, take note of your entrances. . . .

CHAP. V

How a yong Gallant should behaue himselfe in an Ordinary.

. . . By this time the parings of Fruit and Cheese are in the voyder, Cards and dice lie stinking in the fire, the guests are all vp, the guilt rapiers ready to be hangd, the French Lacquey, and Irish Footeboy, shrugging at the doores with their masters hobby-horses, to ride to the new play: thats the *Randeuous:* thither they are gallopt in post, let vs take a paire of Oares, and now lustily after them.

CHAP. VI

How a Gallant should behaue himselfe in a Play-house.

The *Theater* is your Poets Royál-Exchange, vpon which, their Muses (y^t are now turnd to Merchants) meeting, barter away that light commodity of words for a lighter ware than words. *Plaudities* and the *Breath* of the great *Beast*, which (like the threatnings of two Cowards) vanish all into aire. *Plaiers* and their *Factors*, who put away the stuffe, and make the best of it they possibly can (as indeed tis their parts so to doe) your Gallant, your Courtier and your Capten, had wont to be the soundest paymaisters, and I thinke are still the surest chapmen: and these by meanes that their heades are well stockt, deale vpõ this comical freight by the grosse: when your *Groundling*, and *Gallery Commoner* buyes his sport by the penny, and, like a *Hagler*, is glad to vtter it againe by retailing.

Sithence then the place is so free in entertainement, allowing a stoole as well to the Farmers sonne as to your Templer: that your Stinkard has the selfe same libertie to be there in his Tobacco-Fumes, which your sweet Courtier hath: and that your Car-man and Tinker claime as strong a voice in their suffrage, and sit to giue iudgement on the plaies life and death, as well as the prowdest *Momus* among the tribe of *Critick:* It is fit y^t hee, whom the most tailors bils do make roome for, when he comes should not be basely (like a vyoll) casd up in a corner.

Whether therefore the gatherers of the publique or priuate Play-house stand to receiue the afternoones rent let our Gallant (hauing paid it) presently aduance himselfe vp to the Throne of the Stage. I meane not into the Lords roome, (which is now but the Stages Suburbs). No, those boxes by the iniquity of custome, conspiracy of waiting-women and Gentlemen-Ushers, that

5

there sweat together, and the couetousnes of Sharers, are contemptibly thrust into the reare, and much new Satten is there dambd by being smothred to death in darknesse. But on the very Rushes where the Commedy is to daunce, yea and vnder the state of *Cambises* himselfe must our fetherd *Estridge*, like a peece of Ordnance be planted valiantly (because impudently) beating downe the mewes & hisses of the opposed rascality.

For do but cast vp a reckoning, what large cummings in are pursd vp by sitting on the Stage, First a conspicuous *Eminence* is gotten, by which meanes the best and most essenciall parts of a Gallant (good cloathes, a proportionable legge, white hand, the Persian lock, and a tollerable beard) are perfectly reuealed.

By sitting on the stage you haue a signd pattent to engrosse the whole commodity of Censure; may lawfully presume to be a Girder: & stand at the helme to steere the passage of *Scænes* yet no man shal once offer to hinder you from obtaining the title of an insolent ouer-weening Coxcombe.

By sitting on the stage, you may (without trauelling for it) at the very next doore, aske whose play it is: and by that *Quest* of *Inquiry*, the law warrants you to auoid much mistaking: if you know not the author, you may raile against him: and peraduenture so behaue your selfe, that you may enforce the Author to know you.

By sitting on the stage, if you be a Knight, you may happily get you a Mistresse: if a meere *Fleet-street* Gentleman, a wife; but assure your selfe by continuall residence, you are the first and principall man in election to begin the number of *We three*.

By spreading your body on the stage, and by being a Justice in examining of plaies, you shall put your selfe into such true *Scænicall* authority that some Poet shall not dare to present his Muse rudely vpon your eyes, without hauing first vnmaskt her, rifled her, and discouered all her bare and most mysticall parts before you at a Tauerne, when you most knightly shal for his paines, pay for both their suppers.

By sitting on the stage, you may (with small cost) purchase the deere acquaintance of the boyes: haue a good stoole for sixpence: at any time know what particular part any of the infants present: get your match lighted, examine the play-suits lace, and perhaps win wagers vpon laying tis copper, &c. And to conclude, whether you be a foole or a Justice of peace, a Cuckold or a Capten, a Lord Maiors sonne or a dawcocke, a knaue or an vnder Shreife, of what stamp soeuer you be, currant or counterfet, the Stagelike time will bring you to be hunted from thence though the Scar-crowes in the yard, hoot at you, hisse at you, spit at you, yea throw durt euen in your teeth: tis most Gentlemanlike patience to endure all this, and to laugh at the silly Animals: but if the *Rabble* with a full throat, crie away with the foole, you were worse then a mad-man to tarry by it: for the Gentleman and the foole should neuer sit on the Stage together.

Mary let this obseruation go hand in hand with the rest: or rather like a country-seruingman, some fiue yards before them Present not your selfe on the Stage (especially at a new play) vntill the quaking prologue hath (by rubbing) got cullor into his cheekes, and is ready to giue the trumpets their Cue that hees vpon point to enter: for then it is time, as though you were one of the *Properties*, or that you dropt out of yᵉ *Hangings* to creepe from behind the Arras with your *Tripos* or three-footed stoole in one hand, and a teston mounted betweene a forefinger and a thumbe in the other: for if you should bestow your person vpon the vulgar, when the belly of the house is but halfe full, your apparell is quite eaten vp, the fashion lost, and the proportion of your body in more danger to be deuoured, then if it were serud vp in the Counter amongst the Powltry: auoid that as you would the Bastome. It shall crowne you with rich commendation to laugh alowd in the middest of the most serious and saddest scene of the terriblest Tragedy: and to let that clapper (your tongue) be tost so high that all the house may ring of it: your Lords vse it; your Knights are Apes to the Lords, and do so too: your Inne-a-court-man is Zany to the Knights, and (many very scuruily) comes likewise limping after it: bee thou a beagle to them all, and neuer lin snuffing till you haue sented them: for by talking and laughing (like a Plough-man in a Morris) you heape *Pelion* vpon *Ossa*, glory vpon glory: As first, all the eyes in the galleries will leaue walking after the Players, and onely follow you: the simplest dolt in the house snatches vp your name, and when he meetes you in the streetes, or that you fall into his hands in the middle of a Watch, his word shall be taken for you, heele cry, *Hees such a Gallant,* and you passe. Secondly, you publish your temperance to the world, in that you seeme not to resort thither to taste vaine pleasures with a hungrie appetite; but onely as a Gentleman, to spend a foolish houre or two, because you can doe nothing else. Thirdly you mightily disrelish the Audience, and disgrace the Author: mary you take vp (though it be at the worst hand) a strong opinion of your owne iudgement and inforce the Poet to take pitty of your weakenesse, and by some dedicated sonnet to bring you into a better paradice, onely to stop your mouth.

If you can (either for loue or money) prouide your selfe a lodging by the water side: for aboue the conueniencie it brings, to shun Shoulder-clapping, and to ship away your Cockatrice betimes in the morning it addes a kind of state vnto you, to be carried from thence to the staires of your Play-house: hate a Sculler (remember that) worse then to be acquainted with one ath Scullery. No, your Oares are your onely Sea-crabs, board them, & take heed you neuer go twice together w^t one paire: often shifting is a great credit to Gentlemen: & that diuiding of your Fare wil make ye poore watersnaks be ready to pul you in peeces to enioy your custome: No matter whether vpon landing you haue money or no, you may swim in twentie of their boates ouer the riuer, vpon *Ticket:* mary when siluer comes in, remember to pay trebble their fare, & it will make your Flounder-catchers to send more thankes after you, when you doe not draw, then when you doe: for they know, It will be their owne another daie.

Before the Play begins, fall to cardes, you may win or loose (as *Fencers* doe in a prize) and beate one another by confederacie, yet share the money when you meete at supper: notwithstanding, to gul the *Ragga-muffins* that stand a loose gaping at you, throw the cards (hauing first torne foure or fiue of them) round about the Stage, iust vpon the third sound, as though you had lost: it skils not if the foure knaues ly on their backs, and outface the Audience, theres none such fooles as dare take exceptions at them, because ere the play go off, better knaues then they, will fall into the company.

Now sir if the writer be a fellow that hath either epigramd

you, or hath had a flirt at your mistris, or hath brought either
your feather or your red beard, or your little legs &c. on the
stage, you shall disgrace him worse then by tossing him in a
blancket, or giuing him the bastinado in a Tauerne, if in the
middle of his play, (bee it Pastorall or Comedy, Morall or
Tragedie) you rise with a skreud and discontented face from
your stoole to be gone: no matter whether the Scenes be good
or no, the better they are, the worse doe you distast them: and
being on your feete, sneake not away like a coward, but salute
all your gentle acquaintance, that are spred either on the
rushes, or on stooles about you, and draw what troope you can
from the stage after you: the *Mimicks* are beholden to you, for
allowing them elbow roome: their Poet cries perhaps a pox go
with you, but care not you for that, theres no musick without
frets.

Mary if either the company, or indisposition of the weather
binde you to sit it out, my counsell is then that you turne plaine
Ape, take vp a rush and tickle the earnest eares of your fellow
gallants, to make other fooles fall a laughing: mewe at passionate
speeches, blare at merrie, finde fault with the musicke, whew at
the childrens Action, whistle at the songs: and aboue all, curse
the sharers, that whereas the same day you had bestowed forty
shillings on an embrodered Felt and Feather, (scotch-fashion)
for your mistres in the Court, or your punck in the Cittie, within
two houres after, you encounter with the very same block on
the stage, when the haberdasher swore to you the impression
was extant but that morning.

To conclude, hoord vp the finest play-scraps you can get,
vppon which your leane wit may most sauourly feede for want
of other stuffe, when the *Arcadian* and *Euphuird* gentlewomen
haue their tongues sharpened to set vpon you: that qualitie
(next to your shittlecocke) is the onely furniture to a Courtier
thats but a new beginner, and is but in his *A B C* of complement. The next places that are fild, after the Playhouses bee
emptied, are (or ought to be) Tauernes, into a Tauerne then let
vs next march, where the braines of one Hogshead must be
beaten out to make vp another. . . .

II

THOMAS HEYWOOD

An Apology for Actors

This well-known piece has sometimes been discussed as if it were a defense of the drama, something like a dramatic poetry section of Sidney's *Defense of Poesie* or a crude anticipation of Dryden's *Of Dramatick Poesie*. It is neither. Heywood writes not as a dramatist or a critic, but as a committed actor in defense of his profession. In 1612 he had been an actor for a decade and a half; at the time he wrote he was one of the principal sharers of Queen Anne's company at the Red Bull theater, and he dedicated his pamphlet to the former patron of this company and wrote a dedicatory epistle "To my good Friends and Fellowes *the Citty-Actors*." Three of the writers of commendatory verses for the pamphlet (Richard Perkins, Christopher Beeston, and Robert Pallant) were Heywood's fellow actors and sharers in the Queen's company, and a fourth was a dramatist for the company whose principal play for them, *The White Devil*, was published in the same year as Heywood's essay.

Like most Jacobean arguments, Heywood's relies heavily on the example of antiquity, but often he makes statements or implications about contemporary actors and theaters, histrionic ideals, and dramatic values. These passages, which are reprinted here, form one of the more extensive discussions of theatrical affairs by a contemporary of Shakespeare's.

* * *

To my good Friends and Fellowes, *the Citty-Actors*.

OVt of my busiest houres, I haue spared my selfe so much time as to touch some particulars concerning vs, to approue our

From *An Apology For Actors. Containing three briefe Treatises. 1. Their Antiquity. 2. Their ancient Dignity. 3. The true vse of their quality.* Written by Thomas Heywood . . . London. 1612.

*Antiquity, ancient Dignity, and the true vse of our quality.
That it hath beene ancient, we haue deriued it from more then
two thousand yeeres agoe, successiuely to this age. That it hath
beene esteemed by the best and greatest: to omit all the noble
Patrons of the former world, I need alledge no more then the
Royall and Princely seruices, in which we now liue. . . .*

The Author to his Booke.

THe world's a Theater, the earth a Stage,
Which God, and nature doth with Actors fill,
Kings haue their entrance in due equipage,
And some there parts play well and others ill.
The best no better are (in this Theater,)
Where euery humor's fitted in his kinde,
This a true subiects acts, and that a Traytor,
The first applauded, and the last confin'd
This plaies an honest man, and that a knaue
A gentle person this, and he a clowne
One man is ragged, and another braue.
All man haue parts, and each man acts his owne.
She a chaste Lady acteth all her life,
A wanton Curtezan another playes.
This, couets marriage loue, that, nuptial strife,
Both in continuall action spend their dayes.
Some Citizens, some Soldiers, borne to aduenter,
Sheepheards and Sea-men; then our play's begun,
When we are borne, and to the world first enter,
And all finde *Exits* when their parts are done.
If then the world a Theater present,
As by the roundnesse it appeares most fit,
Built with starre-galleries of hye ascent,
In which *Iehoue* doth as spectator sit.
And chiefe determiner to applaud the best,
And their indeuours crowne with more then merit,
But by their euill actions doomes the rest,
To end disgrac't whilst others praise inherit.
    He that denyes then Theaters should be,
    He may as well deny a world to me.

 . . . A Description is only a shadow receiued by the eare but
not perceiued by the eye: so liuely portrature is meerely a forme

seene by the eye, but can neither shew action, passion, motion, or any other gesture, to mooue the spirits of the beholder to admiration: but to see a souldier shap'd like a souldier, walke, speake, act like a souldier: to see a *Hector* all besmered in blood, trampling vpon the bulkes of Kinges. A *Troylus* returning from the field in the sight of his father *Priam,* as if man and horse euen from the steeds rough fetlockes to the plume in the champions helmet had bene together plunged into a purple Ocean: To see a *Pompey* ride in triumph, then a *Cæsar* conquer that *Pompey:* labouring *Hanniball* aliue, hewing his passage through the Alpes. To see as I haue seene, *Hercules* in his owne shape hunting the Boare, knocking downe the Bull, taming the Hart, fighting with Hydra, murdering *Gerion,* slaughtring *Diomed,* wounding the *Stimphalides,* killing the Centaurs, pashing the Lion, squeezing the Dragon, dragging *Cerberus* in Chaynes, and lastly, on his high Pyramides writing *Nil vltra,* Oh these were sights to make an *Alexander.*

To turne to our domesticke hystories, what English blood seeing the person of any bold English man presented and doth not hugge his fame, and hunnye at his valor, pursuing him in his enterprise with his best wishes, and as beeing wrapt in contemplation, offers to him in his hart all prosperous performance, as if the Personater were the man Personated, so bewitching a thing is liuely and well spirited action, that it hath power to new mold the harts of the spectators and fashion them to the shape of any noble and notable attempt. What coward to see his contryman valiant would not bee ashamed of his owne cowardise? What English Prince should hee behold the true portrature of that famous King *Edward* the third, foraging France, taking so great a King captiue in his own country, quartering the English Lyons with the French Flower-delyce, and would not bee suddenly Inflam'd with so royall a spectacle, being made apt and fit for the like atchieuement.

. . . nor do I hold it lawfull to beguile the eyes of the world in confounding the shapes of either sex, as to keepe any youth in the habit of a virgin, or any virgin in the shape of a lad, to shroud them from the eyes of their fathers, tutors, or protectors, or to any other sinister intent whatsoeuer. But to see our youths attired in the habit of women, who knowes not what their intents be? who cannot distinguish them by their names, assuredly knowing, they are but to represent such a Lady, at such a time appoynted?

Do not the Vniuersities, the fountaines and well-springs of all good Arts, Learning and Documents, admit the like in their Colledges? and they (I assure my selfe) are not ignorant of their true vse. In the time of my residence in *Cambridge*, I haue seene Tragedyes, Comedyes, Historyes, Pastorals and Shewes, publickly acted, in which Graduates of good place and reputation, haue bene specially parted: this is held necessary for the emboldening of their *Iunior* schollers, to arme them with audacity, against they come to bee imployed in any publicke exercise, as in the reading of the Dialecticke, Rhetoricke, Ethicke, Mathematicke, the Physicke, or Metaphysicke Lectures. It teacheth audacity to the bashfull Grammarian, beeing newly admitted into the priuate Colledge, and after matriculated and entred as a member of the Vniuersity, and makes him a bold Sophister, to argue *pro et contra*, to compose his Sillogismes, Cathegoricke, or Hypotheticke (simple or compound) to reason and frame a sufficient argument to proue his questions, or to defend any *axioma*, to distinguish of any Dilemma, & be able to moderate in any Argumentation whatsoeuer.

To come to Rhetoricke, it not onely emboldens a scholler to speake, but instructs him to speake well, and with iudgement, to obserue his comma's colons, & full poynts, his parentheses, his breathing spaces, and distinctions, to keepe a decorum in his countenance, neither to frowne when he should smile, nor to make vnseemely and disguised faces in the deliuery of his words, not to stare with his eies, draw awry his mouth, confound his voice in the hollow of his throat, or teare his words hastily betwixt his teeth, neither to buffet his deske like a madman, nor stand in his place like a liuelesse Image, demurely plodding, & without any smooth & formal motion. It instructs him to fit his phrases to his action, and his action to his phrase, and his pronuntiation to them both.

Tully in his booke *ad Caium Herennium*, requires fiue things in an Orator, *Inuention, Disposition, Eloquution Memory*, and *Pronuntiation*, yet all are imperfect without the sixt, which is *Action:* for be his inuention neuer so fluent and exquisite, his

disposition and order neuer so composed and formall, his eloquence, and elaborate phrases neuer so materiall and pithy, his
memory neuer so firme & retentiue, his pronuntiation neuer so
musicall and plausiue, yet without a comely and elegant gesture,
a gratious and a bewitching kinde of action, a naturall and a
familiar motion of the head, the hand, the body, and a moderate
and fit countenance sutable to all the rest, I hold all the rest as
nothing. A deliuery & sweet action is the glosse & beauty of any
discourse that belongs to a scholler. And this is the action be-
hoouefull in any that professe this quality, not to vse any impu-
dent or forced motion in any part of the body, no rough, or
other violent gesture, nor on the contrary, to stand like a stiffe
starcht man, but to qualifie euery thing according to the nature
of the person personated: for in oueracting trickes, and toyling
too much in the anticke habit of humors, men of the ripest
desert, greatest opinions, and best reputations, may breake into
the most violent absurdities. I take not vpon me to teach, but
to aduise: for it becomes my *Iuniority* rather to be pupild my
selfe, then to instruct others. . . .

And amongst vs, one of our best *English* Chroniclers records,
that when *Edward* the fourth would shew himselfe in publicke
state to the view of the people, hee repaired to his Palace at
S. *Iohnes*, where he accustomed to see the Citty Actors. And
since then, that house by the Princes free gift, hath belonged to
the office of the Reuels, where our Court playes haue beene in
late daies yearely rehersed, perfected, and corrected before they
come to the publike view of the Prince and the Nobility. . . .

To omit all the Doctors, Zawnyes, Pantaloones, Harlakeenes,
in which the *French*, but especially the *Italians*, haue beene
excellent, and according to the occasion offered to do some
right to our English Actors, as *Knell, Bentley, Mils, Wilson,
Crosse, Lanam*, and others: these, since I neuer saw them, as
being before my time, I cannot (as an eye-witnesse of their
desert) giue them that applause, which no doubt, they worthily
merit, yet by the report of many iuditial auditors, their performance of many parts haue been so absolute, that it were a

kinde of sinne to drowne their worths in Lethe, and not commit their (almost forgotten) names to eternity. Heere I must needs remember *Tarleton*, in his time gratious with the Queene his soueraigne, and in the peoples generall applause, whom succeeded *Wil. Kemp*, as wel in the fauour of her Maiesty, as in the opinion & good thoughts of the generall audience. *Gabriel, Singer, Pope, Phillips, Sly*, all the right I can do them, is but this, that though they be dead, their deserts yet liue in the remembrance of many. Among so many dead let me not forget one yet aliue in his time the most worthy famous, Maister *Edward Allen.* To omit these, as also such as for diuers imperfections, may be thought insufficient for the quality. Actors should be men pick'd out personable, according to the parts they present, they should be rather schollers, that though they cannot speake well, know how to speake, or else to haue that volubility, that they can speake well, though they vnderstand not what, & so both imperfections may by instructions be helped & amended: but where a good tongue & a good conceit both faile, there can neuer be good actor. I also could wish, that such as are condemned for their licentiousnesse, might by a generall consent bee quite excluded our society: for as we are men that stand in the broad eye of the world, so should our manners, gestures, and behauiours, sauour of such gouernment and modesty, to deserue the good thoughts and reports of all men, and to abide the sharpest censures euen of those that are the greatest opposites to the quality. Many amongst vs, I know, to be of substance, of gouernment, of sober liues, and temperate carriages, house-keepers, and contributary to all duties enioyned them, equally with them that are rank't with the most bountifull; and if amongst so many of sort; there be any few degenerate from the rest in that good demeanor, which is both requisite & expected at their hands, let me entreat you not to censure hardly of all for the misdeeds of some, but rather to excuse vs, as *Ouid* doth the generality of women. . . .

To proceed to the matter: First, playing is an ornament to the Citty, which strangers of all Nations, repairing hither, report of in their Countries, beholding them here with some admiration: for what variety of entertainment can there be in any Citty of Christendome, more then in *London?* But some will say, this dish might be very well spared out of the banquet: to him I answere, *Diogenes,* that vsed to feede on rootes, cannot relish a March-pane. Secondly, our *English* tongue, which hath ben the most harsh, vneuen, and broken language of the world, part *Dutch,* part *Irish, Saxon, Scotch, Welsh,* and indeed a gallimaffry of many, but perfect in none, is now by this secondary meanes of playing, continually refined, euery writer striuing in himselfe to adde a new florish vnto it; so that in processe, from the most rude and vnpolisht tongue, it is growne to a most perfect and composed language, and many excellent workes, and elaborate Poems writ in the same, that many Nations grow inamored of our tongue (before despised.) Neither Saphicke, Ionicke, Iambicke, Phaleuticke, Adonicke, Gliconicke, Hexamiter, Tetramiter, Pentamiter, Asclepediacke, Choriambicke, nor any other measured verse vsed amongst the *Greekes, Latins, Italians, French, Dutch,* or *Spanish* writers, but may be exprest in *English,* be it in blanke verse, or meeter, in Distichon, or Hexastichon, or in what forme or feet, or what number you can desire. Thus you see to what excellency our refined English is brought, that in these daies we are ashamed of that *Euphony* & eloquence which within these 60 yeares, the best tongues in the land were proud to pronounce. Thirdly, playes haue made the ignorant more apprehensiue, taught the vnlearned the knowledge of many famous histories, instructed such as cannot reade in the discouery of all our *English* Chronicles: & what man haue you now of that weake capacity, that cannot discourse of any notable thing recorded euen from *William* the *Conquerour,* nay from the landing of *Brute,* vntill this day, beeing possest of their true vse, For, or because Playes are writ with this ayme, and carryed with this methode, to teach the subiects obedience to their King, to shew the people the vntimely ends of such as haue moued tumults, commotions, and insurrections, to present them with the flourishing estate of such as liue in obedience, exhorting them to allegeance, dehorting them from all trayterous and fellonious stratagems.

Omne genus scripti grauitate Tragedia vincit.

If we present a Tragedy, we include the fatall and abortiue ends of such as commit notorious murders, which is aggrauated and acted with all the Art that may be, to terrifie men from the like abhorred practises. If wee present a forreigne History, the subiect is so intended, that in the liues of *Romans*, *Grecians*, or others, either the vertues of our Country-men are extolled, or their vices reproued, as thus, by the example of *Cæsar* to stir souldiers to valour, & magnanimity: by the fall of *Pompey*, that no man trust in his owne strength: we present *Alexander*, killing his friend in his rage, to reproue rashnesse: *Mydas*, choked with his gold, to taxe couetousnesse: *Nero* against tyranny: *Sardanapalus*, against luxury: *Nynus*, against ambition, with infinite others, by sundry instances, either animating men to noble attempts, or attaching the consciences of the spectators, finding themselues toucht in presenting the vices of others. If a morall, it is to perswade men to humanity and good life, to instruct them in ciuility and good manners, shewing them the fruits of honesty, and the end of villany. *Versibus exponi Tragicis res Comica non vult.*

Againe,

> *Horace, Arte Poëtica.*
> *Et nostri proavi Plautinos & numerous et*
> *Laudavere sales - - - - -*

If a Comedy, it is pleasantly contriued with merry accidents, and intermixt with apt and witty iests, to present before the Prince at certain times of solemnity, or else merily fitted to the stage. And what is then the subiect of this harmelesse mirth? either in the shape of a Clowne, to shew others their slouenly and vnhansome behauiour, that they may reforme that simplicity in themselues, which others make their sport, lest they happen to become the like subiect of generall scorne to an auditory, else it intreates of loue, deriding foolish inamorates, who spend their ages, their spirits, nay themselues, in the seruile and ridiculous imployments of their Mistresses: and these are mingled with sportfull accidents, to recreate such as of themselues are wholly deuoted to Melancholly, which corrupts the bloud: or to refresh such weary spirits as are tired with labour, or study, to moderate the cares and heauinesse of the minde, that they may returne to their trades and faculties with more zeale and earnestnesse, after some small soft and pleasant retirement. Sometimes they discourse of Pantaloones, Vsurers that haue vnthrifty sonnes, which both the fathers and sonnes may behold to their instructions: sometimes of Curtesans, to diuulge their subtelties and snares, in which yong men may be intangled, shewing them the meanes to auoyd them. If we present a Pastorall, we shew the harmelesse loue of Sheepheards diuersly moralized, distinguishing betwixt the craft of the Citty, and the innocency of the sheep-coat. Briefly, there is neither Tragedy, History, Comedy, Morrall or Pastorall, from which an infinite vse cannot be gathered. I speake not in the defence of any lasciuious shewes, scurrelous ieasts, or scandalous inuectiues: If there be any such, I banish them quite from my patronage; yet *Horace, Sermon* I. *Satyr* 4. Thus writes.

> *Eupolis atq; Cratinus Aristophanesq; Poetæ,*
> *Atque alij quorum Comædia prisca virorum est:*
> *Si quis erat dignus describi, quod malus, aut fur,*
> *Quod Mæchus foret, aut sicarius, aut alioqui,*
> *Famosus, multa cum libertate notabunt.*

Eupolis, Cratinus, Aristophanes, and other Comike Poets in the time of *Horace,* with large scope, and vnbridled liberty boldly and plainly scourged all such abuses as in their ages were generally practised, to the staining and blemishing of a faire and beautifull Common-weale. Likewise, a learned Gentleman in his Apology for Poetry, speakes thus: Tragedies well handled be a most worthy kinde of Poesie. Comedies make men see and shame at their faults, and proceeding further amongst other Vniuersity-playes, he remembers the Tragedy of *Richard* the third, acted in Saint *Iohns* in *Cambridge,* so essentially, that had the tyrant *Phaleris* beheld his bloudy proceedings, it had mollified his heart, and made him relent at sight of his inhumane massacres. Further, he commends of Comedies, the *Cambridge Pedantius,* and the *Oxford Bellum Grammaticale;* and leauing them passes on to our publicke playes, speaking liberally in their praise, and what commendable vse may bee gathered of them. . . .

To omit all farre-fetcht instances, we wil proue it by a domestike, and home-borne truth, which within these few yeares happened. At *Lin* in *Norfolke,* the then Earle of *Sussex* players acting the old History of Fryer *Francis*, & presenting a woman, who insatiately doting on a yong gentleman, had (the more securely to enioy his affection) mischieuously and secretely murdered her husband, whose ghost haunted her, and at diuers times in her most solitary and priuate contemplations, in most horrid and feareful shapes, appeared, and stood before her. As this was acted, a townes-woman (till then of good estimation and report) finding her conscience (at this presentment) extremely troubled, suddenly skritched and cryd out Oh my husband, my husband! I see the ghost of my husband fiercely threatning and menacing me. At which shrill and vnexpected out-cry, the people about her, moou'd to a strange amazement, inquired the reason of her clamour, when presently vn-urged, she told them that seuen yeares ago, she, to be possest of such a Gentleman (meaning him) had poysoned her husband, whose fearefull image personated it selfe in the shape of that ghost: whereupon the murdresse was apprehended, before the Iustices further examined, & by her voluntary confession after condemned. That this is true, as well by the report of the Actors as the records of the Towne, there are many eye-witnesses of this accident yet liuing, vocally to confirme it.

As strange an accident happened to a company of the same quality some 12 yeares ago, or not so much, who playing late in the night at a place called *Perin* in *Cornwall*, certaine *Spaniards* were landed the same night vnsuspected, and vndiscouered, with intent to take in the towne, spoyle and burne it, when suddenly, euen vpon their entrance, the players (ignorant as the townes-men of any such attempt) presenting a battle on the stage with their drum and trumpets strooke vp a lowd alarme: which the enemy hearing, and fearing they were discouered, amazedly retired, made some few idle shot in a brauado, and so in a hurly-burly fled disorderly to their boats. At the report of this tumult, the townes-men were immediately armed, and pursued them to the sea, praysing God for their happy deliuerance from so great a danger, who by his prouidence made these strangers the instrument and secondary meanes of their escape from such imminent mischife, and the tyranny of so remorcelesse an enemy.

Another of the like wonder happened at *Amsterdam* in *Holland*, a company of our *English* Comedians (well knowne) trauelling those Countryes, as they were before the Burgers and other the chiefe inhabitants, acting the last part of the 4 sons of *Aymon*, towards the last act of the history, where penitent *Renaldo*, like a common labourer, liued in disguise, vowing as his last pennance, to labour & carry burdens to the structure of a goodly Church, there to be erected: whose diligence the labourers enuying, since by-reason of his stature and strength, hee did vsually perfect more worke in a day, then a dozen of the best, (hee working for his conscience, they for their lucres.) Whereupon: by reason his industry had so much disparaged their liuing, conspired amongst themselues to kill him, waiting some opportunity to finde him asleepe, which they might easily doe, since the sorest labourers are the soundest sleepers, and industry is the best preparatiue to rest. Hauing spy'd their opportunity, they draue a naile into his temples, of which wound immediatly he dyed. As the Actors handled this, the audience might on a sodaine vnderstand an out-cry, and loud shrike in a remote gallery, and pressing about the place, they might perceiue a woman of great grauity, strangely amazed, who with a distracted & troubled braine oft sighed out these words: Oh my husband, my husband! The play, without further interruption, proceeded; the woman was to her owne house conducted, without any apparant suspition, euery one coniecturing as their fancies led them. In this agony she some few dayes languished, and on a time, as certaine of her well disposed neighbours came to comfort her, one among the rest being Church-warden, to him the Sexton posts, to tell him of a strange thing happening him in the ripping vp of a graue: see here (quoth he) what I haue found, and shewes them a faire skull, with a great nayle pierst quite through the braine-pan, but we cannot coniecture to whom it should belong, nor how long it hath laine in the earth, the graue being confused, and the flesh consumed. At the report of this accident, the woman, out of the trouble of her afflicted conscience, discouered a former murder. For 12 yeares ago, by driuing that nayle into that skull, being the head of her husband, she had trecherously slaine him. This being publickly confest, she was arraigned, condemned, adiudged, and burned. But I draw my subiect to greater length then I purposed: these therefore out of other infinites, I haue collected, both for their familiarnesse and latenesse of memory. . . .

The Cardinall at *Bruxels,* hath at this time in pay, a company of our *English* Comedians. The *French* King allowes certaine companies in *Paris, Orleans,* besides other Cities: so doth the King of *Spaine,* in *Ciuill, Madrill,* and other prouinces. But in no Country they are of that eminence that ours are: so our most royall, and euer renouned soueraigne, hath licensed vs in London: so did his predecessor, the thrice vertuous virgin, Queene *Elizabeth,* and before her, her sister, Queene *Mary, Edward* the sixth, and their father, *Henry* the eighth: and before these in the tenth yeare of the reigne of *Edward* the fourth, *Anno* 1490. *Iohn Stowe,* an ancient and graue Chronicler, records (amongst other varieties tending to the like effect) that a play was acted at a place called Skinners well, fast by Clerken-well, which continued eight dayes, and was of matter from *Adam* and *Eue,* (the first creation of the world.) The spectators were no worse then the Royalty of *England.* And amongst other commendable exercises in this place, the Company of the Skinners of *London* held certaine yearely solemne playes. In place wherof, now in these latter daies, the wrastling, and such other pastimes haue been kept, and is still held about *Bartholomew-tide.* Also in the yeare 1390. the 14 yeare of the reigne of *Richard* the second, the 18. of Iuly, were the like *Enterludes* recorded of at the same place, which continued 3 dayes together, the King and Queene, and Nobility being there present. Moreouer, to this day, in diuers places of *England,* there be townes that hold the priuiledge of their Faires, and other Charters by yearely stage-playes, as at *Manningtree* in *Suffolke, Kendall* in the *North,* & others. To let these passe, as things familiarly knowne to all men. Now to speake of some abuse lately crept into the quality, as an inueighing against the State, the Court, the Law, the Citty, and their gouernements, with the particularizing of priuate mens humors (yet aliue) Noble-men, & others. I know it distastes many; neither do I any way approue it, nor dare I by any meanes excuse it. The liberty which some arrogate to themselues, committing their bitternesse, and liberall inuectiues against all estates, to the mouthes of Children, supposing their iuniority to be a priuiledge for any rayling, be it neuer so violent, I could aduise all such, to curbe and limit this presumed liberty within the bands of discretion and gouernment. But wise and iudiial Censurers, before whom such complaints shall at any time hereafter come, wil not (I hope) impute these abuses to any transgression in vs, who haue euer been carefull and prouident to shun the like. I surcease to prosecute this any further, lest my good meaning be (by some) misconstrued: and fearing likewise, lest with tediousnesse I tire the patience of the fauourable Reader, heere (though abruptly) I conclude my third and last TREATISE.

Stultiam patiuntur opes, mihi parvulares est.

III

BEN JONSON

The Induction to *Bartholomew Fair*

Jonson had long been accustomed to write for actors better
established than those of the Lady Elizabeth's company and for
audiences more sophisticated than that at the Hope, a dual-pur-
pose house where bears and bulls were baited part of the week
and where plays were presented on a demountable stage for the
other part. Perhaps he strayed from his normal environment as
a courtesy to his protegé Nathan Field, who apparently had the
role of Littlewit in this play. The comments of the stage-
keeper and articles of agreement between playwright and audience make numerous statements or implications about the normal conduct and expectations of audiences in the public theaters.

* * *

THE INDVCTION.
ON THE STAGE.
STAGE-KEEPER.

Gentlemen, haue a little patience, they are e'en vpon com-
ming, instantly. He that should beginne the Play, Master *Littlewit*, the *Proctor*, has a stitch new falne in his black silk stocking;
'twill be drawn vp ere you can tell twenty. He playes one o' the
Arches, that dwels about the *Hospitall*, and hee has a very
pretty part. But for the whole *Play*, will you ha' the truth on't?
(I am looking, lest the *Poet* heare me, or his man, Master
Broome, behind the Arras) it is like to be a very conceited
scuruy one, in plaine English. When 't comes to the *Fayre*,
once: you were e'en as good goe to *Virginia*, for any thing

From *Bartholomew Fayre: A Comedie, Acted in the Yeere, 1614. By the
Lady Elizabeths Servants. And then dedicated to King Iames of most
Blessed Memorie; By the Author, Beniamin Iohnson* . . . London, . . . 1631,
as edited by Herford and Simpson, *Ben Jonson*, 6:13–17. The original is
full of printer's errors.

there is of *Smith-field*. Hee has not hit the humors, he do's not know 'hem; hee has not conuers'd with the *Bartholomew*-birds, as they say; hee has ne're a Sword, and Buckler man in his *Fayre*, nor a little *Dauy*, to take toll o' the Bawds there, as in my time, nor a *Kind-heart*, if any bodies teeth should chance to ake in his *Play*. Nor a Iugler with a wel-educated Ape to come ouer the chaine, for the *King* of *England*, and backe againe for the *Prince*, and sit still on his arse for the *Pope*, and the *King* of *Spaine!* None o' these fine sights! Nor has he the Canuas-cut i' the night, for a Hobby-horseman to creepe in to his she-neigh-bour, and take his leap, there! Nothing! No, and some writer (that I know) had had but the penning o' this matter, hee would ha' made you such a *Iig-ajogge* i' the boothes, you should ha' thought an earthquake had beene i' the *Fayre!* But these Master-*Poets*, they will ha' their owne absurd courses; they will be inform'd of nothing! Hee has (*sirreurence*) kick'd me three, or foure times about the Tyring-house, I thanke him, for but offering to putt in, with my experience. I'le be iudg'd by you, *Gentlemen,* now, but for one conceit of mine! would not a fine Pumpe vpon the Stage ha' done well, for a property now? and a *Punque* set vnder vpon her head, with her Sterne vpward, and ha' beene sous'd by my wity young masters o' the *Innes o' Court?* what thinke you o' this for a shew, now? hee will not heare o' this! I am an Asse! I! and yet I kept the *Stage* in Master *Tarletons* time, I thanke my starres. Ho! and that man had liu'd to haue play'd in *Bartholomew Fayre,* you should ha' seene him ha' come in, and ha' beene coozened i' the Cloath-quarter, so finely! And *Adams,* the Rogue, ha' leap'd and caper'd vpon him, and ha' dealt his vermine about, as though they had cost him nothing. And then a substantiall watch to ha' stolne in vpon 'hem, and taken 'hem away, with mistaking words, as the fashion is, in the *Stage*-practice.

Booke-holder: Scriuener. To him.

Booke. How now? what rare discourse are you falne vpon? ha? ha' you found any familiars here, that you are so free? what's the businesse?

Sta. Nothing, but the vnderstanding Gentlemen o' the ground here, ask'd my iudgement.

Booke. Your iudgement, Rascall? for what? sweeping the

Stage? or gathering vp the broken Apples for the beares within? Away Rogue, it's come to a fine degree in these *spectacles* when such a youth as you pretend to a iudgement. And yet hee may, i' the most o' this matter i'faith: For the *Author* hath writ it iust to his *Meridian,* and the *Scale* of the grounded Iudgements here, his *Play-fellowes* in wit. Gentlemen; not for want of a *Prologue,* but by way of a new one, I am sent out to you here, with a *Scriuener,* and certaine Articles drawne out in hast betweene our *Author,* and you; which if you please to heare, and as they appeare reasonable, to approue of; the *Play* will follow presently. Read, *Scribe,* gi' me the Counterpaine.

Scr. ARTICLES of Agreement, indented, between the *Spectators* or *Hearers,* at the *Hope* on the Bankeside, in the County of *Surrey* on the one party; And the *Author of Bartholmew Fayre* in the said place, and County on the other party: the one and thirtieth day of *Octob.* 1614. and in the twelfth yeere of the Raigne of our Soueraigne Lord, IAMES by the grace of God *King of England, France, & Ireland;* Defender of the faith. And of *Scotland* the seauen and fortieth.

INPRIMIS, It is couenanted and agreed, by and betweene the parties abouesaid, and the said *Spectators,* and *Hearers,* aswell the curious and enuious, as the fauouring and iudicious, as also the grounded Iudgements and vnderstandings, doe for themselues seuerally Couenant, and agree to remaine in the places, their money or friends haue put them in, with patience, for the space of two houres and an halfe, and somewhat more. In which time the *Author* promiseth to present them by vs, with a new sufficient Play called BARTHOLMEW FAYRE, merry, and as full of noise, as sport: made to delight all, and to offend none. Prouided they haue either, the wit, or the honesty to thinke well of themselues.

It is further agreed that euery person here, haue his or their free-will of censure, to like or dislike at their owne charge, the *Author* hauing now departed with his right: It shall bee lawfull for any man to iudge his six pen'orth, his twelue pen'orth, so to his eighteene pence, 2. shillings, halfe a crowne, to the value of his place: Prouided alwaies his place get not aboue his wit. And if he pay for halfe a dozen, hee may censure for all them too, so that he will vndertake that they shall bee silent. Hee shall put in for *Censures* here, as they doe for *lots* at the *lottery:* mary, if he drop but sixe pence at the doore, and will censure a crownes worth, it is thought there is no conscience, or iustice in that.

It is also agreed, that euery man heere, exercise his owne Iudgement, and not censure by *Contagion*, or vpon *trust*, from anothers voice, or face, that sits by him, be he neuer so first, in the *Commission of Wit*: As also, that hee bee fixt and settled in his censure, that what hee approues, or not approues to day, hee will doe the same to morrow, and if to morrow, the next day, and so the next weeke (if neede be:) and not to be brought about by any that sits on the *Bench* with him, though they indite, and arraigne *Playes* daily. Hee that will sweare, *Ieronimo*, or *Andronicus* are the best playes, yet, shall passe vnexcepted at, heere, as a man whose Iudgement shewes it is constant, and hath stood still, these fiue and twentie, or thirtie yeeres. Though it be an *Ignorance*, it is a vertuous and stay'd ignorance; and next to *truth*, a confirm'd errour does well; such a one, the *Author* knowes where to finde him.

It is further couenanted, concluded and agreed, that how great soeuer the expectation bee, no person here, is to expect more then hee knowes, or better ware then a *Fayre* will affoord: neyther to looke backe to the sword and buckler-age of *Smithfield*, but content himselfe with the present. In stead of a little *Dauy*, to take toll o' the Bawds, the *Author* doth promise a strutting *Horse-courser*, with a *leere*-Drunkard, two or three to attend him, in as good *Equipage* as you would wish. And then for *Kinde-heart*, the Tooth-drawer, a fine oyly *Pig-woman* with her *Tapster*, to bid you welcome, and a consort of *Roarers* for musique. A wise *Iustice* of *Peace meditant*, in stead of a *Iugler*, with an *Ape*. A ciuill *Cutpurse searchant*. A sweete *Singer* of new Ballads *allurant:* and as fresh an *Hypocrite*, as euer was broach'd *rampant*. If there bee neuer a *Seruant-monster* i'the *Fayre;* who can helpe it, he sayes; nor a nest of *Antiques?* Hee is loth to make Nature afraid in his *Playes*, like those that beget *Tales*, *Tempests*, and such like *Drolleries*, to mixe his head with other mens heeles, let the concupisence of *Iigges* and *Dances*, raigne as strong as it will amongst you: yet if the *Puppets* will please any body, they shall be entreated to come in.

In *consideration of which*, it is finally agreed, by the foresaid hearers, and *spectators*, that they neyther in themselues conceale, nor suffer by them to be concealed any *State-decipherer*, or politique *Picklocke* of the *Scene*, so solemnly ridiculous, as to search out, who was meant by the *Ginger-bread-woman*, who by the *Hobby-horse-man*, who by the *Costard-monger*, nay, who by their *Wares*. Or that will pretend to affirme (on his owne *inspired ignorance*) what *Mirror of Magistrates* is meant by the *Iustice*, what *great Lady* by the *Pigge-woman*, what *conceal'd States-man*, by the *Seller* of *Mouse-trappes*, and so of the rest. But that such person, or persons so found, be left discouered to the mercy of the *Author*, as a forfeiture to the *Stage*, and your laughter, aforesaid. As also, such as shall so desperately, or ambitiously, play the foole by his place aforesaid, to challenge the *Author* of scurrilitie, because the language some where sauours of *Smithfield*, the Booth, and the Pigbroath, or of prophanenesse, because a *Mad-man* cryes, *God quit you*, or *blesse you*. In *witnesse* whereof, as you haue preposterously put to your Seales already (which is your money) you will now adde the other part of suffrage, your hands. The *Play* shall presently begin. And though the *Fayre* be not kept in the same Region, that some here, perhaps, would haue it, yet thinke, that therein the *Author* hath obseru'd a speciall *Decorum*, the place being as durty as *Smithfield*, and as stinking euery whit.

Howsoeuer, hee prayes you to beleeue, his *Ware* is still the same, else you will make him iustly suspect that hee that is so loth to looke on a *Baby*, or an *Hobby-horse*, heere, would bee glad to take vp a *Commodity* of them, at any laughter, or losse, in another place.

ANONYMOUS

Præludium for *The Careless Shepherdess*

Though *The Careless Shepherdess* was published as by T[homas?] G[offe?] in 1656, the play proper was thirty or forty years old by that time. The theatrically allusive Præludium and the prologues, however, were written about 1638, much later than the rest of the play, and by another author, possibly Richard Brome. (See *The Jacobean and Caroline Stage*, 4:501–5.)

Whereas Heywood wrote about public theaters and public theater actors, and Dekker had them mostly in mind in the allusions of *The Gull's Hornbook*, the author of the Præludium for *The Careless Shepherdess* has set his action on the stage of a private theater. All his theatrical statements and allusions refer to the physical structure and the production practices at the Salisbury Court in the late 1630's unless he specifically mentions other houses, like the Fortune and the Red Bull.

This Præludium is somewhat reminiscent of Jonson's Induction for *Bartholomew Fair*, but the Caroline author says more about the theater than Jonson did, though he says less about the play which is to follow.

* * *

Præludium:

The Actors.

Spruce, *a Courtier.*
Sparke, *an Inns of Court-man.*
Landlord, *a Country Gentleman.*
Thrift, *a Citizen.*
Bolt, *a Door-keeper.*

From *The Careles Shepherdess. A Tragi-comedy. Acted before the King & Queen, And at Salisbury-Court, with great Applause.* Written by T. G. Mr: of Arts . . . London, 1656.

Præludium for *The Careless Shepherdess*

Prologus.

THE SCENE.

SALISBURY COURT.

*Bolt. A Door-keeper, sitting with a Box on one side of the
Stage.*

To him Thrift *a Citizen.*

THrift. Now for a good bargain, What will you take
To let me in to the play? *Bolt.* A shilling Sir.
   Thri. Come, here's a groat, I'le not make many words.
Thou hast just got my trick for all the world,
I always use to ask just twice as much
As a thing's worth: then some pretend to have
Skill in my wares, by bidding of me half.
But when I meet a man of judgement, as
You have done now, they bid as neer to th' price,
As if they knew my mark. Use me, as you
Do hope to have my custome other times.
   Bolt. In troth Sir I can't take it. *Thri.* Should I go
Away, I know you'd call me back again.
I hate this dodging: What's your lowest price?
   Bolt. I told you at first word. *Thri.* What a shilling?
Why, I have known some Aldermen that did
Begin with twelve pense: and for half so much
I saw six motions last *Bartholomew-Fair*.
   Bolt. When you have seen this play, you'l think it worth
Your money. *Thri.* Well then take this groat in earnest,
If I do like it you shall have the rest.
   Bolt. This is no market or exchange, pray keep
Your aery groat that's thinner then a shadow
To mend your Worships shoes, it is more crackt
Then an old Beaver or a Chambermaid.
   Thri. Well, since you will exact, and stretch your Con-
      science,
Here's a nine pense and four pense half-peny,
Give me the rest again. *Bolt.* There. *Thri.* Now for this
When I come home I'le go unto my book,

And set a figure to each single *Cipher;*
I'le cheat a shilling in a peny, and
A pound in twelve pense. When will it begin?
  Bolt. Presently Sir. *Thri.* Thou once didst tell me so
When the first Act was almost done. *Bolt.* Why then
They presently began to make an end.

Enter Spruce, *a Courtier.*

  Spruce. How oft has't sounded? *Bolt.* Thrice an't please you
    Sir.
  Thri. Sir, by your powdred hair, and gawdy cloaths
I do presume you are a Courtier.
Pray Sir, if I may be so bold to ask,
And, if you go on Tick here too,
What did it cost you to come in? When you
Do buy of us, you of all Gentlemen
Have still the cheapest penyworths. *Spru.* Are you
A Tradesman? *Thri.* Sir, I am a Citizen,
I alwayes do observe that Courtiers
Know Tradesmen when they are a whole street off,
But not when they are neer. *Spru.* 'Tis true, there must
Be a due distance 'twixt the sight and object.
With what variety of wares is your
Shop furnished. *Thri. Imprimis,* with a fair Wife
And Prentice. *Item,* with Knots and Phansies
Of all fashions, and twenty other toyes.
There is a Courtier Sir that owes to me
Two thousand pound for Garters and for Roses.
Faith Sir, and if you would bring a fashion up,
And hang some Ribboning round about your Hat
As well as in one place, you should finde me
And my Wife thankfull. *Spru.* 'Twould be too *Pedlar*-like.

Enter Spark, *an Inns of Court-man.*

  Spar. What's there, a *Courtier* and a *Citizen?*
Such a conjunction is enough to make
A grand *Eclipse.* Sure th' one did never see
Th' other before, 'cause they are now so great.
  Mr. *Spruce.* I am your humble servant.
  Spru. Your Balzack, Mr. *Spark.* What God hath bless'd
Me with this happinesse, the sight of you?
  Spar. Faith Sir fasting night, and I did chuse

Præludium for *The Careless Shepherdess*

Rather to spend my money at a Play,
Then at the Ordnary: I now esteem
My choice as policy, since 'tis my fortune
To sit neer you: If the Play should prove dull
Your company will satisfie my ears.

    Enter Landlord, *a Country Gentleman.*

Landl. God save you Gentlemen, 'tis my ambition
To occupy a place neer you: there are
None that be worthy of my company
In any room beneath the twelve peny.
I've sate with Judges on the Bench, and frown'd
As sowrely upon things I did not know,
As any Lawyer does on a poor Client:
I have found fault with very good Sermons
In my daies, and now I desire that we
May passe our sentences upon this Play.

  Thri. With all my heart. O that I had my Gown!

  Spar. Dare you presume to censure Poetry?
'Tis the Prerogative of the wits in Town,
'Cause you have read perhaps a Statute-Book,
And been High-Constable, do y' think you know
The Laws of Comedy and Tragedy?
Prethee, what kinde of Beast is *Helicon?*
You may have skill in Horse and Sheep, and yet
Know neither *Pegasus*, nor *Pastorals*.
Alas you're ignorant of any stile
But what stands in a hedge; you never heard
Of more then the four humours of the body;
Nor did you ever understand a Plot,
Unlesse that grand one of the *Powder-Treason*.
You've worn perchance a pair of Spatterdashers,
But scarce e're saw a Buskin; and my Nose,
Tells me your feet did never yet wear Socks.

  Spru. And you too would usurp *Apollo's* Chair,
As if th' Exchange did ever breed a wit.
Though you can give words soft and smooth, as is
Your Sattin Ribbon, yet your speech is harsh
To the round language of the Theater,
'Cause you sell *Phansies*, and can cast account,
Do y' think your brain conceives Poetique Numbers?

You cannot tell, if you were ask'd the question,
Whether a *Metaphor* be flesh or fish;
You may perchance have judgement to discerne
What Puppet dances well, or understand
Which Juglers mouth is best at the Bay-leafe,
But who deserves the Lawrell wreath, you know
No more, then you do know which Land i' th' field
Bears Barley, and which Wheat, which Rye, which Oats.

    Spar. 'Cause you will be prodigious, and aim
At Wit, a thing I never heard of, till
I came to th' *Temple*, prethee inform me,
What part you think essentiall to a *Play?*
And what in your opinion is stil'd Wit.

    Landl. Why I would have the Fool in every Act,
Be't Comedy, or Tragedy, I 'ave laugh'd
Untill I cry'd again, to see what Faces
The Rogue will make: O it does me good
To see him hold out's Chin, hang down his hands,
And twirle his Bawble. There is nere a part
About him but breaks jests. I heard a fellow
Once on this Stage cry, *Doodle, Doodle, Dooe,*
Beyond compare; I'de give the other shilling
To see him act the Changling once again.

    Thri. And so would I, his part has all the wit,
For none speaks Craps and Quibbles besides him:
I'd rather see him leap, laugh, or cry,
Then hear the gravest Speech in all the *Play.*
I never saw *Rheade* peeping through the Curtain,
But ravishing joy enter'd into my heart.

    Spar. Ha, ha, ha, ha! To see how their wits jump,
'Tis hard to tell which is the verier Fool,
The Country Gentleman, or Citizen:
Your judgements are ridiculous and vain
As your Forefathers, whose dull intellect
Did nothing understand but fools and fighting;
'Twill hardly enter into my belief
That ye are of this Age, sure ye are Ghosts.
The Poets now have with their heavenly fire
Purg'd their inventions of those grosser follies,
And with sublime conceits enrich'd the Stage:

Præludium for *The Careless Shepherdess*

Instead of loose lascivious mirth, they bring
Ingenious raptures, which do please, not tickle,
And rather move us to admire, then laugh.
The Motly Coat was banish'd with Trunk Hose,
And since their wits grew sharp, the Swords are sheath'd.
   Spru. Then playing upon words is much out
Of fashion here, as Pepper is at Court.
   Landl. Well, since there will be a nere a fool i'th' *Play*,
I'le have my money again; the Comedy
Will be as tedious to me, as a Sermon,
And I do fear that I shall fall asleep,
And give my twelve pense to be melancholy:
   Spar. Nay, ne're fear that, for on my word you shall
Have mirth, although there be no Changlings part.
   Landl. Well, I will stay it out, though't only be
That I may view the Ladies, and they me.
   Thri. Sir, was't a Poet, or a Gentleman
That writ this play? The Court, and Inns of Court,
Of late bring forth more wit, then all the Tavernes,
Which makes me pity Play-Rights; they were poore
Before, even to a Proverb; Now their trade
Must needs go down, when so many set up.
I do not think but I shall shortly see
One Poet sue to keep the door, another
To be prompter, a third to snuff the candles.
Pray Sir, has any Gentleman of late
Beg'd the Monopoly of Comedies?
   Spar. No: But of late the Poets having drown'd
Their brains in Sack, are grown so dull and lazy,
That they may be the subjects of a Play,
Rather then the Authors: They have left to invoke
Thalia now, and only call on Drawers:
They quite neglect *Apollo's* Sacred Reed
Which warbles forth Diviner Harmony,
And use alone the dumb Tobacco-pipe.
Now lest the Stage should only entertain
The Auditors with cold meats, (which are grown
Mouldy and stale, as was the Usurers Pye
Which came to the Table 'bove an hundred times,
Untill at last it crept away it self.)

Some of our Tribe, neither for gain, nor fame,
But out of free and well-meant charity,
Devote their vacant minutes to the Muses,
Preferring them before Balcony-Ladies,
And other fonder vanities of this Age.

Thri. Courtiers, I think, have little else to do;
So to be idle, is in them a vertue:
But I do fear that writing Playes, will make
Our Inns of Court-men Truants in the Law.
Shortly they will be *Ovid*-like, who could
Not chuse but put Indentures into Verse.
E're I am Sheriff, I warrant we shall have
Master-Recorder rhime upon the Bench.

Landl. It was a Comedy, they say, that first
Did make the Lawyer call'd, an *Ignoramus*.

Spar. To put on Sock or Buskin on our feet
Is not our study, but recreation,
When we are tir'd with reading *Littleton*,
Penning a Scene does more refresh our brain
Then Sack, or *Hide-Park* ayr, Poetry is
The sawce that makes severer meats digest,
And turns rude Barbarism into delight.

Thri. Sir, I have heard 'um say, that Poets may
Write without Ink rather then Wine. *Landl.* And I
Have heard that 'tis as hard to make a Play
Without Canary, as it is to make
A Cheese without Runnet: Tobacco leafs
Do more inspire, then all the leafs of books.

Thri. How then does Sack injure our Poets Brains?

Spru. Still are you muffled up in ignorance;
Do you not know too much excesse may turn
The greatest Antidote to deadly poyson?

Spar. Besides, Phylosophers do say, that there's
Antipathy betwixt the Vine and Lawrell;
And since they hate Proximity i'th' Garden,
I scarce believe they do agree i'th' head:
And certain 'tis, that pure Poetique fire
Is not the cause, nor the effect of smoak.

Præludium for *The Careless Shepherdess*

Loud Musique sounds.

But hist, the Prologue enters. *Landl.* Now it chimes
All in, to the Play, the Peals were rung before.

    Pro. Must alwayes I a Hearer only be?

      He being out, is laught at, by { *Spark. Thrift.*
                                { *Spruce. Landl.*

    Pro. Pox take the Prompter. *Exit.*

Enter another to speak the Prologue.

    Pro. Must alwayes I a Hearer only be?
Mayn't a Spectator write a Comedy?
      He being out, looks in his hat, at which an Actor
        plac't in the Pit, laughs.
    Pro. Let him that laughs speak the Prologue for me. *Exit.*
      The Actor in the Pit laughs again, saying:
Faith Gentlemen, I'le leave your company,
Since none will do the Author Justice, I
Will something vent, though't be *ex tempore. Exit.*
    Spar. I do not think but some poor Hackney Poet
Has hir'd the Players to be out upon
Suspition, that they are abus'd i'th' Prologue.
    Spru. Perhaps our presence daunteth them, let us
Retire into some private room, for fear
The third man should be out. *Spar.* A match.   *Exeunt*
                                  Spru. Spar.
    Landl. I'le follow them, though't be into a Box.
Though they did sit thus open on the Stage
To shew their Cloak and Sute, yet I did think
At last they would take sanctuary 'mongst
The Ladies, lest some Creditor should spy them.
'Tis better looking o're a Ladies head,
Or through a Lettice-window, then a grate. *Exit. Land.*
    Thri. And I will hasten to the money Box,
And take my shilling out again, for now
I have considered that it is too much;
I'le go to th' Bull, or Fortune, and there see
A Play for two pense, with a Jig to boot. *Exit.*

35

Enter the Actor that was in the Pit.

Actor. If I too should be out, this answer take,
I do not now so much repeat, as make.

Prologue.

WHen first this Toy was publique, 'twas unknown
To th' Author, and before 'twas feather'd flown;
He now consents, that you should see't once more,
'Cause he hath more faults, then it had before.
He knows there is a snarling Sect i'th' Town,
That do condemn all wit except their own;
Were this Play ne're so good, it should not take,
Nothing must passe that Gentlemen do make.
Whilst I did sit i'th' Pit, I heard one say
There n'ere was poorer language in a Play;
And told his Neighbour, he did fear the vile
Composure would go neer to spoil his stile.
Another damn'd the Scene with full-mouth'd oaths,
Because it was not dress'd in better cloaths;
And rather wish'd each Actor might be mute,
Then he should loose the sight of a fine suit.
   O Wit and Judgement both! what they do raise
To prejudice, is here the chiefest praise:
Would it be proper, think you, for a Swain,
To put on Buskins, and a lofty strain?
Or should a Shepherdess such phrases vent,
As the Spring-Garden Ladies complement;
Should a rough *Satyre*, who did never know,
The thing we call a *Taylor* Lord-like go
In Silks and Sattins? Or a Country Lasse
Wear by her side a Watch or Looking-Glasse:
Faith Gentlemen, such Solecismes as these
Might have done well in the Antipodes:
It argues a strange ignorance to call
Every thing foolish, that is naturall:
If only Monsters please you, you must go
Not to the Stage, but to a *Bartholomew* Show.
The Author aims not to show wit, but Art,
Nor did he strive to pen the Speech, but Part;
He could have writ high lines, and I do know

Præludium for *The Careless Shepherdess*

His pains were double to descend so low:
Nor does he think it infamy, to confess
His stile as *Careless* as the *Shepherdess*.
Good voices fall, and rise, and *Virgil*, who
Did *Georgicks* make, did write the *Æneids* too:
Laurell in woods doth grow, and there may be
Some wit in Shepherds plain simplicity:
The pictures of a Beggar and a King
Do equall praises to a *Painter* bring;
Meadows and Groves in Landskips please the eye
As much as all the City bravery:
May your ears too accept this rurall sport,
And think your selves in *Salisbury Plain*, not *Court. Exit.*

II

ACTORS AND ACTING

V

JOHN RUSSELL BROWN

On the Acting of Shakespeare's Plays

It used to be possible to quote Hamlet's advice to the players, point out that no extravagancies were to be used, and leave the rest to the actor to interpret in the tradition of his art, but today we are told that a completely new technique of acting is needed in order to present Shakespeare's plays in the spirit in which they were written. It is true that not all scholars are agreed on these matters, but even temperate opinion would say that the acting of Shakespeare's contemporaries was "fundamentally formal" and only "shaded by naturalism from time to time."[1] "Formal acting" has not been properly defined but it is generally assumed to be the opposite of "natural," and to make no attempt to give an impression of real life. "Poetry and its decent delivery" are considered "the only real essentials of Elizabethan drama."[2]

The study of Elizabethan acting is comparatively new, and although one book has already been published on the subject,[3] the time is hardly ripe for an authoritative and balanced treatise. But in the meantime, what guidance can scholarship give to actors and producers of Shakespeare's plays? It seems to me that the subject has been approached from an unfortunate angle and that, in consequence, the evidence has been distorted and misapplied. Briefly, I believe that formalism on the stage was fast dying out in Shakespeare's age, and that a new naturalism was a kindling spirit in his theater. This naturalism was not what we understand by the word today, but, in contrast to formalism, it did aim at an illusion of real life. I want to reverse

From *The Quarterly Journal of Speech*, 34 (1953):477–84. Reprinted by permission of the author and *The Quarterly Journal of Speech*.

[1] S. L. Bethell, "Shakespeare's Actors," *R.E.S.*, new ser., 1 (1950):205.

[2] *Ibid.*

[3] B. L. Joseph, *Elizabethan Acting* (1951).

the statement which I have quoted above, and to say that Elizabethan acting aimed at an illusion of life, although some vestiges of an old formalism remained. If this is the case, our modern actors stand a better chance of interpreting Shakespeare than those who were his contemporaries, for the modern tradition is based on a thorough-going naturalism unknown to Elizabethans. If the relics of formalism are properly respected, we can realize the illusion of life with a new delicacy and completeness.

To prove my point, I would have to examine in detail, and in chronological sequence, the whole *corpus* of Elizabethan drama.[4] All I can do here is to counter some of the arguments which might be brought against my statement, and present some evidence which I do not think has been sufficiently discussed.

The earliest advocates of formal acting base their statements on Elizabethan stage conditions; for example, after describing the circled audience and the gallants sitting on the stage, Mr. S. L. Bethell maintains that

> . . . even with the abundance of make-up, scenery, and properties in use to-day, it would have been impossible for actors so closely beset with audience, to create and sustain an illusion of actual life, especially as they performed in broad daylight.[5]

Obviously these conditions made it difficult to sustain an illusion of real life, but nevertheless it was certainly attempted and achieved. Thomas Heywood in his *An Apology for Actors* (1612) writes,

> . . . turne to our domesticke hystories: what English blood, seeing the person of any bold Englishman presented, and doth not hugge his fame, and hunnye at his valor, pursuing him in his enterprise with his best wishes, and as beeing wrapt in contem-

---

[4] Previous work on dramatic technique has generally ignored the question of changing or developing methods; e.g., M. C. Bradbrook's pioneering *Themes and Conventions of Elizabethan Tragedy* (1935) explicitly states that "the development of the conventions has been only slightly indicated" because the subject was too large (p. 1).

[5] *Shakespeare and the Popular Dramatic Tradition* (1944), p. 31. See also M. C. Bradbrook, *Themes and Conventions of Elizabethan Tragedy* (1935), pp. 20–21.

plation, offers to him in his hart all prosperous performance, *as if the personator were the man personated?*[6]

John Webster, the probable author of the Character of "An Excellent Actor" (1615), uses almost the same words; "what we see him personate, we thinke truely done before us."[7] John Fletcher was praised for giving opportunity for a similar illusion:

> How didst thou sway the Theatre! make us feele
> The Players wounds were true, and their swords, steele!
> Nay, stranger yet, how often did I know
> When the Spectators ran to save the blow?
> Frozen with griefe we could not stir away
> Vntill the Epilogue told us 'twas a Play.[8]

Prolonged death speeches must have made the simulation of real life very difficult—*The Knight of the Burning Pestle* ridicules their excesses—but Burbage evidently could achieve it; not only did the audience think he died indeed, but the dramatic illusion extended to the other actors in the scene with him:

> Oft haue I seene him play this part in ieast,
> Soe liuely, that spectators, and the rest
> Of his sad crew, whilst he but seem'd to bleed,
> Amazed, thought euen then hee dyed in deed.[9]

From such descriptions, we must assume that Elizabethan actors aimed at an illusion of real life and that the best of them achieved it.

Even when it is accepted that the Elizabethan actors aimed at an illusion of real life, it is still possible to write down their acting as "formal." So Professor Harbage maintains that

> we are told *what* the actor did (in the estimation of the spectator), but not *how* he did it. Since the conventions of formal acting will be accepted as just while formal acting prevails, testimony like the above is nugatory.[10]

[6] Sig. B4; the italics are mine.

[7] John Webster, *Works*, ed. F. L. Lucas (1927), 4:43.

[8] F. Beaumont and J. Fletcher, *Comedies and Tragedies* (1647), Sig. f2ᵛ.

[9] Quoted from Sir E. K. Chambers, *The Elizabethan Stage* (1923), 2:309.

[10] A. Harbage, "Elizabethan Acting," *PMLA*, 54 (1939):692; the evidence he quotes includes the verses on Burbage quoted above.

But this argument only "explains" the evidence if, on other grounds, the acting is known to be "formal." Even if this could be shown, it does not imply that our actors today should attempt formalism; the fact remains that an illusion of life was attempted. If our actors are more thorough in this respect, may they not be interpreting the plays in the spirit in which they were written?

The arguments for formal acting which are based on the plays themselves are difficult to answer directly; a detailed, chronological study is required. But one may point out, in general, that much of the evidence is taken from early plays, the famous Towton scene in *III Henry VI* (II, 5) being always to the fore.[11] The formal, didactic arrangement of such scenes died out as the Morality plays, on which they seem to be based, disappeared also; it is not representative of the first decade of the seventeenth century. Direct address to the audience is another feature of Elizabethan plays which has been adduced in support of formal acting; such speeches have been thought to shatter "all possibility of dramatic illusion."[12] In this case, it is admitted that Shakespeare's plays do not provide any strikingly clear example,[13] yet even if such were found it would not be an unsurmountable obstacle to the simulation of real life on the stage. There was no gap between the audience and the stage in the Elizabethan theater, and the actors did not address the audience as if it were in another world. There was a reciprocal relationship; the audience could participate in the drama as easily as the actors could share a joke or enlist sympathy. The very fact that it is difficult to distinguish direct address from soliloquy, and soliloquy from true dialogue, shows that the contact with the audience was quite unembarrassed. They shared the illusion of life.

The use of verse in Elizabethan drama has also been taken for a sign that acting was formal; for instance, of the sonnet embedded in the dialogue of *Romeo and Juliet* (I. v. 95 ff.) it has been said,

[11] For instance, see Joseph, *Elizabethan Acting*, pp. 116–22.

[12] Bethell, "Shakespeare's Actors," p. 86.

[13] *Ibid.*, pp. 84–85.

Shakespeare's purpose can only be achieved if his audience is allowed to respond to the figures, the images, and the metrical pattern of these fourteen lines. There is no need to imitate dialogue realistically.[14]

But once more the development of new styles in writing and acting must be taken into account. When Jonson wrote *Timber*, the style of Marlowe already belonged to another age:

> The true Artificer will not run away from nature, as hee were afraid of her; or depart from life, and the likenesse of Truth; but speake to the capacity of his hearers. And though his language differ from the vulgar somewhat; it shall not fly from all humanity, with the *Tamerlanes*, and *Tamer-Chams* of the late Age.[15]

Once the idea of development is accepted, the question about Elizabethan acting ceases to be "Was it formal or natural?" It is, rather, "Which was the new, dominant style, the fashionable mode in which they would strive to produce even old plays or recalcitrant material?" I believe that the comparison between the style of Jonson's age and that of Marlowe's points in one direction only. It had become possible to speak the verse as if it were meant—as if, at that instant, it sprang from the mind of the speaker. Shakespeare's mature style has the best of two worlds; there is the eloquence, precision, and melody of verse, but there is also the immediacy and movement of actual speech. The dramatist has achieved the ideal which Puttenham sought in the courtly poet; he is now

> a dissembler only in the subtilties of his arte, that is, when he is most artificial, so to disguise and cloake it as it may not appeare, nor seeme to proceede from him by any studie or trade of rules, but to be his naturall.[16]

[14] Joseph, *Elizabethan Acting*, p. 129.

[15] *Works*, ed. C. H. Herford and P. and E. Simpson, vol. 8 (1947), p. 587. Jonson's editors date *Timber* between 1623 and 1635, vol. 11 (1952), p. 213, but Professor C. J. Sisson has shown that the work was probably composed as lecture notes while Jonson was acting as deputy for Henry Croke, the Professor of Rhetoric at Gresham College, in 1619, *TLS* (September 21, 1951).

[16] *The Art of English Poesie* (1589); G. Gregory Smith, *Elizabethan Critical Essays* (1904), 2:186–87.

For such dialogue, a formal, rhetorical delivery would destroy the very quality which the poet had striven to attain. The new dialogue needed a new style of acting, and as the verse became less formal and declamatory, so did the acting. Both aimed at an illusion of life.

The internal evidence of the plays has only been hurriedly considered, for its proper treatment would need a greater scope than this present article provides.[17] I would like to turn, therefore, to one piece of external evidence which has been generally accepted as an indication of formal acting. This is the Elizabethan comparison between the actor and the orator. The *locus classicus* is the Character of "An Excellent Actor":

> Whatsoever is commendable in the grave Orator, is most exquisitly perfect in him; for by a full and significant action of body, he charmes our attention.[18]

A later statement is in Richard Flecknoe's *A Short Discourse of the English Stage* (1664) where it is said that Richard Burbage

> had all the parts of an excellent Orator (animating his words with speaking, and Speech with Action).[19]

The comparison between orator and actor is further testified by the use of the word *action* to describe the bodily movements of both artists. From this comparison several deductions might be made; first, the actor used a declamatory voice as distinct from a conversational; secondly, he observed the phrasing, figures, and literary quality of his lines in the manner laid down for the orator; and thirdly, he used "action" to enforce the meaning of his lines rather than to represent the emotion of a character. It has been suggested that John Bulwer's *Chirologia* and *Chironomia*, two books of manual signs for the use of orators, published in 1644, and written by a specialist in the teaching of the deaf, might represent the "actions" used on the

17 Asides, the arrangement of exits, entries, and other stage movement, the use of type costume and characterization are some of the more obvious details which need chronological analysis.

18 Cf. Harbage, "Elizabethan Acting," pp. 701–2; Joseph, *Elizabethan Acting, passim;* and Bethell, "Shakespeare's Actors," p. 202.

19 Quoted from Chambers, *Elizabethan Stage*, 4:370. There has been some argument about the validity of this evidence; see Harbage, "Elizabethan Acting," p. 695, and Bethell, "Shakespeare's Actors," pp. 200–201.

Elizabethan stage.[20] But the deductions can go further, and the actor is sometimes endowed with the intentions of the orator; it is thought that he excited the emotions of his audience rather than expressed those of the character he was representing. Under such conditions a play would be a number of speeches, or, at best, a ritual, rather than an image of actual life. It has even been suggested that, in Johnson's words, an Elizabethan went to the theater in order to

> hear a certain number of lines recited with just gesture and elegant modulation.[21]

Obviously one cannot deny the comparison between actor and orator, but this does not imply that the comparison held at all points; both artists spoke before the people and used gestures—and there the comparison might rest. Distinctions between the two were clearly recognized by Elizabethans. So Abraham Fraunce, speaking of the orator, says that the gesture should change with the voice,

> yet not parasiticallie as stage plaiers vse, but grauelie, and decentlie as becommeth men of greater calling.[22]

The distinction may not be flattering to the actor but that there is one is plain enough. Thomas Wright's *The Passions of the Mind* (1604) makes another distinction; the orator is said to act "really" to "stirre vp all sorts of passions according to the exigencie of the matter," whereas the player acts "fainedly" in the performance of a fiction "onely to delight" (p. 179). These distinctions are quoted by Joseph in his book *Elizabethan Acting*,[23] but he does not seem to accept their implications.

Rhetoric was taught in Elizabethan schools and universities and "pronunciation," or delivery, received its due attention.

---

[20] So Joseph, *Elizabethan Acting*. Even as an indication of an orator's art the books are suspect, for Bulwer himself confesses that "I never met with any Rhetorician or other, that had picturd out one of these Rhetoricall expressions of the Hands and fingers; or met with any Philologer that could exactly satisfie me in the ancient Rhetoricall postures of *Quintilian*" (*Chironomia*, p. 26; quoted from Joseph, pp. 45–47).

[21] *Ibid.*, p. 141.

[22] *The Arcadian Rhetoric* (1588), Sig. I7ᵛ.

[23] Pp. 54 and 58.

Indeed, Heywood in his *Apology* shows that acting was used as a means of training the young orator (Sigs. C3ᵛ–4). If the arts of acting and oratory were truly similar, here was an excellent "school" for actors. But the evidence clearly shows that it was not; the scholars learned a style of acting which was suitable for oratory but condemned on the public stage. So in *II The Return from Parnassus* (c. 1602), Kemp, the professional actor, criticizes the scholar-players as those who

> neuer speake in their walke, but at the end of the stage, iust as though in walking . . . we should neuer speake but at a stile, a gate, or a ditch, where a man can go no further (IV, 3).

Kemp criticizes them because they did not act as men do in real life. Richard Brome makes a similar distinction against scholar-players in *The Antipodes* (1640):

> Let me not see you act now,
> In your Scholasticke way, you brought to towne wi' yee,
> . . . Ile none of these, absurdities in my house.
>
> (II, 2)

The gestures described in Bulwer's books for orators might well be among the scholastic absurdities which Brome inveighs against. In Campion's *A Book of Airs* (1601) the criticism is more precise:

> But there are some, who to appeare the more deepe, and singular in their iudgement, will admit no Musicke but that which is long, intricate, bated with fuge, chaind with sincopation, and where the nature of euerie word is precisely exprest in the Note, like the old exploded action in Comedies, when if they did pronounce *Memeni,* they would point to the hinder part of their heads, if *Video* put their finger in their eye.[24]

Here, the orator's gestures are considered both scholastic ("deepe and singular") and old-fashioned; clearly Campion thought they were not in use in the up-to-date theaters in London.

Perhaps the distinction between actor and orator is most clearly stated in Flecknoe's praise of Burbage which has already been quoted:

[24] To the Reader; *Works,* ed. P. Vivian (1909).

He had all the parts of an excellent Orator . . . , yet even then, he was an excellent Actor still, never falling in his Part when he had done speaking; but with his looks and gesture, maintaining it still unto the heighth. . . .

Flecknoe says, in effect, that though Burbage had the graces of an orator, *yet even then* he was an excellent actor—in spite of some likeness of his art to that of oratory.

Earlier in the same passage, Flecknoe had claimed that Burbage

was a delightful Proteus, so wholly transforming himself into his Part, and putting off himself with his Cloathes, as he never (not so much as in the Tyring-house) assum'd himself again until the Play was done.

Such absorption in one's part has nothing to do with oratory; it is closer to the acting techniques of Stanislovsky. It suggests that an Elizabethan actor sunk himself in his part and did not merely declaim his lines with formal effectiveness. A similar impression is given by the Prologue to *Antonio and Mellida* (first performed in 1599) where actors are shown preparing for their parts and speaking in the appropriate "veins." An incidental image in *Coriolanus* implies a similar technique:

> You have put me now to such a part which never
> I shall discharge to the life.

> (III, 2:105–6)

In the event, Coriolanus was unable to do as Burbage did and wholly transform himself into his part.

There are many extant descriptions of Elizabethan acting but the value of this evidence is commonly belittled because it is written in the same technical language as the criticism of rhetoric and oratory. So Hamlet's advice to the players is dismissed as "a cliché from classical criticism, equally applicable to all the arts."[25] Or again, it is claimed that

the poet has put into the mouth of his Prince nothing that conflicts with the directions normally provided by the teachers of rhetorical delivery.[26]

[25] Harbage, "Elizabethan Acting," p. 690.
[26] Joseph, *Elizabethan Acting*, p. 146.

49

But the fact that the same language was used for acting and oratory does not mean that the same effect was being described. The language of criticism for all the arts was in its infancy and it was perhaps inevitable that acting should be dependent on the technical vocabulary of a more systematic art.

In attempts to interpret descriptions of acting, words and phrases from the criticism of rhetoric and oratory are frequently noted. But their use in another art may give an entirely different interpretation and may be equally pertinent. The phrase *imitation of life* is an example. It is basic to the conception of poetry as an art of imitation, a conception which was not generally understood by Elizabethans—except for Sidney—as referring to the poet's revelation of ideal and universal truth. The usual interpretation is seen in Sir Thomas Elyot's description of comedy as "a picture or as it were a mirrour of man's life"[27] or in Ascham's idea that drama was a "perfite *imitation*, or faire liuelie painted picture of the life of euerie degree of man."[28] The phrase is constantly repeated; Lodge, Jonson, and Heywood all claimed on Cicero's authority that Comedy was *"imitatio vitae, speculum consuetudinis, et imago veritatis."*[29]

The idea of drama as a picture of life suggests a parallel in the art of painting, and here the meaning of imitation is much clearer. For instance it is implicit throughout the description of the pictures offered to Christopher Sly in the Induction of *The Taming of the Shrew:*

> —Dost thou love pictures? we will fetch thee straight
> Adonis painted by a running brook,
> And Cytherea all in sedges hid,
> Which seem to move and wanton with her breath,
> Even as the waving sedges play with wind.
> —We'll show thee Io as she was a maid,
> And how she was beguiled and surprised,
> As lively painted as the deed was done.
> —Or Daphne roaming through a thorny wood,

[27] *The Governor* (1531), ed. H. H. S. Croft (1880), 1:124.

[28] *The Schoolmaster* (1570), *English Works*, ed. W. A. Wright (1904), p. 266.

[29] *A Defence of Poetry* (1579), ed. G. Gregory Smith, *Elizabethan Critical Essays* (1904), I, 81; *Every Man Out of His Humour* (1600), III, 6: 206–7; and *An Apology for Actors* (1612). Sig. F1ᵛ.

> Scratching her legs that one shall swear she bleeds,
> And at that sight shall sad Apollo weep,
> So workmanly the blood and tears are drawn.
>
> (2:51–62)

"As lively painted as the deed was done" is the key to the whole of this description, and "life-likeness" or the "imitation of life" was constantly used in the criticism of the visual arts. So Bassanio exclaims when he finds Portia's picture in the leaden casket, "What demi-god Hath come so near creation?" (*The Merchant of Venice* III, 2:116–17), or Paulina claims that her "statue" can show life "lively mock'd" (*The Winter's Tale* V, 3:19). For an example outside Shakespeare, we may take Thomas Nashe's description of the floor of an Italian summer house; it was

> painted with the beautifullest flouers that euer mans eie admired; which so linealy were delineated that he that viewd them a farre off, and had not directly stood poaringly ouer them, would haue sworne they had liued in deede.[30]

The imitation of life was not the whole concern of Renaissance artists, but their experiments in perspective and light were at first designed to deceive the external eye; their paintings were meant to look like real life.

When the phrase is used of acting, of performing in the "picture" that was the drama, it seems to carry the same implications of deception and the appearance of reality. So Webster praises the Queen's Men at the Red Bull for the acting of *The White Devil* in 1612 or 1613:

> For the action of the play, twas generally well, and I dare affirme, with the Ioint testimony of some of their owne quality, (for the true imitation of life, without striuing to make nature a monster) the best that euer became them.

So also, the imitation of life is praised in *The Second Maiden's Tragedy*, performed in 1611:

> thow shalt see my ladie
> plaie her part naturallie, more to the life
> then shees aware on.[31]

[30] *The Unfortunate Traveller* (1594); *Works*, ed. R. B. McKerrow, vol. 2 (1904), p. 283.

[31] Malone Society Reprint (1909), 2:2015–17.

Shakespeare implies the same standards in *The Two Gentlemen of Verona:*

> For I did play a lamentable part: ...
> Which I so lively acted with my tears
> That my poor mistress, moved therewithal,
> Wept bitterly.
>
> (IV, 4: 171–76)

The idea of a play as a "lively" picture may be seen in Rowley's verses on *The Duchess of Malfy* (1623):

> I Neuer saw thy Dutchesse, till the day,
> That She was liuely body'd in thy Play.

Perhaps most important, the "imitation of life" is implicit in Hamlet's advice to the players: he says that the end of playing is

> to hold, as 'twere, the mirror up to nature; to show virtue her own feature, scorn her own image, and the very age and body of the time his form and pressure (III, 2:25–29).

When he criticizes strutting and bellowing, he invokes the same standard:

> I have thought some of nature's journeymen had made men and had not made them well, they imitated humanity so abominably (ll. 39–41).

Hamlet is applying the same criterion to acting that Bassanio did to Portia's picture—how near is it to creation?

The conception of acting as an imitation of life agrees with the other evidence I have quoted, and suggests that Elizabethan actors aimed at an illusion of real life. It does not explain *all* in the best Renaissance painting or the best Elizabethan acting, but it has an important place in the artists' intentions. To describe the resultant art as formal is to deny this intention; *natural* seems a more appropriate word.

There is probably some reluctance among scholars to admit that naturalism was a keynote of Elizabethan acting. Some critics would obviously wish the plays to be acted in a formal manner. For instance, it is said that a person in a play may be

> first a symbol, second a human being; ... [and the play itself can be] primarily an argument or parable, only secondarily

forced, as it best may, to assume some correspondence with the forms and events of human affairs.[32]

This is an extreme case, but there are other hints of a fear that naturalism would make Shakespeare's plays "smaller," that they would lose the meaning and richness that had been found in the study. Formal acting, on the other hand, seems to offer a declamation in which technical accomplishment could be appreciated and the argument or pattern of the drama could stand revealed. But there is more than one kind of naturalism; there is one for plays set in a drawing-room, and another for plays dealing with kings and soldiers, inspired prophets, and accomplished courtiers. A true naturalism would not disguise the high themes of Elizabethan tragedy or the idealism of their comedy.

We have said that Elizabethan dramatists and actors imitated life, but this does not mean that they tried to make their plays exactly the same as real life; they did not labor, in Marston's words, to "relate any thing as an historian but to inlarge every thing as a Poet."[33] Their plays were more exciting and colorful, more full of meaning, than real life; indeed, compared with them, "Nature never set foorth . . . so rich [a] Tapistry."[34] Yet we may say that they aimed at an imitation of life and the audience was encouraged to take all this as real while the performance was in progress. Within the charmed circle of the theater, a new world might be accepted as real, and what they saw personated could be accepted as truly done before them.

George Chapman once wrote a preface to a play of his which had never been performed, and in it he tried to analyze what this play had missed. Unlike some critics, he believed that

> scenical representation is so far from giving just cause of any least diminution, that the personal and exact life it gives to any history, or other such delineation of human actions adds to them lustre, spirit, and apprehension.[35]

[32] Written of *Timon of Athens;* G. Wilson Knight, *The Wheel of Fire* (1930), p. 274.

[33] "To the General Reader," *Sophonisba* (1606): *Plays*, ed. H. H. Wood (1938), 2:5.

[34] Philip Sidney, *The Defence of Poesie* (1595); *Works*, ed. A. Feuillerat (1923), 3:8.

[35] Dedication, *Caesar and Pompey* (1631); *Tragedies*, ed. T. M. Parrott (1910), p. 341.

A "personal and exact life" was what Chapman expected the actors to give to his play, and these words may serve to describe the naturalism which I believe to be the new power of Elizabethan acting. If actors in today's theater wish to present Shakespeare's plays in the spirit in which they were written, they should respect and enjoy the magniloquence and music of the language, enter into the greatness of conception, and play all the time for an illusion of real life. They must constantly expect a miracle—that the verse shall be enfranchised as the natural idiom of human beings and that all of Shakespeare's strange creation shall become real and "lively" on the stage. Because the Elizabethan actor was capable of working for this miracle, Shakespeare, like other of his contemporaries, dared to "repose eternitie in the mouth of a Player."[36]

36 Thomas Nashe, Preface to Robert Greene, *Menaphon* (1589); *Works*, ed. R. B. McKerrow (1905), 3:312.

VI

MURIEL C. BRADBROOK

The Status Seekers: Society and the Common Player in the Reign of Elizabeth I

The public theater, established in England in the last quarter of the sixteenth century, depended on an "open" audience in London, attending at a regular playing place and paying a regular fee. Although there was much dramatic activity in the provinces, there would have been no Elizabethan drama as we have it had the players continued as strollers. From the coalescence of poets and actors in London the theater evolved as a social institution that existed by public support—and by the ingenuity of the players in evading their enemies.

For hostility to the common players was in this period so strong as several times to threaten to pluck down their wooden galleries and gaily painted scaffolding, leaving only the forlorn shell of an empty ring. Behind the records of the privy council and the City, behind the *Blasts of Retrait* and other published attacks on players there lies a complex social struggle, imperfectly discerned at the time.

Under the protective shield of their lord's badge, invoking a declining form of service—little better than a legal fiction—the players eventually established themselves in the City as purveyors of a commodity for which the public was prepared to put down its cash. Players aspired to the condition of citizens and merchants; to attain it they masqueraded as members of the gentlemanly profession of servingmen; by their enemies

From *The Huntington Library Quarterly*, 24 (1961):111–24. Reprinted by permission of the author and *The Huntington Library Quarterly*. This essay, in considerably altered form, later formed the basis for two chapters of M. C. Bradbrook's *The Rise of the Common Player*, published by Chatto & Windus, Ltd., in conjunction with Harvard University Press, in 1962.

they were constantly confounded with rogues and vagabonds, thieves and cheaters, who lived at fortune's alms. The attempts to put down players, which the city of London pursued so steadfastly throughout the latter part of the sixteenth century, sprang from a variety of feelings. Acknowledged objections were three: pruriency in the plays, pugnacity in the audience, and plague infection. In addition, social prejudice operated against a new and hitherto unrecognized kind of employment, whose position was ambiguous while its profits were alarming.

Moralists preached the immutability of society, the duty of all to remain in the state to which they were born. As Robert Crowley put it:

> For in the worlde ther can not be
> More greate abhomination,
> To thy Lorde God, then is in the
> Forsakeyng thy vocation.[1]

The common player had no fixed place in the commonweal; in spite of his livery, his occupation had developed beyond its traditional limits. He had no room in the scheme of things and, therefore, no place in society. The establishment of the Theatre and the Curtain in 1576 was a turning point; shared with other purveyors of pastimes, such as fencers and bearbaiters, they were the the outward and visible sign of the common player's right. Once a dangerous retainer, he now became a sober householder.

In the earlier part of Elizabeth's reign, merriment and interlude were not sharply distinguished from games and festivities, three-men songs, jigs and feats of "activity," or tumbling. Dramatic art as an independent skill emerged but slowly from the cocoon of playing. The emergence of the art followed the emergence of a new class of men—the position was won by and conceded to one or two "Great Companies,"[2] which achieved a local habitation and a name in the capital, i.e., Leicester's Men in the seventies, the Queen's Men in the eighties,

[1] "The Last Trumpet," in *The Select Works of Robert Crowley*, ed. J. M. Cowper. Early English Text Soc., Extra Ser., 15 (London, 1872):90.

[2] The twelve "Great Companies" of the London liverymen and the horde of lesser companies form a close parallel to the few important acting troops and to the large number of minor, short-lived bands.

the Lord Admiral's and the Lord Chamberlain's Men in the nineties. For polemical purposes these "Great Companies" could still be confused with the crowd of pitiable vagabonds who roamed the countryside with a few tattered, gaudy garments and a half-dozen thumbed old interludes. In practice they established themselves as a new estate, a most difficult thing in a society which demanded that traditional forms should at least be outwardly adhered to, which insisted that new wine should be poured into old bottles. In his triumphant celebration of mercantile greatness, written in 1588, the Armada year, Robert Wilson climaxed the Preface to *The Pleasant and Stately Morall, of Three Lords and Three Ladies of London* with the City's vaunt:

> My former fruites were lovely Ladies three;
> Now of three Lords to talke is *Londons* glee.[3]

The "lords" of this play were gentlemen born and citizens bred, and players who wore the royal badge on their livery did not derive their comfortable incomes from the uncertainties of court favor but from business enterprise.

For about a hundred years before this time, troops of players had been wandering on the roads of England. Servants of a great household who performed a ten-mile circuit in the Christmas season or town players who visited their neighbors were tolerable; but to live permanently by such means was intolerable and dishonest in the eyes of all good citizens. In London in 1565 plays were forbidden in taverns, inns, or victualing houses "wher any money shalbe demaunded or payd for the syght or hyrynge of the same playes."[4] As late as November 1584 the city fathers protested that "It hath not ben used nor thought meete heretofore that players have or shold make their lyving on the art of playeng," but that "men for their lyvings using other honest and lawfull artes, or reteyned in honest services, have by companies learned some enterludes for some encreasce to their profit by other mens pleasures in va-

---

[3] (London, 1590), Sig. A2ᵛ. Among the three lords is Pleasure, representative of players and play lovers.

[4] Order of the court of aldermen, Nov. 29, 1565. In *Collections*, ed. W. W. Greg, Malone Soc., vol. 2 (Oxford, 1931), pt. 3, p. 300. The order is followed by a precept from the lord mayor giving effect to it.

cant time of recreation."[5] As had been done ten years before, in 1574, they demanded that players should appear only at weddings or other festivities "withoute publique or Commen Collection of money of the Auditorie or behoulders theareof."[6]

In 1574 also the Merchant Taylors had observed that when boys from their school played in the livery hall " 'at our comon playes and suche lyke exercises whiche be comonly exposed to be seene for money, everye lewd persone thinketh himself (for his penny) worthye of the chiefe and most comodious place. . . .' "[7] The Merchant Taylors, who were the boys' lords and patrons, had been thrust aside in their own hall instead of being given the place of honor that was their right. They asserted the old form of drama as service by banning any further such presentation of plays.

In October 1575 the vice-chancellor of Cambridge made a plea to the privy council against "badd persons . . . wandringe about the countrye" and was told to beware of "light and decayed persons, who for filthy lucre are mynded, and do seke now Adaies to devise, and sett up in open places shewes of unlawfull, hurtfull, pernicious and unhonest games. . . ."[8] He was ordered to forbid open shows within five miles of the university; in consequence, except for the disturbance provided by their own plays, the students were much less troubled for many years afterward. In 1592 the university's appeal for the renewal of the prohibition was signed by Thomas Legge, the author of *Richardus Tertius*, while William Gager, the chief champion of academic plays at Oxford, could write that he was concerned only to defend the dignity of his college and the fame of the towardly young men, his friends; as for common plays, " 'I can forbeare, and thinke of them as they are. . . .' "[9] He agreed with his opponents that to play for money

5 Reply of the corporation of London to a petition from the Queen's Men. *Ibid.*, vol. 1 (1908), pt. 2, p. 172.

6 Act of common council, Dec. 6, 1574. *Ibid.*, p. 178.

7 From the master's accounts of the Merchant Taylors, printed by E. K. Chambers, *The Elizabethan Stage* (Oxford, 1923), 2:75.

8 Supplication of vice-chancellor and heads of houses, Sept. 18, 1592, with the reply. In *Collections*, 1, pt. 2:192, 195.

9 Letter of July 31, 1592, quoted by Frederick S. Boas, *University Drama in the Tudor Age* (Oxford, 1914), p. 241, from the Corpus Christi College MSS. 352.6.

made men infamous. The chief of these opponents was John Rainolds, who himself in his youth had played before the queen in *Palamon and Arcite* but who continued to denounce plays on moral grounds and with all the lack of charity that moral grounds confer.[10] Meanwhile, common players also continued to visit the universities where they either performed privately or were given some small "reward" to go away peaceably without performing.

Strollers, however grand their livery, were always suspect, for an honest man was expected to have some one place where he belonged and where he earned his bread. He was thus insured proper paternal and authoritative supervision from his pastors and masters. Being without fixed habitation, players were subject to a bewildering variety of control. Socially, the whole problem of the actor in the crucial decades of the 1570's and 1580's turned on the issue of who should control him and in what respects; by social ligaments of control and responsibility he became eventually knit into the community.

To an age like the present, hardened to large-scale unemployment and familiar with the problem of displaced persons, the Elizabethan view that idleness meant guilt and vagrancy meant crime is unfamiliar. By these tenets the strolling players were judged guilty by association and classed with the pickpockets who filched from their spectators. Everyone agreed that the Elizabethan actor should be controlled and ordered, and most of those interested were prepared to do it themselves. Actors thus became involved in struggles larger than their own and were brought between the cross fire of central and local government.

At moments of crisis the central government would put down plays without necessarily feeling hostile to players. The lords of the privy council knew that under the earlier Tudors drama as propaganda had proved a potent, but two-edged, weapon; in the latter part of Elizabeth's reign they were deter-

---

[10] In *Th' Overthrow of Stage-Playes* ([Middelburg], 1599) Rainolds printed and replied to their defense by Alberico Gentili, the Regius professor of civil law, but a note in the copy of this book in the Cambridge University Library (M.* 6.19.3[E]) says that an answer was made by Gentili and printed "wch ye Archb. disliked and sent to ye univers. to burn them." The archbishop in question would be Whitgift.

mined to regulate and, if necessary, suppress inflammatory public comment on risky subjects. Otherwise they were well content that court entertainers should gain their living by amusing the citizens, playing in the innyards, in the open street, or in citizens' houses.

Although forbidden to meddle in matters of state, the players sometimes made the moral claim that they taught good living. This brought them into conflict with the only licensed instructors in virtue, the preachers of the Word. Every attempt to defend players on didactic grounds was met by the retort that plays were the devil's sermons, a hideous mockery or antitype of true instruction. The rhetoric and showmanship of preacher and actor were sufficiently close, but in controversy the player was at a severe disadvantage, for all the authority and prestige lay with his opponents. Moral objections of preachers joined with economic fears of the city tradesmen to produce a powerful opposition.

Between 1574, by which time the city players were well established, and 1584 the privy council and the city fathers tried a series of experiments in control out of which a working compromise emerged. Later, in 1597, when they seemed to unite in a desire to reduce playing, none of the ferocious orders about tearing down of scaffolds had any effect. The bark of the Elizabethan government was very much worse than its bite,[11] especially where large numbers of people were involved. As the executive branch of the government was entirely without a standing army or professional police, its coercive power was by modern standards extraordinarily weak. Consequently, the acts of the privy council seem often to indicate a maximum action that the councilors hope to see approached rather than an order that they expect to find carried out. The council was given to snapping at the city fathers for their slackness in enforcing prescriptions; the city fathers would then turn and threaten the justices of the peace for Middlesex.

The immediate fear of the government was the turbulence of any assembly. London crowds had long been notorious—Froissart had remarked that the commons of England "are the

[11] See William S. Holdsworth, *A History of English Law*, vol. 4 (London, 1924), p. 165.

peryloust people of the worlde, and most outragyoust if they be up, and specialle the Londoners";[12] and Sir William Walworth's treatment of Wat Tyler was a shining example to every lord mayor. The emotional temperature of the Elizabethan audience was much higher than that of a modern crowd, for any assembly was more likely to turn into a mob; and if it did so, there was no way of controlling it. What may appear to modern minds excessive fear of assemblies need not be taken as the reaction either of milksops or tyrants.[13] It was the reaction of responsible and anxious men who knew that in 1549 Kett's Rebellion, in Norfolk, had started at a play and had taken six weeks to subdue, during which time the city of Norwich had been under mob rule. Fear provokes sharp reaction, and Stow recounts an episode of June 1595 when unruly youths, led on by an old soldier with a trumpet, started to throw stones at the warders of Tower Street. They were arrested by the sheriffs; but later, when the lord mayor rode to the spot, he was challenged by the warders of the Tower because the city sword was borne before him, and his sword bearer was wounded. On July 4 the queen appointed a provost marshal to restore order; five of the unruly youths were condemned of treason and executed on Tower Hill.[14] The city fathers' fears of the common players turned out to be unjustified, although the presence of a lord's retainers within the city must always have been a reasonable matter for apprehension. If not with the citizens, the players would quarrel with one another.

The greatest of Elizabeth's subjects was the earl of Leicester. His men, who dominated the scene in the seventies, had been used to trudge the roads with his Bear and Ragged Staff on their sleeves, to perform in London inns during the Christmas

[12] . . . *The Third and Fourth Boke of Sir John Froissart of the Cronycles of Englande* . . . , trans. John Bourchier, Lord Berners (London, 1525), Ch. ccxlii, fol. 312ᵛ.

[13] For a classic example of understatement see Alfred Harbage, *Shakespeare's Audience* (New York, 1941), p. 14. "Elizabethans had a very real fear of the potentialities of a crowd—any crowd. They were less used to crowds than we are, less adept at policing them. . . ."

[14] John Stow, *Annales, or a Generall Chronicle of England . . . Continued . . . by Edmund Howes* (London, 1631), p. 769.

season of festivity, and—if summoned—to wait on their lord and support his dignity. In January 1572, caught by a proclamation against retainers, they wrote to ask for enrollment as his household servants: "not that we meane to crave any further stipend or benefite at your Lordshippes hands but our Lyveries as we have had, and also your honors License to certifye that we are your houshold Servaunts when we shall have occasion to travayle amongst our frendes as we do usuallye once a yere. . . ."[15]

In their lack of any reward from their lord, players bettered the most gentlemanly tradition of servingmen. Their reception in the country depended on whose livery they wore, whereas in London it depended on their talent. A nobleman might demand, and sometimes did demand, special privileges for his players; but the lord mayor of London has the precedence of an earl and could say "No" to Pembroke or Worcester on occasion.

The great rambling households of the nobility included many entertainers, who took to the roads and only occasionally came to court to proffer their services. Elizabeth herself had inherited from her predecessor four interlude players, who, like the lutanists and musicians of her chamber, were feed servants. She had also companies of trumpeters and jugglers, a fool, a minstrel, and a bearward. She might likewise command the Children of the Chapel Royal and of the chapel at Windsor; but for her more expensive Christmas entertainments she looked to the offerings of her loyal subjects, whose privilege it was to amuse her.

By March 1574 it occurred to someone at court, where the ingenious were always looking for new ways of skimming profits from trade, that a patent for licensing playing places in the City would be a useful and rewarding way of control. In reply to a polite request from the lord chamberlain, the City sent a refusal. The power to restrict assembly was vital to

---

[15] Printed in *Collections*, vol. 1 (1911), pts. 4 and 5, pp. 348–49; *The Elizabethan Stage*, 2:86. The proclamation against retainers was but a prelude to the act for the punishment of vagabonds, which appeared later in the year, and which included fencers, bearwards, common players in interludes, and minstrels "not belonging to any Baron of this realm or towards any other honourable person of greater degree."

good government and could not be delegated to individuals. Moreover, the City collected considerable sums for poor relief by granting the privilege of playing within the walls, and these the alderman intended to retain.

Those who contribute to poor relief cannot themselves be considered beggars. The players were no longer shaking a money box hopefully like country mummers; their "gatherers" were stationed at appropriate points upon the entry to the scaffoldage at the innyards, and a fixed price for admission was established.

Yet even subsidies did not prevent the City from hedging its licenses with so many restrictions that on May 10, 1574, by a magnificent gesture the lords of the privy council forced the issue. Letters patent under the great seal of England were granted to the earl of Leicester's Men, James Burbage, John Perkyn, John Laneham, William Johnson, and Robert Wilson

> to use exercise and occupie the arte and facultye of playenge Commedies Tragedies Enterludes stage playes and such other like as they have alredie used and studied . . . to their best commoditie . . . as well within oure Citie of london and liberties of the same as also within the liberties and freedomes of anye oure Cities townes Bouroughes &c whatsoever as without the same . . . Anye acte statute proclamacion or commaundement . . . to the contrarie notwithstandinge Provyded that the said Commedies Tragedies enterludes and stage playes be by the master of oure Revells for the tyme beynge before sene & allowed And that the same be not published or shewen in the tyme of common prayer or in the tyme of greate and common plague in oure said Citye of london.[16]

This gave Leicester's Men a patent of monopoly that overrode the traditional right of the citizens to regulate what happened within their walls. The City could retaliate only by laying down minute regulations requiring all plays as well as playing places to be licensed by the city chamberlain. This was duly effected by the start of the Christmas season, De-

[16] "Dramatic Records from the Patent Rolls," ed. Greg and Chambers, in *Collections*, vol. 1 (1909), pt. 3, pp. 262–63; also in *The Elizabethan Stage*, 2:87–88. See also Virginia C. Gildersleeve, *Government Regulation of the Elizabethan Drama* (New York, 1908), pp. 33–39, for a discussion of this patent.

cember 6, but not without great complaint of affrays and quarrels, incontinency in inns, heiresses allured to secret contracts, withdrawals from divine service, unthrifty waste of the money of poor and fond persons, accidents from the collapse of staging or from the use of gunpowder in plays. This decree exempted performances given for festivity without collection of money in the houses of the mayor and aldermen; and such duplicate control nullified the patent, since the citizens were prepared to enforce it.

Emboldened by the support of the great, the players took the next and decisive step. On April 13, 1576, James Burbage signed the lease of a plot in Holywell in the parish of St. Leonards Shoreditch just outside the walls, on which the first public playhouse for London was built. The history of the London theater had begun.

Not only did "the gorgeous Playing place erected in the fields"[17] give the players a fixed headquarters of their own; in spite of their provision of the Lord's Room as symbol of their patron's natural right, it was the outward and visible sign of their new status. They were no longer common, but city, players; soon they were claiming the academic title of comedians or tragedians. "Some terme them Comedians, othersome Players, manie Pleasers, but I Monsters,"[18] exclaimed William Rankins. There was much in a name.

Instead of seeking out their audience with "Wilt please you to have a fit of our mirth?" the players now summoned crowds to attend their houses at fixed hours. Even more securely than in their accustomed inns, they could build up a wardrobe and a store of properties on a new scale; they rose to be employers of labor. The Theatre and Curtain were the players' livery halls—or something very similar. Later Dekker went so far as to compare the Theatre to the Royal Exchange, the most splendid monument of mercantile greatness.

Theoretically, London performances were justified still as rehearsals for the court. Within four months of the Men's establishment, the Children of the Chapel Royal had ensconced

17 John Stockwood, *A Sermon Preached at Paules Crosse* (London, [1578]), p. 134. This was a sermon for Aug. 24, Bartholomewtide, when revelry would be at its height.

18 *The Mirrour of Monsters* (London, 1587), fol. 2ʳ.

themselves within the city walls in the Liberty of Blackfriars, an ancient religious building, where the secular local government could exercise no control. Yet the keepers of the boys' theater would not have admitted that they were running a common playhouse at all. The city fathers, whose opposition continued unrelentingly and whose fine new houses so prominently displayed their own superfluous wealth, may have sometimes hired the players for a feast, as in the play of *Sir Thomas More*, where Sheriff More entertains the mayor with "My Lord Cardinals players."[19] This nostalgic picture of the good old days may be set against the famous speech on the evils of rioting, where Shakespeare (if it were he), depicting the poor Flemings sent plodding to the coast for transportation, may well have been prompted by the sad and similar fate of poor players sent to trudge the roads for ill behavior not their own. There is, in fact, little evidence of rioting at plays; the city fathers had forgotten to reckon with the fact that those who have paid their penny want their pennyworth. It would be rash, however, to assume that there was no alternative to uproar on the one hand and perfect tranquility on the other. Henslowe's bills for repairs to the Rose Theatre amounted to a very high charge indeed: £108 in 1592 and £108 19s. in 1595. This must must have been partly due to depredations of the audience.

When the players acquired their theaters, their social responsibilities multiplied. They now had to keep roads and ditches in repair as well as to contribute to the poor relief. As soon as they became firmly established, the court began to take its pickings. The energetic Edmund Tilney reorganized the revels office and gained wide powers, which he gradually asserted through his right to license plays. This was in effect a tax on production; and he steadily raised his fees.

Among their many masters the players successfully pursued their audacious career; after every attempt to suppress them, they returned. The compromise that finally emerged has per-

---

[19] This particular part of the MS of the play from the British Museum, Harley MS. 7368—printed by Greg, Malone Soc. (Oxford, 1911)—is in the hand of Anthony Munday; it does not, however, follow that he composed it. See Greg, "The Handwritings of the Manuscript," in *Shakespeare's Hand in the Play of Sir Thomas More,* ed. Alfred W. Pollard (Cambridge, 1923), pp. 41–56.

sisted in some respects to this day: plays were licensed by the lord chamberlain's deputy, the master of the revels, while playing places were licensed by the local authority. The players' lords were still free to exercise any influences they possessed to help their servants, whose incorporation depended on the patronage given them. The death of a lord dissolved his players until they could be taken over by his heir or find another patron.

The opening of the playhouses provoked the organized opposition of city preachers and pamphleteers, some of whom were renegade playwrights. From the work of John Northbrooke in 1577 to that of William Rankins in 1587, the great companies were confounded with the lowest vendors of pastime or singled out only as being exceptionally dangerous and successful. In his pseudonymous *Second and Third Blast of Retrait from Plays and Theaters* (London, 1580), Anthony Munday[20] went so far as to criticize the players' lords:

> since the reteining of these Caterpillers, the credite of Noble men hath decaid, & they are thought to be covetous by permitting their servants, which cannot live of themselves, and whome for neernes they wil not maintaine, to live at the devotion or almes of other men, passing from countrie to countrie, from one Gentlemans house to another, offering their service, which is a kind of beggerie. . . . For commonlie the goodwil men beare to their Lordes, makes them drawe the stringes of their purses to extend their liberalitie to them; where otherwise they would not (pp. 75–76).

This was hardly an argument that could be pursued when in March 1583 the queen herself extended her patronage to a troop of common players—without emolument. So in his *Anatomie of Abuses*, published that year in London, Philip Stubbs is content to call players "buzzing dronets" once more, adding "Goe they never so brave, yet are they counted and taken but for beggars

[20] The work is described on the title as by "Anglo-phile Eutheo." Munday's authorship was first suggested by J. Dover Wilson in both "Anthony Munday, Pamphleteer and Pursuivant," *Modern Language Review*, 4 (1909):484–87; and "The Puritan Attack upon the Stage," in *The Cambridge History of English Literature*, ed. A. W. Ward and A. R. Waller, vol. 6 (New York, 1910), p. 441.

. . . live they not upon begging of every one that comes?"
(Sigs. M1ʳ,ᵛ).

That playing was industry was a paradox which for many
years could not gain acceptance. For William Rankins, the last
and most heated of the opponents, the queen's livery was no
protection and the queen's example no precedent:

> The Prince must be pleased, therefore the subject be diseased.
> For that is poison to some, which is medicinable to other, and
> of a perticular good, by abuse maye spring a generall evill.
>
> *The Mirrour of Monsters* (fol. 2ᵛ)

Common players were in no position to put their case.
Stephen Gosson found it easy to confute their *Play of Plays*,
where Delight was separated from Life by Zeal; he had only
to distinguish between Delight Spiritual and Delight Carnal.
The reasoning of the schools was not designed to cope with
genuinely new phenomena but only with the logical ordering
of a limited set of known facts and the views of accepted
authorities.

In *Kind Harts Dreame* (1592) Henry Chettle hinted that
economic motives might underlie the City's opposition, but he
put this base argument into the mouth of Tarlton the Clown.

On paper the Puritans won the scolding match; the real vic-
tory, as before, went to the players. By their mere existence
the Queen's Men demonstrated the dignity of their art. When
in the nineties they gave place to the Admiral's and Lord
Strange's (afterward the Chamberlain's) Men, the position was
so secure that the last-named company in 1592 could petition
for leave to reopen at the Rose in August, although a riot had
closed the theaters in June. The great size of the company,
they asserted, made traveling impossible; they added that their
opening would benefit the poor watermen, whose livelihood
depended on rowing the audience to the Bankside. A petition
was enclosed, headed by that toiling sculler, Philip Henslowe.
The company were allowed to come back from Newington
Butts.

In the previous March a feeler had been put out to see if the
city companies would be prepared to pay Edmund Tilney a
handsome annuity for suppressing plays. The answer was that
the payment of annuities was a dangerous precedent, which

the companies would not wish to set up; they knew that the enforcement of such a ban would have fallen upon themselves.[21]

At the end of the century another storm blew up, and the privy council ordained two playhouses only: the Fortune on the north bank for the Admiral's Men and the Globe on the south bank for the Lord Chamberlain's Men. Nevertheless, the Rose and the Curtain remained standing, and soon a third company of players was officially allowed to appear. Before the turn of the century at least one of the common players had taken up the general challenge of contempt and had become a gentleman. William Shakespeare's acquisition of coat armor was treated as a jest by some of the players, but "Not without right" seems a motto which the situation called for.

The official location of players' establishments received its fullest acknowledgment in the letters patent by which James I constituted Shakespeare and his fellows the King's Men, which authorized them to play "within theire nowe usual howse called the Globe within our County of Surrey" and elsewhere; it requested "to allowe them such former Curtesies as hath bene given to men of theire place and quallitie."[22]

Their place and quality! Such a term sounds almost respectful. It recognizes both the players' dignity and the value of their art. The right to license being henceforth limited to the royal family, the Lord's Room became completely forgotten; in 1610, Ben Jonson described its dark recesses as the haunt of "the shops *Foreman*, or some such *brave sparke*" with his "*Pusil*."[23] Yet the title of lord's servants had served its purpose in smoothing a way for the new estate; and such was the rigidity of social habit that, long after the protective power of a livery had passed, it was possible for the author of *The Character of a Common Player* (1615) to taunt the actor with his dependence on popular support as something both deceptive and improper:

[21] See *Collections*, ed. Jean Robertson and D. J. Gordon, vol. 3 (1954), p. 166.

[22] *Ibid.*, 1, pt. 3:264–65.

[23] "To the worthy Author, *M. John Fletcher*." This poem was prefixed to Fletcher's *The Faithful Shepheardesse* (London, n.d.). Reprinted in *Ben Jonson*, ed. C. H. Herford, and Percy and Evelyn Simpson, vol. 8 (Oxford, 1947), pp. 370–71.

howsoever hee pretends to have a royall Master or Mistresse, his wages and dependence prove him to be the servant of the people. When he doth hold conference upon the stage; and should looke directly in his fellows face; hee turnes about his voice into the assembly for applausesake, like a Trumpeter in the fields, that shifts places to get an eccho.[24]

However, in this year, Sir George Buc, master of the revels, in his "Discourse or Treatise of the Third University," which was eventually printed with Stow's *Annales*, adduces among London's claims to be considered a university city that dramatic poetry is "lively expressed and represented" there, and that in his own office the art of revels "hath a setled place within this Cittie."[25]

[24] By J. Cocke; reprinted in *The Elizabethan Stage*, 4, Appendix C:256.

[25] Stow, chaps. 38, p. 1082, and 47, p. 1086. These chapters treat "Of Poets and of Musicians" and "Of the Art of Revels."

VII

MICHAEL JAMIESON

Shakespeare's Celibate Stage

The Problem of Accommodation to the Boy-Actors in *As You Like It, Antony and Cleopatra,* and *The Winter's Tale*

> The Characters of Women, on former Theatres, were perform'd by Boys, or young Men of the most effeminate Aspect. And what Grace, or Master-strokes of Action can we conceive such ungain Hoydens to have been capable of? This Defect was so well consider'd by *Shakespear*, that in few of his Plays, he has any greater Dependance upon the Ladies, than in the Innocence and Simplicity of a *Desdemona*, an *Ophelia*, or in the short Specimen of a fond and virtuous *Portia*.
>
> Colley Cibber,
> *An Apology for the Life of Mr. Colley Cibber, Comedian*

> Much could be said for the restoring of the celibate stage; but the argument, one fears, would be academic.
>
> Harley Granville-Barker,
> *Prefaces to Shakespeare*

A discussion like the present one, which is concerned less with literary values than with stage practice, has to be conjectural in its method and tentative in its conclusion. The theatre is—notoriously—ephemeral, a fact on which certain of its chroniclers and remembrancers have improvised that slow, sad, eschatological music which is typified by these generalizations of Maurice Baring's:

> The actor's art dies with him; but the rumour of it, when it is very great, lives on the tongue and sometimes in the soul of

From *Papers Mainly Shakespearian* Collected by G. I. Duthie. Published by the University of Aberdeen (Edinburgh and London, 1964). Reprinted by permission of the author and the University of Aberdeen.

man, and forms a part of his dreams and of his visions. The great of old still rule our spirits from their urns. . . .[1]

The most enduring monuments, the most astounding miracles of beauty achieved by the art and craft of man, are but as flotsam, drifting for a little while upon the stream of Time; and with it now there is a strange russet leaf, the name of Sarah Bernhardt.[2]

The art of the Elizabethan boy-actresses, unlike that of Bernhardt, may not have been "very great," and the rumours which have been preserved, both of their art and of their lives, are confused and scanty. My purpose is to discuss the effects, as far as they are still discoverable, which the enforced presence of boy-actresses in the Lord Chamberlain's/King's Men had on Shakespeare's presentation of women in three plays—*As You Like It, Antony and Cleopatra* and *The Winter's Tale*. I am not concerned with the child-actors, who played *all* the parts—boys, women, and old men[3]—in such companies as the Children of the Chapel, but with those few boys in the adult companies who specialized in women's parts and for whom Granville-Barker coined the useful term "the boy-actress."[4] To speak at this stage of Shakespeare's "accommodation" to the boy-actress would be to beg the question, and I make no such initial assumption. What my approach does assume—and it is no longer revolutionary[5]—is that William Shakespeare, as house-

[1] Maurice Baring, *The Puppet Show of Memory* (London, 1922), p. 227.

[2] Maurice Baring, *Punch and Judy* (London, 1924), p. 42.

[3] Hence the image of the Parcae's mistake in Ben Jonson's epitaph for the thirteen-year-old Salomon or Solomon Pavy who "acted old men so truly" that he was carried off long before his time. See Epigram CXX reprinted by C. H. Herford and Percy and Evelyn Simpson in *Ben Jonson* (Oxford, 1925–52), vol. 7, p. 77. This should not be taken to mean that boys ever played old men *in the adult companies*. See note 10, below.

[4] Harley Granville-Barker, *Prefaces to Shakespeare*, 1st ser. (London, 1927), p. xxvii.

[5] See, for instance, the "placing" of Shakespeare by G. E. Bentley: ". . . of all the swarm of Elizabethan dramatists who made the English theater great, Shakespeare is the one most intimately and continuously associated with actors and theaters. Actors were his professional colleagues and his daily associates." *The Swan of Avon and the Bricklayer of Westminster* (Princeton, 1946), p. 6. Or Professor J. Dover Wilson's declaration that Shakespeare wrote "not books but prompt-books, or, if you will,

keeper, company-sharer, actor, and dramatist-in-ordinary to his company, planned his plays with his fellow-actors constantly in mind for the parts he was writing, and that his views of their capabilities conditioned the parts as they survive today.

Plays are complex mechanisms, and a speech, a device, or a situation which seems, at first glance, to have a *theatrical* origin may, in fact, owe its existence to a literary tradition or may have been present already in Shakespeare's source. C. E. Montague, for instance, showed theatrical perception when he wrote:

> In the "seven ages" speech in *As You Like It* you see Shakespeare meeting the technical difficulty that Orlando has just gone off to fetch Adam, and that something or other must be done to give him time to reach Adam and come back; you see Shakespeare timing the action, watch in hand as it were . . .

So far, excellent; but Montague proceeded:

> and possibly giving man an extra age or two, lest Orlando and Adam should seem to come incredibly soon.[6]

These last words altogether overlook the fact that the Seven—not Five or Six—Ages of Man was a commonplace of medieval philosophy. In trying to discover what effects the presence of boy-actresses had on Shakespeare's presentation of his women, a critic has to be cautious. *As You Like It*, *Antony and Cleopatra*, and *The Winter's Tale* represent three Shakespearian *genres*, comedy, tragedy, and romance, and between them they give a wide range of Shakespearian women, but a further reason for selecting these plays is that each has a single and unusually full source in Thomas Lodge, Sir Thomas North, and Robert Greene, respectively. Shakespeare can thus be glimpsed in the process of adapting material for the stage, and one aspect of his dramaturgy, his presentation of women, can be studied in detail.

---

theatrical scores for the performance of moving pageants of speech, action, and colour, upon a particular stage by a particular troupe of actors for a particular audience." Quoted (without reference) by Allardyce Nicoll, "Studies in the Elizabethan Stage since 1900," *Shakespeare Survey*, vol. 1 (Cambridge, 1948), p. 13.

[6] *A Writer's Notes On His Trade* (London, 1930), pp. 229–30.

It would be possible to proceed directly to the three plays and make (rash) deductions about the boy-actress from them, but, mindful of Miss Bradbrook's warning that "there is little that can be directly inferred from the plays about the style of acting at the Globe,"[7] I find it necessary to decide, at some length, from slight contemporary references, quaint rumours, and sound scholarship, just which assumptions can legitimately be held about the boy-actress as the only solid basis for further deductions from the text.

I

What assumptions are we justified in making about the qualities of the boy-actresses who played Shakespeare's women? One set of notions was uncompromisingly stated by Sir Sidney Lee who, in 1906, wrote:

> In Shakespeare's day boys or men took the part of women, and how characters like Lady Macbeth and Desdemona were adequately rendered by youths beggars belief. But renderings in such conditions proved popular and satisfactory. Such a fact seems convincing testimony, not to the ability of Elizabethan or Jacobean boys—the nature of boys is a pretty permanent factor in human society—but to the superior imaginative faculty of adult Elizabethan or Jacobean playgoers.[8]

The Toryism of this Boys-will-be-boys view was challenged by George Pierce Baker in these words:

> Much of the current wonder that Shakespeare's heroines could have been adequately represented by boys and youths vanishes if one knows the contemporary evidence as to their exceeding skill and realises how long, thorough, and varied the training of an Elizabethan actor could be.[9]

Certainly Professor Baker, by directing students to contemporary testimony, is more illuminating than is Mr. Ronald Watkins, when, in an attempt to be helpful, he remarks:

[7] M. C. Bradbrook, *Elizabethan Stage Conditions* (Cambridge, 1932), p. 105.

[8] Sidney Lee, *Shakespeare and the Modern Stage* (London, 1906), p. 19.

[9] George Pierce Baker, *The Development of Shakespeare as a Dramatist* (New York, 1907), pp. 56–57.

> Anyone who has seen *Poil de Carotte*, . . . *Shoe Shine* or *The Fallen Idol* will be ready to believe that the acting of the Globe boys was not the least moving part of the performance . . . ,[10]

a modern analogy which is false on at least five counts, since in these films (*a*) *young* boys were playing *boys of their own ages* within (*b*) a convention of realistic acting and in (*c*) a non-continuous performance later given continuity in a cutting-room, with (*d*) directors of genius—Duvivier, de Sica, Reed—constantly at their sides engaged in (*e*) the most mechanised and easily-faked medium of artistic expression. Filmgoers who imagined in 1948 that young Master Bobby Henrey was consciously acting in *The Fallen Idol* should consult his fond mother's record of Sir Carol Reed's directorial chicanery, *A Film Star in Belgravia*. In recent years schoolmaster-producers like Mr. Watkins and Mr. Guy Boas have published records[11] of their own successful productions of Shakespeare's plays with schoolboy casts, tacitly suggesting that these performances have more nearly recaptured Shakespearian acting conditions than those of the professional theatre. But it is one thing for a schoolboy Lady Macbeth to hold his own with a Macbeth from the Sixth Form, quite another for a trained boy-actress to play, on a weekly roster, the great women's roles of Shakespeare and of his fellow playwrights for the King's Men, professionally harnessed to a star-actor, Burbage, who was thirty-three[12]

[10] Ronald Watkins, *On Producing Shakespeare* (London, 1950), p. 165. Mr. Watkins's film-list also includes *Mädchen in Uniform*. I fail to see the present relevance of this drama of Freudian growing pains in a Potsdam school for the daughters of impoverished officers. Mr. Watkins's basic point is the ability of children to express strong emotions. He might, more happily, have cited H. N. Hillebrand's study *The Child Actors* (Urbana, 1926), which shows the prevalence *in Shakespeare's own day* of juvenile acting in pageants, royal progresses, pre-Reformation church rituals, grammar- and choir-schools, and boys' companies. It was on this long-established tradition of juvenile acting that the professional theatres drew, rather than on vague capacities to express emotion.

[11] Mr. Watkins described his production of *A Midsummer Night's Dream* (at Harrow) in *Moonlight at the Globe* (London, 1946); Guy Boas some surprising selections (e.g. *Troilus and Cressida*) for performance by the boys of the Sloane School, Chelsea, in *Shakespeare and the Young Actor* (London, 1955).

[12] Burbage's age is discussed by Thomas Whitfield Baldwin, *The Organization and Personnel of the Shakespearean Company* (Princeton, 1927), pp. 238–39.

when he created Macbeth in 1605–6 and who relinquished the part only at his early death. I do not mean to disparage school performances of Shakespeare, but I suspect that their real purpose is to broaden the children's interests rather than to enable the masters who direct the productions to make scholarly points. Occasionally, of course, a gifted boy may give a performance of Portia or Katherina which is striking enough to refute as jaundiced a view of juvenile acting as Sir Sidney Lee's. Of Master Laurence Olivier's performance as Kate in a school production of *The Taming of the Shrew* in 1922, when he was fifteen, Dame Ellen Terry wrote in her diary:

> This gives us an idea of what the boy-actors in Shakespeare's time were like, yet people assume they were clumsy hobbledehoys.[13]

In general, however, to accept the phenomenon of juvenile amateur acting as anything but a shaky analogy for Elizabethan practice would be to ignore the essential issues of long training, established acting style, and professional disciplines which are involved.

It is not only the attitude of boys to acting which has changed, but that of an audience to the notion of such acting, so that where, by some trick of stage history, professional boy-actresses made a late survival, the Elizabethan attitude could never be recaptured. In 1788 Goethe saw a performance in Italy of Goldoni's *La Locandiera* in which men played the women's parts. Professor Nagler, in reprinting his reactions, suggests an analogy with the responses of Shakespeare's audience:

> After the initial strangeness had disappeared, Goethe experienced the unique aesthetic pleasure which Elizabethan playgoers must have felt when they watched boys playing Juliet and Cressida.[14]

It is significant, however, that the performance prompted Goethe to this philosophical discussion on the nature of theatrical illusion:

[13] *Ellen Terry's Memoirs*, ed. by Edith Craig and Christopher St. John (New York, 1932), p. 326.

[14] A. M. Nagler, *Sources of Theatrical History* (New York, 1952), p. 433.

I found [at the Roman comedies] a pleasure to which I had hitherto been a stranger . . . in the particular kind of representation we witnessed, the idea of imitation, the thought of art was called forth vividly, and . . . only a kind of self-conscious illusion was produced.

We . . . experience a double charm from the fact that these people are not women, but play the part of women. We see a youth who has studied the idiosyncrasies of the female sex in their character and behaviour; he has learned to know them, and reproduces them as an artist; he plays not himself, but a third, and in truth, a foreign nature.[15]

The performance *was* analogous to an Elizabethan one, but Goethe's attitude was sophisticated; he was over-conscious of "the thought of art." What he enjoyed was akin to the Brechtian alienation-effect. That "initial strangeness" differentiates him from the Elizabethans; and one wonders if what worked for comedy would, in Goethe's late day, have worked for tragedy also.

The Elizabethan practice of casting boys in women's parts was a theatrical convention like any other; more serious, for instance, than that of British pantomime, where the Principal Boy is a strapping and obvious girl and the Dame is a red-nosed comedian in skirts, less rigid and rarefied than the dynastic mysteries of female impersonation practised by gentlemen of Peking like Mr. Mei Lan-fang. The measure of a convention is that it goes unquestioned, so that Thomas Coryat recorded the shock, both moral and aesthetic, of seeing this convention shattered by foreigners. Of a Venetian theatre visit of 1608, he wrote:

Here I observed certaine things that I never saw before. For I saw women acte, a thing that I never saw before, . . . and they performed it with as good a grace, action, gesture, and whatsoever convenient for a Player, as ever I saw any masculine Actor.[16]

Coryat seemed quite content with the way things were ordered in England: his highest praise of Italian actresses is that they

[15] From *Goethe's Travels in Italy*, trans. Charles Nisbeth (London, 1883), pp. 569–70. Reprinted by Nagler, pp. 433–34.

[16] *Coryat's Crudities* (London, 1611), p. 247, new ed., 2 vols. (Glasgow, 1905), 1:386.

were as good as English boys. This impression of the quality of Shakespeare's boy-actresses is reinforced by such stray allusions as Ingine's speech in *The Devil is an Ass*[17] in which he mentions the boy Richard Robinson passing as a woman at a gossips' feast,[18] but critical comments on boy-actresses came at a later, better-documented period of stage history. In two passages Pepys refers to female impersonations by the last of the boy-actresses, Edward Kynaston (born 1640?),[19] the only boy-actress whose portrait survives:[20]

(*a*) *August 18, 1660*. [Saw] "The Loyall Subject," where one Kinaston, a boy, acted the Duke's sister, but made the loveliest lady that ever I saw in my life, *only her voice not very good.*[21]

(Some scholars who have reproduced this passage have omitted the last six words to avoid the question of Kynaston's poor voice, but by Miss McAfee's reckoning, Kynaston, whose training in the clandestine theatricals of the interregnum must have been spasmodic, would have been around twenty by this time, and, in more normal circumstances, would have graduated from women's parts by then. There is no reason for supposing Elizabethan boy-actresses' voices were poor, or that they habitually acted women's roles once their voices had broken. Hamlet and the players threatened by the Closing of the Theatres knew the value of a boy-actress's voice.)

(*b*) *January 7, 1660–61*. Among other things here [in *The Silent Woman*], Kinaston, the boy, had the good turn to appear

[17] Ben Jonson, *The Divell is an Asse*, II, 8, Herford-Simpson, *Ben Jonson*, 6:208.

[18] Professor Harbage mentions that Robinson could "pass as a woman off the stage," and adds the warning "but notice this is off the stage *on the stage.*" Alfred Harbage, "Elizabethan Acting," *PMLA*, 54 (1939):691, n. 15. The paper is reprinted in *Theatre for Shakespeare* (Toronto, 1955).

[19] Conjectural date by Helen McAfee, *Pepys on the Restoration Stage* (New Haven, 1916), p. 225.

[20] Mezz. pl., engraved by R. B. Parkes after R. Cooper, to Colley Cibber's *Apology*, 7th ed., ed. Lowe, 2 vols. (London, 1889), vol. 1, facing p. 122. Reproduced by W. Robertson Davies, *Shakespeare's Boy Actors* (London, 1939).

[21] McAfee, p. 225. Italics added.

in three shapes: first, as a poor woman in ordinary clothes, to please Morose; then in fine clothes as a gallant, and in them was clearly the prettiest woman in the whole house, and lastly, as a man; and then likewise did appear the handsomest man in the house.[22]

Praise of Kynaston appears more authoritatively in a passage by John Downes in which that retired prompter attributes "several," and by name four, women's parts to Kynaston who (he adds):

. . . being then very Young made a Compleat Female Stage Beauty, performing his Parts so well, especially *Arthiope* and *Aglaura*, being Parts greatly moving Compassion and Pity; that it has since been Disputable among the Judicious, whether any Woman that succeeded him so Sensibly touch'd the Audience as he.[23]

It is tempting to take at face value a passage from a play of 1676 which contains the line "Besides I can never endure to see Plays since Women came on the Stage; Boys are better by half,"[24] but, in the context of the play,[25] it is clear that the speaker Snarl (an "old pettish fellow, a great Admirer of the last Age and A Declaimer against the Vices of this, and privately very vicious himself") is a fault-finding hypocrite whose nostalgia is meant to carry no critical weight.

There is one kind of contemporary evidence which suggests that the Jacobean boy-actresses were effeminate. Puritan pamphleteers unleashed unambiguous accusations of homosexual re-

---

[22] McAfee, p. 225. But the part of Epicene makes this case of female impersonation a special one, a point well made in a letter to *The Times* of 22 February 1909, reprinted—and attributed to William Poel—by the editors of the Oxford *Ben Jonson*, 9:220, in which the correspondent [Poel?] insists that "the essential thing is that the principal female character must be played by a boy or youth."

[23] John Downes, *Roscius Anglicanus* (London, 1708); new ed., ed. Montague Summers (London, n.d.), p. 19.

[24] Thomas Shadwell, *The Virtuoso, a comedy acted at the Duke of York's Theatre* (London, 1676), Act I (p. 16). Reprinted, for biographical purposes, by Professor Bentley, *The Jacobean and Caroline Stage* (Oxford, 1941), 2:588, where, of course, no theatrical inference is drawn.

[25] *Ibid.*, "Drammatis Personae," B 4ᵛ. See also Albert S. Borgman, *Thomas Shadwell: His Life and Comedies* (New York, 1928), pp. 163–64.

lations between the boys and the adult players,[26] but gossip, to be credited, must have proven grounds, and such hysterical statements by Zeal-of-the-Land Busies cannot be checked at this date.

What we know of the organization and training of Elizabethan boy-actresses is sufficient to indicate that Kynaston was no solitary phenomenon. Boys joined the company under arrangements analogous to apprenticeship[27] from the age of ten upward;[28] they probably played first children's, then women's parts; each was boarded out with a company-sharer or hired-man who was responsible for the boy's further training.[29] Thus, although the acting life of each boy-actress must have been relatively short,[30] each was highly trained in speech, movement, music (if he had a voice), and in such arts as fencing which would equip him for an adult career, should he prove worthy, in his company. The stiff, brocaded, highly decorous costume of the Elizabethan lady may have contributed to successful female impersonation, but boy-actresses also had to play less decorously clad women like Doll Tearsheet and Dol Common. This is not the place to review scholarly debate on the nature of Elizabethan acting. The Elizabethans freely mingled extreme conventionalism and extreme realism in dramatic writing. Doubtless they did so in their acting, though it is safe to say that Elizabethan acting would seem formal by present-day

[26] Passages from Philip Stubbs, Stephen Gosson and William Prynne are reprinted, and inconclusively discussed, by Davies, *Shakespeare's Boy Actors*, pp. 9–18.

[27] Professor Baldwin in *Organization and Personnel*, pp. 32–33, argued that the boys "would be taken under the provision of the apprentice law . . . (5 Eliz. c. 4)," but ignores the fact that, as there was no actors' guild, legal apprenticeship was impossible.

[28] Baldwin, p. 35, leaned heavily towards ten as the entering age (which would square with his notions of an *actual* apprenticeship) but confessed that ". . . of eight *fairly* definite cases *one* apprentice entered at ten and five others *almost certainly* did; all were certainly taken *before they were thirteen*." My italics emphasize the vagueness of the evidence Baldwin brought to his thesis.

[29] Talk of master and boy survives in Wright's *Historia Histrionica* of 1699 in which Truman speaks of Hart as "Robinson's Boy or Apprentice." Reprinted by Bentley, *Jacobean and Caroline Stage*, 2:692.

[30] See Hamlet's speech and *The Actors Remonstrance*, quoted p. 80.

standards. Indeed Professor Harbage has found in the success of the boy-actresses a further clue to Elizabethan acting style:

> My explanation of the apparent adequacy of the Elizabethan boy-actor is simply *formal acting*.[31]

The qualities Coryat commended in the British boy-actresses —*grace, action, gesture and whatsoever* [is] *convenient for a player*[32]—may seem odd alongside truth to life, spontaneity, conviction, or the concepts of Stanislavski or Mr. Lee Strasberg, but they were probably among the criteria by which Shakespeare's boy-actresses were judged in the parts he wrote for them. Shakespeare's one revealing comment on the problem of the boy-actress's short career, Hamlet's lines—

> What, my yong Lady and Misstris? Byrlady your Ladiship is neerer Heauen then when I saw you last, by the altitude of a Choppine. Pray God your voice like a peece of vncurrant Gold be not crack'd within the ring[33]—

chime exactly and sympathetically with the old stagers' professional concern voiced, at the time of the Closing of the Theaters, in *The Actors Remonstrance:*

> Our boyes, ere wee shalle have libertie to act againe, will be growne out of use, like crackt organ-pipes and have faces as old as our flags.[34]

[31] Harbage (n. 18 above), p. 703. The case for extremely formal acting has been put by B. L. Joseph in *Elizabethan Acting* (London, 1951) and elsewhere. For a rebuttal of Joseph see J. F. Kermode in *Review of English Studies*, n.s., 4 (1953):70–73. See also S. L. Bethell, "Shakespeare's Actors," *Review of English Studies*, n.s., 1 (1950):193–205; R. A. Foakes, "The Player's Passion: Elizabethan Psychology and Acting," *Essays and Studies*, n.s., 7 (1954):62–77; A. M. Nagler, *Shakespeare's Stage* (New Haven, 1958); Marvin Rosenberg, "Elizabethan Actors: Men or Marionettes?" *PMLA*, 69 (1954):915–27. (A lecture-demonstration by Dr. Joseph and a band of players who visited the University of Sussex with him on February 23, 1964, convinced me that I have misrepresented his views above, or that he has modified them. See the new edition of *Elizabethan Acting* [1964].)

[32] Coryat, quoted p. 76.

[33] *Hamlet*, II, 2:444–49. Oo 4. Act, scene and line references are to G. L. Kittredge's one-volume edition (Boston, 1936). Signatures refer to the First Folio, against which spelling has been checked.

[34] *The Actors Remonstrance, or Complaint for the silencing of their profession* (London, 1643). Reprinted by W. C. Hazlitt, *The English*

In the three plays themselves, the basis for deciding the questions of Shakespeare's accommodation to his juvenile interpreters must be this image of the boy-actress as a youthful, highly trained, assured, and valuable performer, who, in stature and still-unbroken voice, would contrast effectively with the adult members of the Shakespearian company.

II

Of the three plays *The Winter's Tale* makes the simplest demands of the boy-actresses and, disregarding chronology, I take this late play first. The play has one star part, Leontes, whose 682 lines[35] went possibly to Burbage, and a group of important subsidiary roles, three of which, Paulina (325), Hermione (207), Perdita (128), required boy-actresses. The divided action of the play made doubling peculiarly feasible. Mamillius and the ladies of the court could be doubled with Mopsa, Dorcas, and other shepherdesses; it is possible that Mamillius and Perdita, in the interests of a family likeness, were played by one boy, and that the boys who played Hermione and Paulina "walked on" as shepherdesses in the sheepshearing interlude. Thus the play met the basic requirement of the King's Men—it did not tax the numerical strength of their boy-actresses.[36] Of the important characters not in Greene's novel[37]—Antigonus, the Young Shepherd, Autolycus, Paulina—only one is a woman, and this new character was not a dramatic indulgence on Shakespeare's part, but the second character in the play and the one through whom Shakespeare effected and made credible the one significant deviation from his source, the resurrection of Hermione from cold storage which closes the play.

The *genre* to which this work belongs was indicated by John

Drama and Stage under the Tudor and Stuart Princes 1543–1664 (London, 1869), p. 263.

[35] The figures throughout are from Professor Baldwin's tables, *Organization and Personnel*, between pp. 228 and 229.

[36] "From three to five boys would normally have been sufficient for the female parts." E. K. Chambers, *William Shakespeare: A Study of Facts and Problems* (Oxford, 1930), 1:82.

[37] *Pandosto. The Triumphe of Time* (London, 1588). Reprinted, *New Variorum Edition* (Philadelphia, 1898), pp. 324–52.

Donne, who once spoke in a sermon of the Book of Job as "a representation of God in a Tragique-Comedy, *lamentable beginnings comfortably ended*."[38] Shakespeare, by plunging straight into such lamentable beginnings, seems to have required of the boy-actress playing Hermione the simplest effects, which—on a stage dominated by the insanely jealous Leontes—would have been the more telling in dignity and calm:

> I must be patient, till the Heauens looke
> With an aspect more fauorable. Good my Lords,
> I am not prone to weeping (as our Sex
> Commonly are) . . .[39]

a speech which would have helped the boy-actress unemphatically to establish Hermione's womanliness. The hobbledehoy theory[40] is belied by Hermione's advanced pregnancy which (though Elizabethan costume might preclude its representation) is graphically pointed out by Leontes:

> . . . and let her sport her selfe
> With that shee's big-with, for 'tis *Polixenes*
> Ha's made thee swell thus,[41]

in lines which would have defeated an inadequate boy-actress. All that is asked of Hermione in the Trial is ringing sincerity ("Sir,/You speake a Language that I vnderstand not":[42]) and a spectacular faint at the news of Mamillius' death. She does not reappear until, in the play's "comfortable ending," the boy-actress, made up as an older woman and splendidly dressed, was ceremonially revealed in a statuesque silent pose well within his abilities.

The part of Paulina, that female Kent, is spiritedly conceived along outspoken lines. Her function is primarily that of observer, commentator, and critic. It is Paulina who opposes Leontes, who refuses to be silenced:

> *Pau.* Let him that makes but trifles of his eyes
> First hand me . . .[43]

---

[38] Sermon VII, St. Paul's, Christmas Day 1629. *Complete Poetry and Selected Prose*, ed. John Hayward (London, 1929), p. 592.

[39] II, 1:106–9; Aa 3ᵛ.

[40] See n. 13 above.

[41] II, 1:60–62; Aa 3ᵛ.

[42] III, 2:80–81; Aa 6.

[43] II, 3:62–63; Aa 4ᵛ.

who too accusingly announces Hermione's death ("Alas, I haue shew'd too much/The rashnesse of a woman: He is toucht/To th' Noble heart"[44]), who brings the king to repentance, and who, in a double sense, stage-manages the ceremonial reconciliation:

> *Pau.* Musick; awake her: Strike:
> 'Tis time: descend: be Stone no more: approach:
> Strike all that looke vpon with meruaile,[45]

an invocation which demands impressive delivery by the boy-actress, just as her would-be exit line demands graciousness:

> ...I (an old Turtle)
> Will wing me to some wither'd bough, and there
> My Mate (that's neuer to be found againe)
> Lament, till I am lost.[46]

Paulina, despite her occasional shrewishness and even violence, personifies loyalty and commonsense, and the part would have fitted the capacities of a boy.

Perdita, the play's romantic heroine, is no realistic shepherdess. She makes a late and highly formal entrance, symbolically dressed as the goddess of flowers and fertility, to this accompanying speech of Florizel's:

> *Flo.* These your vnvsuall weeds, to each part of you
> Do's giue a life: no Sheperdesse but *Flora*
> Peering in Aprils front.[47]

The love-plot is presented, not through amorous action, but in such poetry as this transfiguration of the original meeting in the novel:[48]

> *Flo.* I blesse the time
> When my good Falcon, made her flight a-crosse
> Thy Fathers ground.[49]

---

[44] III, 2:221–23; Aa 6ᵛ.

[45] V, 3:98–100; Cc 1ᵛ.

[46] V, 3:132–35; Cc 2.

[47] IV, 4:1–3; Bb 2.

[48] "...Dorastus (who all that daye had bene hawking ...)" *Variorum*, p. 339.

[49] IV, 4:14–16; Bb 2.

or Florizel's:

> When you do dance, I wish you
> A waue o' the Sea, that you might euer do
> Nothing but that.[50]

Perdita's formal distribution of the flowers is part of a design through which the flower-freshness of the heroine is suggested. Here, as so often in Shakespeare, the verse when well-spoken does its own work upon an audience, and a trained boy-actress would have paired well here with an older boy as Florizel.

In Bohemia, Perdita and Florizel dominate the serious action. In the reconciliations and recoveries of the final act Perdita is mostly silent and an onlooker (which explains how a nineteenth-century stage beauty contrived to play Hermione *and* Perdita, with a stand-in for Act V), while Paulina controls and directs the scene in which the statue of Hermione warms to life.

Shakespeare's presentation of this trio of women, the two mature ladies of the court and the foundling-princess, accords well with the conventional assumptions of vivacity, skill, and subordination to an adult male player which are made about Shakespeare's boy-actresses.

III

A reading of *As You Like It*, however, forces a reconsideration of this conception of the boy-actress's task as subordinate (*a*) because in Rosalind Shakespeare gave the boy-actress twice as many lines (747)[51] as any other character in the play, and made the part, moreover, twice as long as that of Viola, and markedly longer than either Macbeth (704) or Prospero (665); and (*b*) because the virtuosity of Rosalind's two-fold impersonation within the play seems to have assumed a virtuosity in the original boy-actress.

Rosalind and Celia belong, with Portia and Nerissa, Beatrice and Hero, Viola and Olivia, to a series of paired heroines in which the first, the taller, takes the initiative while the second is placid and conventional. The text of *As You Like It*, follow-

[50] IV, 4:140–42; Bb 2ᵛ.

[51] Baldwin's figures, between pp. 228 and 229.

ing Lodge's novel,[52] confirms this physical contrast, on which indeed, is based the disguise—the woman as page—which Rosalind adopts for most of the play's action:

> *Ros.* Were it not better,
> Because that I am more then common tall,
> That I did suite me all points like a man . . .[53]

This led Granville-Barker to point out what has become a cliché in discussions of this play, that "through three-parts of the play a boy [as opposed to a modern actress] would have the best of it."[54] This judgment I accept with considerable reserve. If, as commentators more ingenious than Barker imply, Shakespeare's frequent recourse to this device of disguise was dictated by a need to put at ease his inadequate boy-actress (whose daily business, I would object, was female impersonation), how was the boy-actress first to impose himself on the audience as a great lady? Certainly a boy Rosalind would have made a more credible Ganymede and have justified Phoebe's infatuation, but Shakespeare did not use this device for purposes of credibility. Rosalind's essential femininity is revealed through (not in spite of) this disguise with such delicacy and dramatic skill that, in his fully documented examination of forty contemporary English plays containing the female page, Dr. Freeburg did not seem to find a subtler exploitation of this then-

[52] *Rosalynde. Euphues golden legacie* (London, 1590). Reprinted, *New Variorum Edition* (Philadelphia, 1890), pp. 317–87.

[53] I, 3:116–18; Q 5. All other references to Rosalind's height agree with this, except one line of Le Beau's (I, 2:283; Q 4ᵛ) in which Celia is described: "But yet indeede the taller is his daughter." This has led Professor Dover Wilson to argue in the New Cambridge edition of the play (Cambridge, 1926), p. 103, that in the first performances Rosalind was played "by a short boy, shorter than the boy who played Celia" but that, in the later performances for which the text (as we have it) had been revised, Rosalind was played by a much taller boy—or by the same boy grown taller. The one word "taller," which is a likely printer's error for "smaller," hardly warrants such a theory—particularly as Rosalind's height is emphasized by Lodge: "I (thou seest) am of a tall stature, and would very well become the person and apparell of a page . . ." *Variorum*, p. 331—but Professor Wilson's theory usefully reminds us that, even in Shakespeare's lifetime, a succession of boys must have played these parts in the stock company of the King's Men.

[54] *Prefaces*, 1st ser., p. xxvii.

prevalent device.[55] Shakespeare and the boy-actress had therefore a technical problem which no woman Rosalind would have, for, the moment an audience accepts Ganymede *as a boy*, instead of as a credibly disguised woman, the drily romantic irony of Rosalind's scenes with Orlando evaporates. A convention of fairly formal acting and the unquestioning acceptance of the boy-actress (by which a regular playgoer could presumably say to himself "That's the woman" just as, looking at Kempe, he could say "That's the funny man") made this evaporation less likely, but, once Rosalind was disguised, Shakespeare's concern was constantly to stress that femininity breaks through Rosalind's strident (and on the Elizabethan stage possibly *too* manly) pose.

This femininity Shakespeare stressed in three ways. First, he made a comic theatrical point of Rosalind's falling short of that pose in such speeches as this:

> *Ros.* I could finde in my heart to disgrace my mans apparell, and to cry like a woman: but I must comfort the weaker vessell, as doublet and hose ought to show it selfe coragious to pettycoate; therefore courage, good *Aliena*.[56]

Or the dialogue following Rosalind's faint at the sight of the napkin stained with Orlando's blood:

> *Oli.* Be of good cheere youth: you a man?
> You lacke a mans heart. . . .[57]
> Well then, take a good heart, and counterfeit to be a man.
> *Ros.* So I doe: but yfaith, I should haue beene a woman by
> right.[58]

Secondly, Shakespeare fully exploited the passive Celia as confidante—Rosalind's scenes with her are revealingly girlish, and in them she constantly speaks of herself *as a woman*:

> . . . dost thou think though I am caparison'd like a man, I haue a doublet and hose in my disposition?[59]

[55] Victor Oscar Freeburg, *Disguise Plots in Elizabethan Drama* (New York, 1915), pp. 98–99.

[56] II, 4:4–8; Q 6.   [58] IV, 3:174–77; R 6.

[57] IV, 3:164–65; R 6.   [59] III, 2:204–6; R 2ᵛ.

Later in this scene Rosalind, on learning of Orlando's presence, stresses her assumed boy's clothes four times in some seventy lines of the First Folio text:

(*a*) *Ros.* Alas the day, what shall I do with my doublet & hose?[60]
(*b*) *Ros.* But doth he know that I am in this Forrest, and in man's apparrell?[61]
(*c*) *Ros.* Do you not know I am a woman, when I thinke, I must speake.[62]
(*d*) *Ros.* I wil speake to him like a a sawcie Lacky, and vnder that habit play the knaue with him.[63]

And after the mock love-scenes, it is to Celia that Rosalind's genuine involvement is revealed in the excited and infectious speech:

Ros. O coz, coz, coz: my pretty little coz, that thou didst know how many fathome deepe I am in loue: but it cannot bee sounded . . .[64]

Thirdly, the essentially feminine Rosalind was depicted in those scenes with Orlando in which the complex *theatrical* situation was that of a boy-actress playing a girl, Rosalind, who, while disguised as a boy, Ganymede, openly mimics herself in his character. Shakespeare at the outset cunningly suggested to his audience the close association of boys and women ("for the most part, cattle of this colour"[65]) and contrived to show both Ganymede's impersonation of Rosalind and the real woman:

Orl. But will my *Rosalind* doe so?
Ros. By my life, she will doe as I doe.[66]

A Bradleian critic would argue (rightly) that such glimpses of the female in the male as Rosalind's faint are psychologically true. They are also, in the acted context of the play, theatrically necessary. They represent a conscious, and successful, attempt by Shakespeare to ensure that Rosalind's virtuosity steadily advances the play's romantic action. In scenes of comedy, con-

[60] III, 2:231–32; R 2ᵛ.
[61] III, 2:242–43; R 2ᵛ.
[62] III, 2:263–64; R 2ᵛ.
[63] III, 2:313–15; R 3.
[64] IV, 1:209–11; R 5ᵛ.
[65] III, 3:434–35; R 3.
[66] IV, 1:158–59; R 5.

fidences, and unorthodox courtship, Shakespeare anticipated, and compensated for, a boy's shortcomings and, by exploiting his advantages, planned the part so that it could be played by a boy and yet not lose its womanliness. The other women in this play are conventional and minor characters, but of all the Shakespearian women who disguise as pages, Rosalind, more than Viola, more than Imogen, more even that Portia, is Shakespeare's gesture of faith in the boy-actress. What happens at the end of *As You Like It* confirms this view. Nothing comparable happens elsewhere in Shakespeare; and I do not recall parallels in other plays of the period. The play ends on a daring break with tradition, as Rosalind comes forward:

> *Ros.* It is not the fashion to see the Ladie the Epilogue: but it is no more vnhandsome, then to see the Lord the Prologue.

And her farewell to the audience reveals that essential pretence on which all boy-actresses' performances were based:

> *If I were a Woman,* I would kisse as many of you as had beards that pleas'd me, complexions that lik'd me, and breaths that I defi'de not: And I am sure, as many as have good beards, or good faces, or sweet breaths, will for my kind offer, when I make curt'sie, bid me farewell. *Exit.*[67]

It is the cue for the boy-actress, as star of this comedy, to take a solo "curtain."

IV

If depicting Rosalind in terms of the boy-actress's ability was a challenge to Shakespeare, what of Cleopatra? His handling of this great part might itself be the subject of a single paper. Once more there is the simple problem of sheer length—Cleopatra's 670 lines come second only to Antony's 813, which makes her part formidable, but the disposition of the scenes makes the part more demanding than is Antony's since (*a*) within the divided worlds of Rome and Egypt Cleopatra has no physical part in the Roman scenes, and (*b*) once Antony is dead, the whole of Act V with the great climax of the play's ending—the high-water mark of Shakespeare's dramatic poetry —had to be borne by the boy-actress alone, a signal assumption

[67] [Epilogue] 1–3 and 19–25; S2. Italics added.

of authority in that unknown player. Yet critics have expressed their amazement, not at the theatrical assumptions which lie behind such apportioning and emphasis, but at the very idea that *any* boy-actress *ever* attempted the part. Sir Sidney Lee recorded his incensed feelings on this matter thus:

> *It seems almost sacrilegious* to conceive the part of Cleopatra, the most highly sensitised in its minutest details of all dramatic portrayals of female character,—*it seems almost sacrilegious* to submit Cleopatra's sublimity of passion to interpretation by an unfledged representative of the other sex.[68]

It was with overcoming prejudices such as these that Granville-Barker was concerned in that part of his preface in which he developed the following argument:

> Shakespeare's Cleopatra had to be acted by a boy, and this did everything to determine, *not his view of the character, but his presenting of it.*[69]

This antithesis of view and presentation is admirable, but, it seems to me, that Barker, who saw the play as "a tragedy of sex without one single scene of sexual appeal"[70] containing a maximum of three embraces, a play in which "the best evidence . . . of Cleopatra's physical charms" is "a description of them by . . . the misogynist Enobarbus—given us, moreover, at a time when she has been out of our sight for a quarter of an hour or so,"[71] took minimal account certainly of both the attested competence of boy-actresses and the formalism of their acting, and possibly also of Shakespeare's complex response to Plutarch.[72]

The part of Cleopatra, in variety of mood, makes exhausting demands on its interpreter. Even within the conventions of Elizabethan acting, the part must have demanded temperament

---

[68] Sidney Lee (n. 8 above), p. 42. Italics added.

[69] *Prefaces to Shakespeare,* 2d ser. (London, 1930), p. 203. Italics added.

[70] *Prefaces,* 1st ser., p. xxviii.

[71] *Prefaces,* 2d ser., p. 204.

[72] *Plutarch's Lives, translated out of French into English by Thomas North* (London, 1595). Abridged version of North's life of Antony, *New Variorum Edition* (Philadelphia, 1907), pp. 388–409.

in its performer. Cleopatra is not merely regal. She must be, by turns, ferocious ("Ile vnhaire thy head"[73]), bawdy ("I take no pleasure/In ought an Eunuch ha's"[74]), brilliantly malicious (the superb, instantaneous dismissal of Octavia as "dull of tongue, and dwarfish"[75]), utterly feminine in impulse ("If you finde him sad,/Say I am dauncing"[76]). She must both match Antony's "You haue been a boggeler euer"[77] and rise to the great keening speeches at his death:

> Oh wither'd is the Garland of the Warre,
> The Souldiers pole is falne: young Boyes and Gyrles
> Are leuell now with men: The oddes is gone,
> And there is nothing left remarkeable
> Beneath the visiting Moone.[78]

Cleopatra, as Granville-Barker has shown, is frequently presented through the speeches of others (notably Enobarbus), but, in overstating the inferences from this fact, Barker suggested, perhaps unconsciously, that *tact* is Shakespeare's most conspicuous accommodation in this play. If physical embraces were embarrassing—though it is impossible now to know what Burbage did on the words "the Noblenesse of life/Is to do thus . . ."[79]—how was a boy-actress expected to bring off the scene in which Cleopatra seems to smother the dying Antony in kisses:

> Dye when thou hast liu'd,
> Quicken with kissing: had my lippes that power,
> Thus would I weare them out.[80]

The boy-actress had to back up the poetic allusions to Cleopatra's allure ("this great Faiery"[81]) not contradict them. What Plutarch—or North—called Cleopatra's flickering enticement is suffused throughout the speeches of the play, as is Antony's god-like stature, in images which, with the persistence of a leitmotif in opera, raise the standing of Antony and Cleopatra as

[73] II, 5:64; [x]x 4ᵛ.
[74] I, 5:9–10; [x]x 2ᵛ.
[75] III, 3:19; [x]x 6ᵛ.
[76] I, 3:3–4; [x]x 1ᵛ.
[77] III, 13:110; [y]y 3.
[78] IV, 15:64–68; [y]y 6–6ᵛ.
[79] I, 1:36–37; vv 6ᵛ.
[80] IV, 15:38–40; [y]y 6.
[81] IV, 8:12; [y]y 4ᵛ.

persons tragically involved in the play's action. These allusions to the legendary Cleopatra are both a booster to the boy-actress and an indication of how greatly Shakespeare, engaged in the necessary compressions of dramatizing his source, was imaginatively stimulated by Plutarch. They are dramatically necessary because Cleopatra is uniquely incapable of a full representation on the stage, as Miss Tallulah Bankhead, Miss Vivien Leigh, Miss Katharine Hepburn, and other glamorous actresses have discovered in our own day, not because an embarrassed boy-actress was basically inadequate.

The inspired solo of the play's end reinforces this. Shakespeare clearly had great confidence in his boy-actress to have given him, in the deeply serious scene in which Cleopatra resolves on suicide, the daring lines:

> . . . and I shall see
> Some squeaking *Cleopatra* Boy my greatnesse
> I'th' posture of a Whore.[82]

While the psychology of the Elizabethan playgoer was such that the boy-actresses were accepted without question, this deliberate reminder, which has no precedent in Plutarch, would, on the lips of an inadequate or awkward boy, be a fatal preparation for the ceremony of purification which follows:

> I am Fire, and Ayre; my other Elements
> I giue to baser life.[83]

And how (to overstate the case) could a blushing, embarrassed, flat-chested boy carry that penultimate speech:

> *Cleo.* Peace, peace:
> Dost thou not see my Baby at my breast,
> That suckes the Nurse asleepe.[84]

Shakespeare used devices of imagery and rhetoric in an essentially dramatic way, seizing on every suggestion he found in Plutarch, to make Cleopatra playable on the Jacobean stage, but, in accommodating himself to the boy-actress, he did not sacrifice a single emotional effect.

[82] V, 2:219–21; zz 1ᵛ.

[83] V, 2:292–93; zz 2.   [84] V, 2:311–13; zz 2.

V

Shakespeare's texts, as they survive, are a guide to his theatrical intentions and to the artistic effects which were available to him, but playscripts, especially those in which stage-directions are few, can be a tantalizingly incomplete record of the original performances. A discussion like the present one is really concerned not only with what Shakespeare did as a writer, but what he did as a producer also—not only with the words he gave the actors of his company (over whom he had, for a dramatist, special authority) but with how he wanted them to speak, to move, to express emotion. Since our knowledge of the Elizabethan theatre, and of techniques of acting and of presentation there, is incomplete and based in part on conjecture, conclusions have to be tentative. What effects, then, of the presence of the boy-actress are still discernible in the women's parts as they survive today?

These three plays do not give a fully representative cross-section of Shakespearian women, but a reading of them allows some valid generalization on the question of accommodation to the boy-actress. Shakespeare kept his cast of women small. He often planned women's parts to be brief also, less because his boy-actresses were inadequate than because the whole drift of Elizabethan drama, particularly in the history plays which were Shakespeare's dramatic apprenticeship, was virile. Ophelia and Lady Macbeth are supporting parts, not in accommodation to the boy-actress, nor even in deference to Burbage, but in accordance with Saxo-Grammaticus who was concerned with Hamlet and with Holinshed whose theme was Macbeth. It is true that there are aspects of female character which Shakespeare did not ask his boy-actresses to explore, but I cannot agree with Miss Margaret Webster who believes:

> It is easy to see *what Shakespeare refrained from doing* because of this limitation [the boy-actress], if such he considered it, but not so easy to define what *positive* effect it had on the great women's parts.[85]

[85] Margaret Webster, *Shakespeare Without Tears* (New York, 1942), p. 93.

The first part seems dangerously mistaken, because no one can ever know why Shakespeare chose *not* to do the things he did not do, or even that the question of choice arose. The lesson of *Antony and Cleopatra* is that when Shakespeare decided to tackle a tragedy of sexual infatuation, he achieved his aim within the capabilities of the boy-actress. It is difficult to define the positive effects of the boy-actress's presence, because a particular play so often shatters our limiting assumptions, but chief among these positive effects in the depiction of *young* women is an exploitation of the boy-actress's natural qualities of youth. In comedy, where Rosalind is the exemplar, Shakespeare drew on the boy's resources of gaiety, impudence, high spirits, fresh, ringing tones and youthful self-confidence and swagger. In tragedy or romance (Perdita is an incomplete example) he drew on complementary resources of innocence, openness of disposition, and an elusive selflessness. Such an explanation of the character of these women has been condemned by Professor Stoll as too mechanistic and materialistic;[86] it is not meant as a complete explanation.

Each of the women's parts, particularly the unconventional ones (which are never the first that the generic term "Shakespearian Women," with its feminist overtones of Mrs. Jameson, brings to mind), posed its own problems in technique, exposition and accommodation, but the inference from Rosalind and Cleopatra is that once Shakespeare was aware what problems the boy-actress would have to face, his view of the character remained unaltered and he denied himself no single legitimate effect in presenting his great succession of women on the celibate stage.

[86] E. E. Stoll, *Shakespeare's Young Lovers* (London, 1937), p. 54.

VIII

MARVIN ROSENBERG

Elizabethan Actors: Men or Marionettes?

A good deal of critical energy has gone in recent years into the attempt to demonstrate that even the best Elizabethan actors were some kind of human marionettes.[1] Some twenty years ago Miss M. C. Bradbrook wrote: the "general consensus of opinion on Elizabethan acting" was this: "There would be comparatively little business, and gesture would be formalised. Conventional movement and heightened delivery would be necessary to carry off the dramatic illusion."[2] Since then various articles in learned journals and sections of scholarly books have

From *PMLA*, 69 (1954):915–27. Reprinted by permission of the author and of the Modern Language Association. The author comments: "Since the publication of this essay several of the scholars cited who took the formalist point of view have indicated their agreement with the attitude expressed here. Waldo McNeir did so in correspondence with me; Bertram Joseph in correspondence and in his book *The Tragic Actor* (London, 1959), and Alfred Harbage in a review (*Shakespeare Quarterly*, October, 1951, pp. 360–61). Mr. Harbage deserves special mention: he was one of the readers for *PMLA* when this essay was submitted, and though it then disagreed so clearly with his own view he passed it for publication. Scholarship is nourished on this kind of open-mindedness. Further support of the essay's point of view was published in a note in *PMLA*, vol. 71 (March, 1956) by David Klein, who quoted, from his extensive knowledge of the contemporary literature, several other references to 'natural' acting."

[1] Alfred Harbage was willing to call them puppets, "Elizabethan Actors," *PMLA*, 54 (September, 1939):703. Harbage has since altered some of his beliefs about Elizabethan acting, as will be noted. His 1939 arguments for formal acting are explored hereafter only when they represent opinions not known to be altered, or when they are representative of the formalist case generally. Harbage observed, in 1939, that Sir Edmund Chambers had left us, in the area of Elizabethan acting style, "a playground—one precinct free for untrammeled guessing" (p. 685). Harbage entered himself as a player in the "game," which I am happy to join.

[2] *Elizabethan Stage Conditions* (Cambridge, 1932), p. 109.

supported the "formalist" attitude, which now comes to this: that the Elizabethan dramatist's words were all that really counted, and that his actors were trained to be graceful, mannered mouthpieces who recited the dramatic poetry without letting their personalities or their personal ideas of the part played color the performance in any way; they acted formally, not naturally; they did not portray character, they symbolized it. Formalism has tended toward a rigid orthodoxy, although, as we shall see, one of the modern champions of the single style, Professor Harbage, seems to have moved away from his first strict view in the direction of a more liberal formalist attitude of the kind represented by S. L. Bethell. Bethell, frankly facing the rich and lively variety of the Elizabethan plays, noted scenes demanding something like "natural" treatment, and so he allowed a second, relaxed style subordinate to a conventional technique, or sometimes mixed with it. He also saw, as separate modes, the clowning, which he regarded as non-naturalistic, and the elements of vaudeville. But for the regular drama, he argued, "the poetry and its decent delivery were the only real essentials" and "I have no doubt that the formal manner of delivery was used." The depersonalized actors, Bethell felt, could have made no "addition of 'personality' or 'creativity' " to their lines; they let the lines tell what the character was, instead of trying to be the character.[3]

The orthodox formalist movement culminated in a 1951 book by B. L. Joseph, who writes: "In the theatre, as in the study, the poet's words are all that count. . . . We must be prepared to respond to Elizabethan drama in the same attitude of mind as we respond to opera or ballet before we can hope to criticize the dramatists' techniques justly . . . given two actors of equal talent, each would be able to perform the same speech in exactly the same way, apart from differences of voice and personal appearance."[4]

Now this is a kind of acting like nothing known in the available history of the later British theatre. Nothing there

[3] "Shakespeare's Actors," *RES*, n.s., 1 (July, 1950):193–205. Bethell says his reading of Joseph's MS before publication (see next note) convinced him that the Elizabethans used formal delivery (p. 202).

[4] *Elizabethan Acting* (London, 1951), pp. 123, 151–52, 153.

nourishes the conception of great actors as interchangeable as machine parts in character interpretation and in voluntary resignation of personality. Inevitably, the leading figures of the theatre have not only differed in style and personality and originality of interpretation; they have even gone out of their way to emphasize the differences, for the purposes of both artistic pride and commercial competition.[5] This striving toward uniqueness belongs to a great actor as much as it does to any artist. He has never been the passive instrument through which the playwright's score might be forever duplicated; his nature, and the nature of his art, have demanded that he contribute creatively to a play's dormant lines the dimensions of speech, movement, and emotion—"the soule of lively action" —that he uniquely could provide.[6] But the formalists ask us to believe that things were different in Elizabethan times, that men like Edward Alleyn and Richard Burbage, recognized as artists by their contemporaries, were willing, in an age of individualists, to extinguish their vanity and conform their great talents to stock acting patterns;[7] that they were, in fact, a different breed of man and artist from the great English actors who followed them. Let us consider the reasoning that led the formalists to these conclusions which history and present experience seem to invalidate.

The most significant single argument has been the supposed influence on Elizabethan drama of the "boy actor." Most of

[5] To give a single instance: Garrick, with his "new style," was unmistakably unlike old Quin; but we are told that he underlined the contrast by reintroducing the trance scene into his production of *Othello*, chiefly because his rival was too fat to perform it. See *Memoirs of the Life of Charles Macklin* (London, 1789), 2:260.

[6] Marston, in his preface to *The Malcontent*, wrote: "onely one thing afflicts me, to thinke that Scaenes invented, meerely to be spoken, should be inforcively published to be read. . . . but I shall intreate . . . that the unhansome shape which this trifle in reading presents, may be pardoned, for the pleasure it once afforded you, when it was presented with the soule of lively action."

[7] Harbage took the orthodox formalist view when he wrote, in a comment on J. Cocke's uncomplimentary "A Common Player" (1615), "Cocke's . . . word *common* means 'typical' and does not exempt such actors as Alleyn and Burbage, whose method—not skill—was probably quite typical" (Harbage, p. 687).

the modern believers in formalism[8] have concluded that Shakespeare could not hope to get naturalistic acting from the boys, and that therefore the acting of his time must have been either entirely or predominantly formal.

This is hardly fair to the actors who were good enough to play some of the tremendous women's roles of Shakespeare's day. First of all, they were not necessarily "boys." They were as likely to be young men, and are sometimes so referred to in legal documents of the time. Some were mature men. T. W. Baldwin mentions two actors playing women's parts in 1635 who must, from other figures he gives, have been between 24 and 28.[9] From post-Restoration theatre history we get further hints: Colley Cibber tells how Charles II complained of the lateness of a first curtain, only to be fairly told that "the queen had not shaved yet."[10] There was probably much jest, but not all jest, in the prologue spoken before the first appearance of an Englishwoman in *Othello* on the professional stage:

> For (to speak truth) men act, that are between
> Forty and fifty, Wenches of fifteen;
> With bone so large, and nerve so incomplyant,
> When you call *Desdemona*, enter Giant.[11]

We know, too, that these adult male actors of women's parts were artists in their own right.[12] We might guess this from

[8] See Bradbrook, p. 113; Harbage, pp. 702–3; Robert H. Bowers, "Gesticulation in Elizabethan Acting," *So. Folklore Quart.*, 12 (December, 1948):270; Bethell, p. 205; Ronald Watkins, *On Producing Shakespeare* (New York, 1950), pp. 168–69.

[9] *The Organization and Personnel of the Shakespearean Company* (Princeton, 1927), p. 36. They had been with Beeston at the Cockpit in 1621, and the usual starting age, according to Baldwin, was 10–14.

[10] *Apology for the Life of Colley Cibber* (New York, 1888), I, 179.

[11] Thomas Jordan, in *Shakespere Allusion Book* (London, 1909), II, 87.

[12] We have skilled actors playing women's parts excellently in furtive theatres in our major cities today. Their easy verisimilitude, that sometimes creates nervous embarrassment in modern audiences, was apparently taken for granted by the Elizabethans and post-Elizabethans—except those of Prynne's persuasion. Here I think even Granville-Barker allowed his Victorian background to confuse him, when he wrote: "it is Shakespeare's constant care to demand nothing of a boy-actress that might turn to unseemliness or ridicule" (*Prefaces*, London, 1927, 1st ser., p. xxviii). Appar-

the tremendous demands the playwrights made of them; but we have further assurance from observers.

The Restoration's famous Kynaston[13] was one of the few we know by name; John Downes, a wise old theatre head, wrote of him: "it has been Disputable among the Judicious, whether any Woman that succeeded him so Sensibly touch'd the Audience as he."[14]

Shakespeare, fifty years earlier, surely had equally skilled artists to play his great gallery of women. Consider this description of a performance of *Othello* by the King's Men at Oxford in 1610.[15] It was contained in a Latin letter from one of the spectators; I will translate the significant part: "They also had tragedies, well and effectively acted. In these they drew tears, not only by their speech, but also by their action. Indeed Desdemona, killed by her husband, in her death moved us especially when, as she lay in her bed, her face alone implored the pity of the audience."

Here is a description of accomplished acting as we ourselves know it. The players added to the lines their own creative art of interpretive physical movement and speech; they made the sophisticated Oxford audience weep by their acting as well as by their words. And note that while this was the great Burbage's own company, what most touched the observer was the power of the actor playing the heroine to convey emotion, simply through facial expression. We can gauge the completeness of the illusion from the fact that the "boy actor" himself is not even mentioned; Desdemona it is who was pitied. Are

---

ently the audiences forgot the "boys" were male—see the description, further in my text, of the performance of *Othello* at Oxford. In the 16th and early 17th centuries men who wanted to act like women must have seen the stage as a kind of natural home. I certainly do not mean to say here that most—or even many—of Shakespeare's "boy actors" were homosexual; but there may well have been some grains of truth in Prynne's furious assaults upon the "Sodomiticall" theatre.

[13] See, e.g., Pepys's diary, 7 January 1661, where "Kinaston" is described as "clearly the prettiest woman in the whole house."

[14] *Roscius Anglicanus* (London, 1708), ed. Montague Summers (London, 1927), p. 19.

[15] Geoffrey Tillotson, "*Othello* and *The Alchemist* at Oxford," *TLS*, 20 July 1933, p. 494.

we not entitled to assume from this, in the absence of contrary evidence, that the men who played women could act anything demanded of them, without the need to formalize or symbolize their actions to disguise their age or their sex?

What else impels the formalists to find a non-personal, stereotyped acting in Shakespeare's time? Passages in the plays have been singled out which suggest that actors were stilted and conventional; typical is Buckingham's speech in *Richard III:*

> Tut, I can counterfeit the deep tragedian,
> Speak, and look back, and pry on every side,
> Tremble, and start at wagging of a straw,
> Intending deep suspicion. Ghastly looks
> Are at my service, like enforced smiles;
> And both are ready in their offices
> At any time to grace my strategems.
>
> (III, 5:5)[16]

I cannot imagine better proof that good Elizabethan acting was anything *but* such hackneyed stuff. How could Shakespeare establish more clearly the relative naturalness of his players than by deliberately pointing out again and again the stereotyped work of second-raters? That there were such second-raters was of course inevitable. There are always hacks where there is art. We have similar hack actors on our own stages. George Jean Nathan has described the stereotyped gestures of one of them, a well-known actress; here is her routine for "panic"—and note its family resemblance to Buckingham's histrionics: "Panic: Rapid looks to left and right, nervous paddling of thighs, wild brushing of hair up from ears, more rapid looks from right to left, execution of a few steps of the rhumba, and rapid inhalations and exhalations as if uncomfortably anticipating the imminent approach of a glue factory."[17] Here, as in Shakespeare's lines, the recognition of hack acting clearly implies that more natural acting is known and valued. Note that Shakespeare could speak a kind word for actors, too, as in the induction to *The Taming of the Shrew,* where a Lord says of a player:

[16] Miss Bradbrook quotes several such satirical passages to support her formalist view. M. C. Bradbrook, *Themes and Conventions of Elizabethan Tragedy* (Cambridge, 1935), pp. 21 ff.

[17] *Theatre Book of the Year* (New York, 1944), p. 27.

> This fellow I remember
> Since first he play'd a farmer's eldest son.
> 'Twas where you woo'd the gentlewoman so well.
> I have forgot your name; but, sure, that part
> Was aptly fitted, and naturally performed.
>
> (Induction, 83)

Some minor formalistic arguments, based on deduction, may be considered briefly. Miss Bradbrook has suggested that stage directions may be taken as indications of regular acting conventions. Thus, we are told firmly that "Joy was expressed by cutting capers"[18] because in Chapman's *Charlemagne* an actor cuts capers to show he is unaffected by bad news. We can hardly suppose that this reaction, in quantity and quality, could be extended to other characters, other plays: that Lear might caper when reunited with Cordelia, or Othello with Desdemona at Cyprus. The mind reels a little at the thought. What we have in *Charlemagne*, of course, is one playwright's use, in a particular context, of a familiar piece of business to communicate emotion. Sometimes these bits of business are indeed quite universal: Shakespeare has Othello "gnaw his nether lip" in rage, as Eugene O'Neill has Mildred Douglas, in a stage direction in *The Hairy Ape*, "biting her lip angrily"; but in neither case need we suppose that the actor concerned was necessarily trained to act in patterned movement.

Another minor formalist deduction is based on the theory of speed: that the plays had to move in patterns because they were actually presented whole in something like "two houres traffic."[19] From my review of the arguments, I am satisfied that the phrase did not denote, literally, 120 minutes acting time, but, in most cases, two to three hours; besides, there was probably unrecorded cutting of the texts we have, and this would have prevented mere races against time. Surely we are not to suppose that the actors moved like clockwork and spoke in measured rhythms to meet deadlines. In the absence of hard evidence I see no reason to accept a notion so foreign to known theatre practice.

It has also been suggested that the nature of the Elizabethan

[18] *Themes and Conventions*, p. 22.

[19] Bowers (see n. 8), p. 270.

theatre demanded formal acting; and we read that probably Burbage "was part of a statuary group, rather than part of a picture. His attitudes must have been statuesque, and his gestures such as would convey meaning to the considerable portion of the audience who could not see his face. . . ."[20] Miss Bradbrook deduced that "to maintain attention it would be necessary to exaggerate movement or statuesqueness, to use inflated delivery and conventional posture."[21] But we must remember that the Globe and the other outdoor theatres were comparatively small. The Globe itself had apparently an outside diameter of no more than 85 feet. The *farthest* spectator would not be more than about 75 feet away from the rear of the stage. To some extent, the Globe would correspond to what one might expect from a "theatre in the round" today. In such theatres, as we know, players need not shout, or resemble statuary. To return momentarily to that *Othello* performance at Oxford, there the actor clearly relied on an expressive face to help communicate the emotion the playwright intended. We have no reason to suppose the technique was changed for the public theatres.

Finally, one of Joseph's deductions needs considering. He cites references to indicate that bets were made on the skill of rival actors, and argues that this must show they had a "generally accepted body of rules as to what was a fault."[22] To me the vision this conjures up of skilled automatons competing in the manner of fancy divers or trained seals is intolerable. My guess, without further evidence, is that any such competitions would have been judged by the reactions each player could draw from his audience through the individual quality of his work.

We come now to the chief source of external evidence for formal Elizabethan acting. It is the foundation for Joseph's whole book on the subject, and it has supported the arguments of others. It is this: actors were probably trained in formal

[20] Harbage, p. 704.

[21] *Themes and Conventions*, p. 21.

[22] Joseph, pp. 152–53. See also, for a fuller account of these wagers, Murray Bromberg, "Theatrical Wagers," *N&Q*, CXCVI (8 December 1951):533–35.

patterns because they were occasionally likened to orators, who presumably exemplified stereotyped techniques.

The supporting evidence is not convincing. No genuine acting manual is extant that sets out rote procedures for Elizabethan players. The nearest thing, probably, is Professor Harbage's find of the preface to the anonymous *Cyprian Conqueror*. It gives such instructions as: "in a sorrowful parte, ye head must hang downe; in a proud, ye head must bee lofty; in an amorous, closed eies, hanging downe lookes, & crossed armes . . . " et cetera.[23]

This find is still in manuscript, and dated some time after 1633; but most against it was Harbage's own refusal, with scholarly honesty, to admit it as firm evidence for the case he was then making for formal acting. He noted that it might easily have been an amateur's work; and he found, as has many another scholar, that up through the nineteenth century other stereotyped acting manuals appeared at times when, history indicates, players were acting with spontaneity.[24]

What remains, then, as evidence of formal acting? Basically, the deduction that actors were another kind of orator. Joseph argues: "That what is applied to acting in oratory also applied to acting on the stage is evident in the description of *An Excellent Actor* (in the Overbury 'characters,' perhaps written by Webster), . . . [it] states categorically: 'Whatsoever is commendable to the grave Orator, is most exquisitly perfect in him'" (p. 1). Joseph also cites Richard Flecknoe's statement (of 1664) that the great actor of Shakespeare's company, Richard Burbage, "had all the parts of an excellent orator."

This really is the whole base of Joseph's case. He goes on to show that general Elizabethan education was rhetorical, that much attention was given to the control and decorum of speech and movement—but he never offers any real evidence of stereotype training of actors. For supporting data Joseph chiefly

[23] Harbage (p. 698) in 1939 described this as a "Preface to a play still in manuscript, *The Cyprian Conqueror*, or the *Faithless Relict*," and added that it probably appeared "after, but not long after, Prynne's attack of 1633." In Harbage's review of the Joseph book—*SQ*, 2 (October, 1951), 360–61—the find is described as "the anonymous *Cyprian Conqueror* with preface drawn from the *Onomasticon* and similar works. . . ."

[24] Harbage (*PMLA*), pp. 698–99.

relies on a 1644 manual of rhetorical delivery by John Bulwer, a teacher of the deaf and dumb, who provided drawings showing how the hand, arm, and fingers might be used in speech.[25] Bulwer was trying to describe fairly universal gestures useful for orators;[26] he had nothing to say to actors. Indeed, a contemptuous phrase of his suggests how very differently he regarded actors and orators. Of the striking of the forehead with the hand, he wrote: "my Author concurs in opinion with *Quintilian* and adjudgeth it worthy of banishment from the Hand of an Oratour, and to be confined to the Theater, and the ridiculous Hands of Mimicks" (Joseph, p. 57).

To return to Flecknoe and the Overbury character, it is interesting to note what Joseph does *not* quote from those sources. Flecknoe also wrote: Burbage "was a delightful *Proteus,* so wholly transforming himself in to his Part, and putting off himself with his Cloathes, as he never (not so much as in the Tyring-house) assum'd himself again until the Play was done. . . ."[27] This sounds rather like an earlier Stanislavski—"wholly transforming himself in his part." And consider this, from the Overbury character: the actor "doth not strive to make nature monstrous, she is often seene in the same Scaene with him, but neither on Stilts nor Crutches. . . ."[28] Is not this a precious way of saying that his acting should be, in fact, natural and unstilted?

In denying that such descriptions as these do point to "natural" acting, the formalists clearly depend on subjective interpretation. Sometimes these interpretations are hard to square with the basic formal approach itself. Thus Waldo McNeir, quoting from Edmund Gayton's *Pleasant Notes upon Don Quixote* (1654), offers this item in support of conventional acting:

[25] *Chirologia* and *Chironomia,* 2 works which appeared together and shared the same title page, 1644.

[26] And even for orators, Bulwer left room for variation. See Joseph, pp. 56–57.

[27] Richard Flecknoe, preface to *Loues Kingdom* (1664), in *Critical Essays of the Seventeenth Century,* ed. J. E. Spingarn (Oxford, 1908), 2:95.

[28] *New and Choice Characters* (1615), ed. W. J. Paylor (Oxford, 1936), pp. 76–77.

> Some passions counterfeited long, whether of griefe or joy, have so alter'd the personaters, that players themselves . . . have been forc'd to fly to Physick, for cure of the disaffection, which such high penn'd humours, and too passionately and sensibly represented, have occasion'd. I have knowne my selfe, a Tyrant comming from the Scene, not able to reduce himselfe till Sack made him . . . forget he was an Emperour, and renew'd all his old acquaintance to him. And it is not out of most men's observation that one most admirable Mimicke in our late Stage so lively and corporally personated a Changeling, that he could never compose his Face to the figure it had, before he undertook the part.[29]

McNeir finds the phrases "too passionately and sensibly represented" and "lively and corporally personated" as "perhaps . . . more descriptive of a formal than a natural style of acting." On matters of impressions of this sort, it is really impossible to argue; I don't see how these actors could have *been* their characters more—and this is one of the formalists' marks of natural acting.

A further approach of the formalists is to insist that when the word "natural" itself is used to describe Elizabethan acting it doesn't really mean natural, but something else. Joseph says, "To act 'naturally' in Shakespeare's time was no more to act naturalistically than to sing naturally in opera is to sing naturalistically" (p. 149). Such a conception collides headlong with the Elizabethan attitude as expressed, for instance, in Hamlet's advice to the players. This seemed aimed precisely at attacking the kind of performance that might indeed pass in operatic singing as "natural"—if this adjective can be applied in the same way to an art form that often deliberately departs from the verisimilitude the theatre so deliberately seeks to capture. The formalist critics can make nothing of Hamlet's speeches, particularly his criticism of hacks who "imitate nature so abominably." Joseph barely skirts the passages. When he comes to another championship of the natural style, Heywood's *Apology for Actors*, Joseph leaps to this curious conclusion: ". . . if Heywood is to be believed . . . rhetorical acting would provide the audience with an experience as intense as anything we are likely to know today" (p. 153). For evidence, he offers

[29] *PMLA,* 56 (June, 1941), 581–82.

this quotation: "To turne to our domesticke hystories, what English blood seeing the person of any bold English man presented and doth not hugge his fame, . . . offers to him in his hart all prosperous performance, as if the Personator were the man Personated, so bewitching a thing is liuely and spirited action, that it hath power to new mold the harts of the spectators and fashion them to the shape of any noble and notable attempt."

Neither here nor anywhere else does Heywood praise "rhetorical" acting; nowhere does he suggest that good acting is in any way artificial, non-"naturall." The key to the above quotation is the phrase, "as if the Personator were the man Personated." Far from wanting actors to copy any artificiality in rhetoricians, Heywood urges the orators themselves to use "a naturall and familiar motion of the head, the hand, the body" and he echoes the earlier phrase in his general advice to "qualifie everything according to the nature of the person personnated." He specifically warns against "oueracting trickes."

The formalists who seek to strengthen their arguments with Heywood's references to oratory miss the real point of his *Apology*. Heywood, "moved by the sundry exclamations of many seditious Sectists in this age," was using every argument he could think of to appease the attackers of the stage. He probably would have claimed the theatre cured the pox, if he could have made even a remote case. As it was, he demonstrated the drama's power for good by solemnly relating, in considerable detail, how plays had at various times brought two women spectators to confess the murders of their husbands, and how a performance helped warn a British community of a surprise attack by Spanish commandos. Rhetoric simply offered Heywood another weapon of argument; rhetoric was a respectable tool of society, and by showing that acting was related to it, he could make the stage shine in reflected respectability. But having adopted this gambit, Heywood went on to say how much more valuable acting was than oratory—in comparison, a mere "speaking picture," as painting was but "dumbe oratory"; what really brought history and morality to life, Heywood wrote, was the stage, where only could be seen—and here, clearly stated, is Heywood's conception of natural acting

—"a souldier, shap'd like a souldier, walke, speake, act like a souldier."[30]

It may be that the Elizabethan idea of "natural acting" was not exactly the same as ours; but we have no real evidence to suggest that, in its developed form, it was studiously patterned. If it was so in the early days of the endless rhymed couplet speeches, then acting must have shared with the drama its progress toward artistic maturity, and the increasing power to communicate valid experience. The late Elizabethan criticism of acting is directed mainly against rhetorical, inflated techniques, as they would be manifested in strained, hackneyed, artificial performance; when the Elizabethans praised a "natural" performance they obviously meant acting recognizably close to human behavior. Of course different types of human behavior demanded different modes of communication. Plain citizens behaved differently from kings; clowns were different from ordinary people making a joke. When various types were mixed, what counted on Shakespeare's stage was what counts on our own; each in his own way had to imitate nature well. The long oratorical speeches, when properly designed, were not insets of elocution, but tangible manifestations of the person who spoke them. If the character and his message were oratorical, the speeches would be so, but they were not therefore "rhetorical" as opposed to "natural." Anyone who has watched players as skilled as those appearing in our own time at Stratford knows how "natural" some of the longest and most formal of Shakespeare's speeches can sound, when properly handled.

It would have been impossible for the later Elizabethans to hold to any single form of realism in their acting, as it would be for us. Action, then as now, had to be suited to the word—and the word, in different plays, was pitched at various levels above that of phonographic naturalism. A recent judgment of Harbage's is significant here. Some thirteen years ago his forceful arguments for a single, formal acting style gave impetus to the formalist movement. Since then—as all scholars should, and too few do—he has reconsidered the evidence. In a review, he has observed that there must, indeed, have been a variety in the

[30] Thomas Heywood, *An Apology for Actors* (1612), in the Scholars' Facsimiles and Reprints edition (New York, 1941), n. p.

acting to suit the variety in the plays. He wrote: "Different parts of Elizabethan plays are different, sometimes intimate, sometimes the reverse; sometimes 'realistic,' sometimes the reverse, sometimes in verse, sometimes in prose. The dialogue is sometimes an alternation of orations, sometimes snatches of conversation with every commonplace intonation preserved."[31]

So clearsighted an empirical view seems inevitable when one reads the Elizabethan plays carefully. The drama of Shakespeare's time was an explosion of art in which the artists—the playwrights—shaped their conceptions of human nature and human dreams into acting materials much too rich and diverse to fit into fixed categories. The plays are textured with every mood and mode that came to the dramatists' minds: the rough and tumble of native drama, farce, fantasy, melodrama, fable, tragedy of all kinds, comedy of all kinds, historical drama, pastoral, pastoral-historical-comical-tragical—is there any wonder poor Polonius could not keep up? And each play, as it differed from other plays, and sometimes as it varied within itself from scene to scene, demanded from the actors constant creative adjustments. If men like Burbage were the artists we are told they were, they were able in all forms, from low comedy to high tragedy, so to represent the natures of the persons personated as to convey the necessary sense of humanity in action.

The job was easiest in the clearly designed character parts, especially where the language and its implied action was the kind that was moved on to the stage from the neighboring streets and houses. Jonson's London types, for instance, oversimple as they sometimes were, must have been easy studies for the repertory actors, quick to seize and fix on popular, recognizable characterization. The parts of Falstaff and his noisy associates, the latter particularly cut in clear, homespun outline, must have been comfortable and easy garments to put on for the company's short, intermittent runs. We can learn something about more elegant acting, too, from Falstaff and his friend Pistol. The knight's very mocking of the king hints to us that monarchs then often did speak formally and weightily, indeed as they—and senators and presidents—often do now; and we can accept the fact that Shakespeare's play-kings who sound

[31] Harbage (*SQ* review), pp. 360–61.

formal and oratorical were supposed to sound that way. They were imitating nature well. But Pistol's rantings tell us further that beyond the suitably regal dramatic heroes there were others, whom he imitates, who sawed the air much too much, and out-Heroded a legion of Herods. We and the Elizabethans both laugh at them; they imitated nature abominably.

The hard parts for the Elizabethan actors—as for today's actors—were those that were complex, that ranged widely in emotional experience, that demanded sharp changes of tempo and technique. Consider, for instance, the tremendous challenge Shakespeare presented to some boy actor with the role of Cleopatra. She is a queen, and speaks like a queen to Caesar; with Antony she is amorous, coy, dignified, furious, but always the great paramour; alone with her maidens, and especially in the marvellous scenes when she scolds the messenger for bringing news of Antony's marriage, and then forgives him because of his report of Octavia's ugliness, she is simply and wonderfully a woman. Shakespeare had to depend on the actor, who played so many parts in one, to communicate through the lines a continuous personality in which all the changing moods could seem natural and plausible.

Shakespeare's dependence on the actor is a hard fact for the formalist to accept. For back of the formalist attitude, I believe, is a wishful preconception that Shakespeare must be fixed and immutable, never subject to the varying interpretations of mercurial actors.[32] In many cases, the formalist is a sensitive, imaginative man who cannot tolerate theatre characterizations of Shakespeare different from his own soaring conceptions; and he is angered by the mangling the great plays sometimes undergo on the stage. So he looks wishfully back to Shakespeare's own time, and postulates a theatre in which the poetry was all, was never-changing, and had to be conveyed through depersonalized mouthpieces.

[32] T. S. Eliot has expressed this attitude in its raw form: "I rebel against performances of Shakespeare's plays because I want a direct relationship between the work of art and myself, and I want the performance to be such as will not interrupt or alter this relationship any more than it is an alteration or interruption for me to superpose a second inspection of a picture of a building upon the first" (*Elizabethan Essays* [New York, 1934], p. 15).

Elizabethan Actors: Men or Marionettes?

What kind of a theatre would this be? No one respects the great Elizabethan lines more than I do; I know that Shakespeare's plays would not have lasted in the theatre without the great poetry; but in the theatre the poetry, the lines, do not stand by themselves. They must be gathered into focus through the projection of a human personality. The formalists tell us that the players did not try to *be* characters, that they let the lines tell what the character was; but what *do* the lines tell us the character is? What *is* Hamlet, Othello, Macbeth? What two scholars will agree? Yet these scholars are only seeking what the actors have always sought—to find a frame of reference in which the character's experiences may be organized.

A Shakespearean character must be *somebody*—some recognizably human combination of emotions, desires, actions. The playwright left it to the actor to give an identity to that combination. The great actor's special genius for this task was his sensitivity to the poetry's meaning and emotion as it could be expressed through voice and movement. This sensitivity is not mechanical; it matures, and is refined, so that an actor, like a scholar, continually discovers new riches in Shakespeare; thus Laurence Olivier told recently how, after years of playing, a minor phrase of Hamlet's suddenly became meaningful to him. Burbage was a lucky actor, because he could ask the playwright about subtleties of interpretation; but Shakespeare was lucky too that he knew he had, in Burbage, an artist inspired to sense and express in a total characterization meanings which even the playwright may not have recognized when he wrote them.

With all the magic in Shakespeare, there was never this magic, that the lines, merely by being spoken well, would create a personality for whom spectators might weep, as they wept for Desdemona at Oxford in 1610. But there *was* this magic: that the lines evoked superlatively a creative form-drive in the actor, as a piece of eloquent marble does in a sculptor; and it was by the actor's organization of the poetic material, his endowing it with the soul of lively action, that he moved people in the theatre to tears and laughter as Shakespeare intended them to be moved, and as they can be moved in no other way.

IX

WILLIAM A. RINGLER, JR.

The Number of Actors in Shakespeare's Early Plays

I

It has by now become a commonplace to assert that Shakespeare wrote his plays, not to be read but to be performed; and to lament at what has been lost from them, because only in their Elizabethan and Jacobean productions was the full range of their effects realized. The closing of the theaters in 1642 caused a break in the continuing acting traditions of earlier days, and the printed Quarto and Folio texts of Shakespeare's plays that survive to us in many places fail to preserve notes of stage business and special effects that are necessary for realizing the full import of the scenes. Their stage directions are unfortunately often deficient, because Shakespeare himself, as an actor and shareholder in his own company, was available to supervise the casting of his plays and to instruct his fellows in their roles, so that he did not feel it necessary to write down all the details of his productions.

Often it is possible to deduce important details of production from the dialogue itself. We know that Cleopatra dies, not on her throne but on her bed (an important detail for an understanding of the play); because Caesar says,

> Take up her bed,
> And bear her Women from the Monument.
> [V, 2:357]

But there are other details that have been lost to us, and that can be recovered, if they can be recovered at all, only by indirect means. One example of stage business that would have been otherwise lost is provided by a contemporary reference to the

This essay has not been printed before.

acting of *A Midsummer Night's Dream*. In that play the words of the burlesque Pyramus and Thisbe scene are perhaps sufficiently humorous by themselves, for when Pyramus kills himself he says:

> Come tears, confound, out sword, and wound
> The pappe of *Pyramus:*
> I, that left pappe, where heart doth hoppe.
> Thus dy I, thus, thus, thus.

And Thisbe, when she finds Pyramus dead and kills herself, delivers a similarly ludicrous dying speech:

> Asleep, my love? What, dead, my dove?
> . . . .
> Tongue, not a word: come, trusty sword:
> Come, blade, my breast imbrew:
> And farewell, friends: thus *Thysby* ends:
> Adieu, adieu, adieu.

But the words were not the only humorous part of Shakespeare's original production; for, according to the report of Edward Sharpham,[1] Thisbe stabbed herself, not with Pyramus' sword, but with the scabbard! Unfortunately, this is the only recorded certain reference to contemporary stage business in any of Shakespeare's plays, so that to re-create his original productions we must develop other techniques of analysis.

One promising line of investigation has been to examine the composition of the company for which Shakespeare wrote all but the earliest of his plays, the Lord Chamberlain's–King's Company, first organized in June, 1594, for which he wrote exclusively during the rest of his dramatic career. We know the names of the principal shareholders and of some of the hirelings of this company, but we have only a little direct evidence about the roles each actor played. Contemporary references tell us that Richard Burbage played the parts of Richard III, Hamlet, Othello, and Lear. Occasional actors' names in speech prefixes show that Kemp played Peter in *Romeo and Juliet* and Dogberry (with Cowley as Verges) in *Much Ado;* and that

---

[1] *Shakspere Allusion-Book*, ed. E. K. Chambers, 1:174. Another possible, but not certain, allusion to stage business in a contemporary production is the suggestion that Hamlet in the graveyard scene not only held the skull of Yorick in his hand but also stroked it (*ibid*, pp. 160–61).

Sinklo, a hireling, played the keeper in *Henry VI Part III*, and other minor parts in *The Shrew* and *Henry IV Part II*. A few other actors' names have been identified, or imagined, in speech prefixes; but all are for extremely minor parts, and some derive from later rather than from the original productions (such as Tawyer, who announces the play of the rude mechanicals with his trumpet in the Folio text of *A Midsummer Night's Dream*).[2] Shakespeare himself is named in the three extant actor lists, but we have no contemporary evidence whatever to indicate the parts he played.

Professor T. W. Baldwin, in his *Organization and Personnel of the Shakespearean Company* (1927), has made the most exhaustive study of the actors of Shakespeare's plays undertaken to date, and has attempted to assign roles to particular actors for all the important parts in the plays. But his analyses, it seems to me, are deficient and lack probability, because he assumes that each of the principal actors in Shakespeare's company specialized in a particular character "line" (whereas it is more probable that they were virtuosos who delighted in exhibiting their acting skills by playing a great variety of roles—as Sir Laurence Olivier today at one time plays the lead in *Hamlet* and at another time in *The Entertainer*), and because he fails to take into account the well-established Elizabethan practice of doubling and assigns each character to a different actor.

Doubling of roles was the universal practice on the professional stage from the beginning of the sixteenth century until the closing of the theaters. William J. Lawrence published an important pioneering article on the subject in his *Pre-Restoration Stage Studies* (1927), and more recently David M. Bevington has produced a masterly study of the effects of the practice on earlier dramatists in *From Mankind to Marlowe* (1962), but he did not extend his analyses to Shakespeare. J. Engelen, "Die Schauspieler-Ökonomie in Shakespeares Dramen," in *Shakespeare Jahrbuch*, volumes 62 (1926) and 63 (1927), and M. Sack, *Darstellerzahl und Rollenvertheilung bei Shakespeare* (1928), have made preliminary studies of doubling in Shakespeare's plays, but their results are inconclusive because they concentrate on the major speaking parts and pay inadequate

---

[2] References are collected by A. Gaw, "Actor's Names in Basic Shakespearean Texts," *PMLA,* 40 (1925):530–50.

attention to the entire company, which must also include the mutes.

My object in this paper is far less ambitious than the studies of Baldwin, Engelen, and Sack, who attempt to apportion the roles in Shakespeare's plays. I do not at this time wish to guess which actors played what parts. I wish to ask only one question: how many actors were available to Shakespeare for his earlier plays? And if a definite answer to that question is possible, and I think it is, I then wish to consider briefly whether or not that information will shed new light on the contemporary production of the plays and reveal aspects of their performance that were unguessed at before, and I think it will.

II

Analysis of the shareholders of Shakespeare's company, the actor lists, and the occasional names of actors in the texts of the plays, will not by itself give us precise information about the size of Shakespeare's company, because the lists give us the names of only the principal actors, and we have no direct information about the number of hirelings or about the number of boys who played female roles and other parts. The size of Shakespeare's company must be determined by making a casting analysis of each of the plays separately. But there is one piece of external evidence.

The German visitor, Thomas Platter, recorded seeing, on 21 September 1599, in the thatched playhouse across the Thames (the new Globe), a performance of *Julius Caesar* "mitt ohngefahr 15 personen . . . agieren."[3] This was undoubtedly Shakespeare's play, but the only text, the Folio, has 45 speaking parts. Since a member of the audience would not ordinarily be able to identify the individual actors who doubled in the various parts, someone must have told Platter that the Chamberlain's Company numbered "about fifteen" in September 1599. Let us test the validity of Platter's information by analyzing the text of the play itself.

Our analyses must be based upon the original good Quartos, or upon the Folio where no Quartos are available (though we

[3] E. K. Chambers, *Elizabethan Stage*, vol. 2 (1923), pp. 364–66, first printed by G. Binz, "Londoner Theater und Schauspiele im Jahre 1599," *Anglia*, 22 (1899):456–64.

must bear in mind that the Folio texts sometimes represent later productions rather than the original performances, and may be adapted to somewhat larger casts). Currently available edited texts of the plays are misleading in many small details, because their stage directions and speech prefixes are influenced by the emendations of many generations of editors, from the early eighteenth century onward, several of whom were less well informed about Elizabethan conditions of stage production than they should have been. Therefore the unedited original texts, even though they contain scribal and compositorial corruptions, provide a sounder basis for analysis than do improperly edited modern texts.

We must also analyze the casting in accordance with what we can learn of the production procedures of Shakespeare's own company. The Quartos make it clear that the action of a Shakespearean play is continuous, and that the structural unit of production is not the act but the scene. A scene is marked by a momentary clearing of the stage, and one convention from which Shakespeare never deviates is that an actor who exits at the end of one scene never reenters at the beginning of the following scene (except that in the "alarms and excursions" of battle scenes the action is continuous). If an actor is needed in two consecutive scenes, Shakespeare always arranges for him either to exit before the end of the preceding scene or to reenter after the beginning of the following scene. Thus in *Julius Caesar*, Caska, who appears in both I, 2 and I, 3, exits 28 lines before the end of I, 2 in order to reappear at the beginning of I, 3. But the interval between exit and reentry can be quite brief, as in the case of Flavius and Murellus, who exit at the end of I, 1 and reenter in I, 2 immediately after Caesar and the others have assembled on the stage.[4] Thus though modern edi-

---

[4] A similar device is used in *Shr.* V, 1–V, 2 and *R3* III, 3–III, 4 where the pause before reentry is provided by bringing in a table. The only apparent exception to this rule is in the *Tempest* where Prospero and Ariel exit at the end of IV, 1 and immediately reenter in the following V, 1, which has led Dover Wilson to suggest quite properly that an intervening scene has been cut from the original text at this point. Another apparent exception is in *The Winter's Tale* where Camillo and Archidamus exeunt at the end of I, 1 and where Camillo is named as immediately reentering in the massed stage direction at the beginning of I, 2; but he is not addressed until line 209 and it is clear that he does not reenter until Leontes exclaims, "What? *Camillo* there?"—therefore the massed

tors divide *Julius Caesar* into five acts and eighteen scenes, it was originally composed in 15 scenes, for IV, 2–3, V, 1–2, and V, 3–4 are each single continuous scenes rather than two. It is fascinating to observe step by step the skilful generalship with which Shakespeare marshals his characters, observes the convention of scene breaks, and arranges the entrances and exits of characters in one scene so that those needed in the following scene are available for their parts, and where doubling is required have adequate time for changes of costume and makeup. The scene must be the unit of analysis in determining the casting of the plays.

In calculating the size of the cast the speaking parts are easy to identify; the main problem is to ascertain the number of mute attendants and others who are supposed to be on stage in each particular scene. In this we must depend upon references in the text itself, and upon often vague and imprecise stage directions. When writing Shakespeare probably left the specific determination of the number of mutes to be used in a particular scene to be worked out in production, and sometimes used phrases such as "three or foure followers" (of Morocho in the *Merchant of Venice* II, 1) or "as many as can be" (*Titus Andronicus* I, 1:69); though analysis of the casting reveals that he usually kept remarkably accurate track of the personnel of his company and of the number of actors available to him in any particular scene. My experience in analyzing the casting of the plays indicates that a plural for mute "attendants," "soldiers," etc., should usually be interpreted as no more than two, unless there is evidence in the text to the contrary, for on the Shakespearean stage two is a crowd, and "four or five most vile and ragged foils" are enough to represent the opposing armies at Agincourt. Thus in *Julius Caesar* the "certaine Commoners" in I, 1 need be represented only by the Carpenter and Cobbler specified in the speech prefixes (though it is logical to assume that they are identical with the first two of the four plebeians

---

stage direction needs emending, though I have not noticed its being emended in recent texts. Many of Shakespeare's stage directions need emending, for indications of entrance are sometimes misleading and necessary exits are frequently lacking altogether—he apparently depended on his veteran actors' getting off stage at the proper time on their own initiative without needing a direction written in their parts.

specified in III, 2 and III, 3—and later analysis of the doubling possibilities shows that actors are available to play the parts of two additional mutes in I, 1).[5]

The text of the dialogue as well as the stage directions should be examined minutely for indications of the presence or absence of characters. Thus when Brutus at V, 3:108 says, "Labio and Flavio set our Battailes on," he may just as well be giving information rather than uttering a command, and there is no necessity to assume that Labio and Flavio are present on the stage (the comma before "set," which is inserted in modern editions, does not appear in the Folio, and I do not think it should be inserted). We must also always be alert for possible errors in speech prefixes, which occur more frequently than modern editors are often aware. Editors have frequently expressed puzzlement over the absence of Ligarius from the assassination scene, but have not been disturbed by the equally puzzling presence of the mute Lepidus. Ligarius would be recognized by the "kerchief" on his head (II, 1:315). He does not have to speak to make his presence known; Shakespeare has been at considerable pains (by repetition at II, 1, II, 2, and II, 3) to identify him as one of the eight conspirators, to indicate by his speech with Brutus at the end of II, 1 that he will take an active part in the conspiracy, and after the murder the citizens name him as one of the assassins (III, 3:43). It is clear that Shakespeare intended him to be present at the assassination, and I think he is present; for names were often abbreviated in dramatic manuscripts in stage directions as well as in speech prefixes, and the printed form "Lepidus" could have resulted from the compositor misreading "Li" as "Le" (a common graphical confusion) and so improperly expanding his misreading to "Lepidus" instead of "Ligarius" which Shakespeare had intended.

I mention these details merely to indicate the frequent textual difficulties facing the investigator attempting to determine the casting of Shakespeare's plays and to illustrate the kinds of

[5] Shakespeare made considerable use of groups of characters, usually of similar numbers, who reappear at intervals and sometimes take on an almost symbolical significance. Thus Bushy, Bagot, and Green, though they are not specifically mentioned in *Richard II* until I, 3, are probably those who "attended" Richard in his initial entrance at I, 1.

decisions he sometimes has to make. Indeed, one of the by-products of analyzing the casting is that it brings to light a number of textual and production problems that were hereto-fore unsuspected. However, in constructing the complete list of characters for a play, both speakers and mutes, the analysis should be made as conservatively as possible from the evidence available, and allowance should be made for all possible variant interpretations. Therefore, in my final List of Characters in the Order of Their Appearance for *Julius Caesar* (Fig. 1), I have set down only the definitely present Carpenter and Cobbler in I, 1 (though in the later casting list actors are available for two more); have retained the name Lepidus, but marked it with a question mark in III, 1; and have omitted Labio and Flavio in V, 3 (though in the later casting list actors are available for their parts if their presence is insisted upon). The resulting list enumerates 49 distinguishable characters, of whom four are mutes (the two soldiers of Cassius in IV, 2, the third soldier of Octavius and Antony in V, 1 to V, 5, and the ensign of Cassius in V, 3). It should be noticed that there are never more than 16 characters in any one scene, and never more than 14 on stage at any one time.

The List of Characters in Order of Their Appearance graph-ically shows Shakespeare's technique in adapting a play with a large number of speakers to the capabilities of a small acting troupe. Scenes opening with a large number of characters are always preceded by scenes or ends of scenes with only a few characters, so that adequate time is allowed for the shifting around of the small cast and for doubling. Though there are 49 characters in the play as a whole, only 29 of these appear in the first part of the play (through III, 3). In the remaining scenes 20 new characters appear; but only five of the original characters continue (and two of these are reduced to bit parts). Only the three principals—Brutus, Cassius, and Antony—hold the two halves of the play together. This technique is also typical of Shakespeare's other English and Roman history plays, which are his only ones that have exceptionally large casts of characters.

After the total number of characters is determined, the next problem is to calculate the minimum number of actors neces-sary to produce the play. A preliminary calculation can be

FIGURE 1

JULIUS CAESAR

(Characters in Order of Appearance)

	I,1	I,2	I,3	II,1	II,2	II,3	II,4	III,1	III,2	III,3	IV,1	IV,2	IV,3	V,1	V,2	V,3	V,4	V,5
Flav.	x-																	
carp.	x	-0-																
Mure.	x-	-0-																
cobb.	x-																	
Caesar.		x-			x-0			x-					x					
Caska.		x-	x					x-		x								
Calphurnia.		x-			x													
Antony.		x-						x-	x-0-		x			x			-x	x
Soothsay.		x-					-x	x-										
Brutus.		x-		x-				x-	x-0-			x-	x-	-x	x	x-	x	x
Cassius.		x	-x	-x				x-		x		x	x-	-x		x		
Portia.				-x			-x											
Decius.		0-		-x	-x			x-										
Cicero.		0-	-x															
Cinna.			-x					x-										
Lucius.				x-			x					-x	x-					
Metellus.				-x				x-										
Trebonius.				-x				x-										
Ligarius.				-x				x-?										
svt. Caesar.					-x			x-										
Publius.					-x			x-										
Artemidorus.						x		x-										

x = speaker   0 = mute (* indicates mute on Figs. 2–4)   - = enters after beginning or exits before end of scene

FIGURE 1—*Continued*

	I,1	I,2	I,3	II,1	II,2	II,3	II,4	III,1	III,2	III,3	IV,1	IV,2	IV,3	V,1	V,2	V,3	V,4	V,5
Popilius Lena								x-										
Lepidus								0-?			x-						o-	
svt. Antony								-x										
svt. Octavius									-x-									
plebeian 3									x-									
plebeian 4										x								
Cinna the poet										x								
Octavius										x	x			x-		x	-x	-x
Lucillius												x	-x					
Varro													x					
Claudius													x					
Pindarus												x				x		
Titinius												x	-x			x-x		
sold. Cassius												x						
sold. Cassius												o						
poet.													x					
Messala												o	-x	-o		o-		-o
sold. O & A														x				-o
sold. O & A														o				-o
sold. O & A														o				-o
messenger O & A														o				
ensign of Cassius																o		
Young Cato																x	x	
Strato																		x
Voluanius																		x
Dardanius																		x
Clitus																		x

made by analyzing the scenes consecutively in pairs. In *Julius Caesar* at the end of I, 1 two characters exeunt, and at the beginning of I, 2 ten new characters enter; up to this point a minimum cast of twelve is needed. If we continue in this fashion, we find the critical point at II, 4–III, 1; for at the end of II, 4 Portia and Lucius exeunt, and at the beginning of the following III, 1 fourteen actors enter—a cast of sixteen is needed at this point. In no other part of the play are so many actors needed at any one time. In other plays the critical point may occur early—at I, 1:72 in *Romeo and Juliet*, and in still others not until late—at IV, 2–V, 1 in *Much Ado* (in both these plays the maximum number is again sixteen).

We are now ready to test our hypothesis of the size of Shakespeare's company by making up a detailed doubling chart for the entire play, in which we assign all the roles to available actors and so calculate how many actors are needed to produce the play. In assigning roles we again should adhere to practicable principles of dramatic production and the evidence of the texts. We should start with the major speaking parts, and seldom or never assign more than one role to an actor with a large number of lines to memorize. It soon becomes evident that Shakespeare himself was careful to distribute the number of lines among the members of his cast according to their capacities. None of his early plays has more than six roles with 200 lines or more; in *Julius Caesar* only Brutus, Cassius, Antony, Caesar, and Caska have more than a hundred lines each—all the rest are minor parts. In assigning roles attention should be paid to physical characteristics indicated by the text (tall or short, fat or thin, singer or nonsinger); and parts appropriate for adults should be distinguished from those appropriate for boys (boys should be assigned women's and children's parts, and they can also play pages and mute attendants such as soldiers and servants). I place the boys' parts at the bottom of the chart.

After the major roles have been assigned, the possibilities for doubling should be investigated. Adequate time should always be allowed for costume changes, though on the Elizabethan stage these changes were apparently executed with considerable celerity. In *The Merchant of Venice* Jessica exits in her woman's costume at the end of II, 5, and enters "above" in boy's clothes after II, 6:24; since it takes her seven lines to descend

(51-7), it must have taken her the same time to ascend, which leaves only 17 lines, or about a minute of acting time, for her costume change. Changes involving a complete change of identity probably took somewhat longer, but not much longer. Elizabethan actors apparently prided themselves on being quick-change artists, and like some actors today—such as Alec Guinness—delighted in playing multiple roles.

In assigning multiple roles, I assume that each speaking part must always be played by the same actor (thus though Caesar is killed in III, 1, the same actor must play the part of his ghost in IV, 3). However, actors may play one part, double in a second part, and after an interval reassume the first part (thus the boy who plays Lucius in II, 1 and II, 4 can double as the servant of Antony at the end of III, 1, reassume the part of Lucius in IV, 2—IV, 3, and after the final exit of Lucius, double as young Cato in V, 3—V, 4).

The results of the assignments of roles made in accordance with these principles can be seen in Figure 2, the Doubling Chart for *Julius Caesar*. This I believe represents approximately the assignment of roles to actors of the Chamberlain's Company that would have been made by the bookkeeper or by Shakespeare himself. The chart, however, is approximate only, because there is often a variety of alternate possibilities for doubling. Though there is not so great a variety as is often assumed, for Shakespeare usually constructed his plays very tightly and made maximum use of all the actors available to him. It may be that in mounting his play he introduced even more mutes than are specified by a conservative interpretation of his text. For example, in I, 1 actors 15 and 16 are available to represent additional mute commoners, and additional mute plebeians in III, 3 and III, 4; and full use could be made of the entire cast to swell the final scene by having actors 13, 14, and 16 appear as additional mute soldiers of Antony. At any rate, what is clearly established by the Doubling Chart is that *Julius Caesar*, with 49 distinguishable roles, can easily be produced by a company of sixteen actors, and cannot be produced with less than sixteen. So Platter's informant, who told him the play was produced by a company of "about fifteen," was approximately correct.

The next problem is to determine whether this number of

FIGURE 2
JULIUS CAESAR
(Doubling Chart)

Actor	I,1	I,2	I,3	II,1	II,2	II,3	II,4	III,1	III,2	III,3	IV,1	IV,2	IV,3	V,1	V,2	V,3	V,4	V,5	No. of Lines
1		Brut-		Brut	Brut			Brut-	Brut-			Brut	Brut	-Brut	Brut	-Brut	Brut-	Brut	721
2		Cass	-Cass	-Cass-				Cass-	*Cass-			-Cass	Cass-	-Cass		Cass			482
3		Anto-			Anto			Anto	Anto		Anto			Anto			-Anto	-Anto	324
4		Caes-			Caes			Caes	*Caes				-Caes-	*solA			-IsolA	-solA	156
5		Casc-	Casc	Casc-	*Casc			Casc-			Octa			Octa-				-Octa	174
6		*Deci-		Deci-	Deci			Deci-	ple3-	ple3		Luci	Luci	-Luci		*Luci	Luci	-Luci	97
7	cobb		Cinn	Cinn-	Cinn			Cinn-	ple2-	ple2		*Mess	-Mess	-Mess	*Mess	-Mess	*Mess	-Mess	106
8	carp				Treb			Treb-	ple1-	ple1		Pind				Pind-	-2solA		54
9	Mure	*Mure-		Liga-	Liga			Liga-		CinP		*Titi	Titi-	*Titi-		Titi			95
10	Flav	*Flav-		Mete-	*Mete			Mete-	ple4-	ple4							*Flav-		69
11		soot-					soot-	soot-			Lepi-		-poet-			-Stra		Stra	38
12		*Cio-	Cic-		Publ			Publ-				Varr	-Varr					Clit-	69
13						Arte		Arte-				Clau	-Clau	-mesA				Dard-	103
14		Port-		Port-			Port	Popi-				*solC				-Cato	Cato		29
15		Calp-			Calp			svtA-				-solC				*Volu		Volu-	56
16				Luci	svtC		Luci	svtO	svtO			Luci	Luci	-ensi		*ensi			5

* indicates mute   - enters after beginning or exits before end of scene

16 represents the usual size of the Chamberlain's Company. I have analyzed all 18 of the pre-Globe plays (even those composed before the formation of the Chamberlain's Company), and I believe that it does. Starting in 1599 and working backward, we find that *Henry V* with 45 speakers and 6 mutes can be acted by 14 men and 2 boys, or 12 men and 4 boys; that *Much Ado* with 22 speakers and 4 mutes can be acted with 11 or 12 men and 4 boys; and that indeed all the 18 pre-Globe plays, with two exceptions, can be produced with a standard cast of 16 (12 men and 4 boys). Even the play with the largest cast, *Richard III* with 55 speakers and 17 mutes, can with doubling easily be acted by a cast of 16.[6]

The two exceptions are *Titus Andronicus* and *Two Gentlemen of Verona*. *Titus Andronicus* requires only 16 actors for speaking parts and mutes after the first scene; but in the opening scene some seven to nine additional mutes, "as many as can be," are called for. But *Titus Andronicus* was composed before the formation of the Chamberlain's Company in June 1594; for Henslowe's Diary records its being performed as "ne" by Sussex's men on 23 January 1594; later in June it was produced

[6] I have in each case analyzed the plays and constructed the doubling charts to determine the *minimum* number of actors required by the text, without any preconceptions of what that number should be and without any forcing of the evidence. The results of my analyses are that nine of the pre-Globe plays require 16 actors (*2H4, H5, 1H6, 2H6, R2, R3, Merch, Ado, Rom*), four require 15 (*3H6, LLL, MND, Shr*), and three require 14 (*Err, 1H4, John*). Impressions based on hasty analyses are often misleading. *The Merchant of Venice*, for example, has only 20 speaking parts and 8 or 9 distinguishable mutes, and all the speaking parts can easily be performed by a cast of 13 without doubling any of the major roles. But more careful analysis reveals that this is also a play of pageantry which requires several mutes to fill the stage at Belmont, the Venetian court, and the finale. If we follow the stage directions, which specify "three or foure followers" of Morocho and a "traine" for Portia at II, 1 and II, 7, and other mutes elsewhere, the minimum cast possible is 16 if we give Morocho three mute followers and Portia one mute and Nerissa as her train. The critical points are II, 1 and II, 7, where only three actors are available as followers of Morocho and only Nerissa and one other as the train of Portia. Though seven of the plays *can* be produced with a minimum of 14 or 15 actors, they could in each case be conveniently produced with a cast of 16. The small range of these figures is remarkable, and shows that when Shakespeare sat down to write a play he usually had in mind a cast of 16 to produce it, and in almost every case he made maximum use of the cast available to him.

by the Lord Admiral's and Lord Chamberlain's Men playing in combination, and it was printed the same year with a statement on the title page that it had been acted by the companies of Derby, Pembroke, and Sussex. It is obvious that it was written in the uncertain and difficult period during which the Elizabethan acting companies were being re-formed, when some of them went bankrupt and others temporarily joined together. The printed text of the play reflects performance by a combined company, when Shakespeare could indulge himself in the unusual luxury of having more than 16 actors available, and so could crowd his stage with the pageantry of additional mute characters.

The second exception, *Two Gentlemen of Verona*, is quite short and has the smallest cast of any Shakespearean play. There are only sixteen speaking parts, which with the musician who sings in IV, 2 and the mute Ursula in IV, 4 provide only eighteen identifiable roles. Nine actors appear in the final scene; but the play requires a total of ten (seven men and three boys) for production; though if it were not for the specified speaking parts of the second and third outlaws in IV, 1, V, 3, and V, 4, it could easily be produced with a cast of eight (five men and three boys). But no matter how the doubling is rearranged, the use of the actors remains extremely inefficient (unlike their use in Shakespeare's other plays), because there are no other parts for the second and third outlaws to take in the first three acts. The Folio provides our only text of this play, and it may be that the version we have is one hastily and carelessly cut down for production by a small travelling troupe; but it seems to me more likely that *Two Gentlemen of Verona* is Shakespeare's earliest play, written before he had become acquainted with the casting requirements of a professional repertory company.

The only plays other than Shakespeare's known to have been acted by the Chamberlain's Men before their move to the Globe in 1599 are Jonson's *Every Man in His Humour* and the anonymous *A Warning for Fair Women*. The latter play, printed in 1599 as "acted for the Lord Chamberlains men," proves on analysis to be designed for a cast of exactly twelve men and four boys. Jonson's play was acted in 1598, and the earliest unrevised text, the 1601 Quarto, lists sixteen named characters on the reverse of the title page, though an unnamed servant also speaks in I, 1 and in V, 1 one or possibly two mute servants are needed. The interesting thing about the structure of Jonson's play is that, contrary to Elizabethan practice, none of the named characters can be doubled except Cob, and possibly Peto. In the last scene fifteen named characters appear on the stage, the entire cast except Cob, and his absence is explained by the fact that he is required to play the part of the unnamed servant who handles Clement's armor and ushers other characters on and off the stage. So it is clear that when Jonson wrote *Every Man in His Humour* for the Chamberlain's Men in 1598, he also tailored his script to a cast of 16.

We can now identify the adult actors of Shakespeare's company by name, for Jonson's 1616 Folio version of *Every Man in His Humour* (revised for a slightly larger cast, because Cob and Tib now converse in the final scene) lists the names of the ten "principall Comoedians" who acted in the original performance of 1598 as Will. Shakespeare, Aug. Philips, Hen. Condel, Will. Slye, Will. Kempe, Ric. Burbadge, Ioh. Hemings, Tho. Pope, Chr. Beeston, and Ioh. Duke. The first eight of these ten names reappear either as shareholders in the Globe lease of 21 February 1599, or as members of the company when it received its patent as the King's Men on 19 May 1603 (by which time Armin had succeeded to the place of Kemp). Beeston and Duke were probably hirelings, and the other hirelings in 1598 were probably Richard Cowley (who probably succeeded George Bryan, who was a payee until 1596), who played the minor part of Verges in *Much Ado*, was a payee in 1601, and became a shareholder in 1603; and John Sinklo (or Sincler), who acted minor parts in *Henry IV Part II* and other plays. These were the twelve adult actors of the company in 1598, to whom we must add four boys for our total of sixteen. It is probable that, except for the boys, who would have to be dropped from women's parts as their voices changed, the personnel of the company remained relatively stable between 1594 and 1599.[7]

[7] The custom of having twelve adult actors as the normal complement of an Elizabethan acting company may have been established in 1585 with the formation of the Queen's Company, several of whose twelve members later joined the Chamberlain's Company. So possibly from the very beginning of his professional career, Shakespeare may have become accustomed to writing plays for a cast of twelve adult actors and perhaps four boys.

Shakespeare's later plays also show admirable craftsmanship in adapting the cast of characters to the requirements of a comparatively small acting company. All of his plays composed after the move to the Globe in 1599 can also be produced with a cast of 16 for speaking parts; but several of these later plays require in addition a group of 6 or 8 masquers or dancers, who may have been hired soon after the move to the Globe and certainly by the time the Blackfriars was opened. It is significant that, except for these masquers, Shakespeare to the very end of his writing career adhered to his original basic pattern of a cast of 16 actors (except that in *Henry VIII*, written in collaboration, a different technique appears).

In the seventeenth century Shakespeare's company continued to prosper and its size gradually increased, until in 1624 at least 35 men and an unknown number of boys were listed in its employ.[8] These later records have led scholars to assume that Shakespeare could always depend upon a flexible number of actors—shareholders, hirelings, extras—ranging from 16 to 25 and including musicians and stage-keepers;[9] but the present analysis has, I hope, proved that during the early years of the Chamberlain's Company before the move to the Globe, that is between 1594 and 1599, Shakespeare *never* wrote a play for more than 16 actors including mutes, that the composition of his company during that period appears to have remained stable with 12 adults and 4 boys, that the actors who appeared on the boards even in bit parts were all full-time professionals, and that stage-keepers and other untrained extras need never have been drafted for the exigencies of a scene.

III

What has been written above may be of some slight interest to textual critics struggling with the minutiae of stage directions and speech prefixes, or to the technical investigators of Elizabethan stage conditions and the chroniclers of dramatic history.

[8] G. E. Bentley, *Jacobean and Caroline Stage*, 1:16.

[9] G. E. Bentley, *Shakespeare: A Biographical Handbook* (1961), p. 123, and *Shakespeare and His Theater* (1964), pp. 32–45. Bentley has made the most careful analysis of the size of Shakespeare's company to date, and his figures remain valid for the later career of the company in the seventeenth century. Chambers (*William Shakespeare*, 2:86) calculated a company of about 18 adults with an unspecified number of boys.

But of what use is it to present-day producers who are not limited by a circumscribed cast in mounting the plays; what use is it to the theater-goer who will not be able to recognize doubling if it is properly executed and will be annoyed by it if it is carried out too obviously; and of what use is it to the reader to know that Shakespeare had only sixteen actors with which to mount his plays, which when read have separate names for each character and each speech? Is to ask how many actors were in the company for which Shakespeare wrote as senseless and irrelevant a question as "How Many Children Had Lady Macbeth"?

It may be replied that analyses like those above will heighten the appreciation of producers, theater-goers, and readers for the cunning of Shakespeare's scenes, and may correct misstatements, such as the suggestion of some textual critics that the Bad Quarto of *Hamlet* was reported by the actor who played Marcellus and later Voltemand (the two parts cannot be doubled), or that Puck was "a cousin of Moth in *Love's Labour's Lost,* and no doubt played by the same small, agile boy" (Puck was played by a full grown man). But these are minor matters, even though of some interest. Much more important are radically new interpretations of the tone and atmosphere of some of the plays that are brought to light by an analysis of their casting. It is here that the techniques described in this paper can recover aspects of Shakespeare's own productions, his plays as performed under his own direction rather than as read, which have been lost and cannot be rediscovered by examination of the text alone. Let us look briefly at two pre-Globe plays, *Love's Labour's Lost* and *A Midsummer Night's Dream*, and see what an analysis of their casting will reveal.

Love's Labour's Lost has only 22 distinguishable roles: 19 speaking parts (counting Boyet as one of the "three Lordes" who accompany the Princess in II, 1) and three mutes (the third Lord in II, 1 and probably IV, 1, and the two Blackmoores in V, 2). The play could almost be produced with 14 actors; but that would necessitate Boyet's doubling as Dull (which would leave only nine lines for a costume change between his exit as Boyet before the end of IV, 1 and his entry as Dull at the beginning of IV, 2, an impracticably short time for a major shift in character), so the probable minimum cast is 15.

Only four actors with minor roles have to double: the mute third Lord as Holofernes and a mute Black-moore, the second Lord as Nathaniel and a mute Black-moore, Dull as the Forester and Marcade, and the boy who plays Jaquenetta and Maria.[10] None of these combined parts runs over 185 lines, and there are always 40 or more lines for costume changes.

At least 17 distinct characters appear in the long last scene (941 lines); but though the action is continuous, the scene is broken into three parts (1–309 when the Princess and her three ladies exeunt and leave Boyet momentarily alone on the stage, 310–734 when the Worthies exeunt, and 735–941, the company finale).[11] The quickest costume change is made by Costard, who exits at 512 and returns as Pompey at 549 (37 lines). After the disguises of the Prince and his courtiers and the Worthies, all 15 actors gather together on the stage for the company finale in the roles in which they first appeared. The Princess and her three ladies and the King and his three lords have remained with Boyet on stage after the exits of Marcade and the Worthies (730 and 734); then Armado returns at 888 in his braggart captain's costume, and three lines later "Enter all"—whom I take to be Moth, Holofernes, Nathaniel, Costard, and Dull in their original costumes, bearing stage symbols for spring and winter. And so the play is returned to its beginning, for "Jacke hath not Gill."

[10] A sixteenth actor would have very little to do (about the only parts available for him would be the second or third Lord, a mute Black-moore, and Marcade)—did Shakespeare construct the play in this fashion to relieve himself of an acting part?

[11] As in most Shakespearean plays, a number of stage directions are wanting in this scene. There is "Exit Cu[rate]" at 590, though Nathaniel should exit at 584; and there is "Exit Boy" for Moth at 598, but though he speaks at 707 no reentry is indicated. In order to give effect to Costard's announcement at 678, "The party is gone, fellow Hector, . . . she is two months on her way," he should burst upon the stage. Therefore he should exit at 591, Moth should exit as indicated at 598, and both Costard and Moth should run back upon the stage in great excitement at 678— their exits and excited return will suggest to the audience that they have had opportunity to learn about Jaquenetta's condition (I think this improves on the stage business suggested in the Furness *Variorum*, p. 293; Dover Wilson's *New Cambridge*, p. 180; and Richard David's *New Arden*, p. 175). There is no exit for Marcade indicated, but he probably leaves immediately after his "tale is told" at 730; it is on this assumption that I have given his part to Dull.

One apparent difficulty in casting *Love's Labour's Lost* is the large number of roles that seem to require boy actors. Women's parts were ordinarily played by boys, and the tiny page Moth, the sweet singer of the company, must also be played by a boy. Thus we have Jaquenetta, the Princess and her three ladies, and Moth, a total of six apparent boy's parts. Jaquenetta and Maria never appear on stage together and can easily double; but at V, 2:158 the Princess and her three ladies and Moth are on stage at the same time, which apparently requires five boys, though our analyses have indicated that only four boys were ordinarily available.

This has led one recent editor of the play to suggest that "the large number of parts for which boy-players would be required—the Princess and her ladies, Jacquenetta, Moth—points away from the regular actors' companies to some great household where a troupe of choristers was maintained."[12] But these parts require a high degree of professional competence, scarcely to be expected of household choristers; and the First Quarto of 1598 states that it was "presented before her Highnes this last Christmas," presumably by the Chamberlain's Company. A closer examination of the text will show that only the usual four boy actors are needed.

The King and his three courtiers fall in love with the Princess and her three ladies, and most of us imagine that the Princess and her ladies are the usual beauties of romance—at least I have not come upon any editor or commentator who has hinted the contrary. But notice that, when the Princess first enters, Boyet says:

> Be now as prodigall of all Deare grace,
> As Nature was in making Graces deare,
> When she did starve the generall world beside,
> And prodigally gave them all to you.
>
> [II, 1:9]

And when the clown Costard, delivering Berowne's letter, wants to know who is the head lady, the greatest lady, he says:

> *Clow.* Which is the greatest ladie, the highest?
> *Quee.* The thickest, and the tallest.
> *Clow.* The thickest, and the tallest: It is so, trueth is trueth.

[12] Richard David, *New Arden* (1951), p. 1.

> And your waste M[i]str[e]s were as slender as my wit,
> One a these Maides girdles for your waste should be fit.
> Are not you the chiefe woman? You are the thickest heere.
>
> [IV, 1:46]

The humor of these two passages, and of other parts of the play besides, resides in the fact that the Princess, far from being a young, lithesome heroine of romance, is actually intended by Shakespeare to be represented on the stage as a portly Amazon, like Katisha in the *Mikado*. Her part, then, is taken not by a small graceful boy, but by a large ungainly man (see Fig. 3). And so by an analysis of the casting, and the text, we get a clue to a visual dimension of the play and a source of comedy unsuspected before, for Navar's courtship of the Princess has an entirely different effect upon an audience that perceives her as portly and probably gruff-speaking.[13]

Analysis of the casting of *A Midsummer Night's Dream* also sheds new light on the original production. The First Quarto of 1600, which is closest to Shakespeare's autograph and represents the earliest state of the text, contains 22 speaking parts (counting the "Fairie" who speaks at II, 1:1 as distinct from the other four fairies, which is required by the casting pattern), and one mute attendant of Theseus (Theseus enters with "others" at I, 1:1—Philostrate is one and the plural requires a second, and he addresses an unnamed attendant at IV, 1:107), for a total of 23. These are all the characters distinguishable, because I assume that the "traine" of Oberon and of Titania whose members enter at II, 1:60 are the four named fairies, two and two; and that the "two of our company" who dance the Bergomaske at V, 1:369 are two of the mechanicals, probably Quince and Snout.

Twentieth-century producers of *A Midsummer Night's Dream* have striven to bring out its "dream-like, fairy-like atmosphere," represented for example by the 1935 film of Max

---

[13] An adult male actor can, of course, be made up to look like a beautiful woman, though his voice is usually a disadvantage. In 1660 Pepys saw Edward Kynaston, who was famous for his female impersonations, act Olympia in *The Loyal Subject* when he was in his upper teens or about twenty, and remarked that he was "the lovliest lady that ever I saw in my life, only her voice not very good" (*Diary*, August 18, 1660). That Shakespeare did not intend the Princess to appear beautiful is shown by the text itself which emphasizes her excessive height and portliness.

FIGURE 3

LOVE'S LABOUR'S LOST

(Doubling Chart)

Actor	I, 1	I, 2	II, 1	III, 1	IV, 1	IV, 2	IV, 3	V, 1	V, 2a	V, 2b	V, 2c	No. of Lines
1	Biron		-Biron-	-Biron			Biron		Biron	Biron	Biron	619
2	King-		-King-				-King		-King	King	King	314
3			Prin		Prin-				Prin	Prin	Prin	283
4		Arm		Arm-				-Arm		-Arm Hect	-Arm	261
5			Boyet		Boyet-				-Boyet	Boyet	Boyet	230
6	-Cost	-Cost-		-Cost-	-Cost-	-Cost-	-Cost-	-Cost		-Cost Pomp	-Cost	205
7			*3 Ld		*3 Ld-	Hol		Hol	-*Bl-	Hol Jud	Hol	185
8	-Dum-		Dum-				-Dum-		-Dum-	Dum	Dum	86
9	-Long-		-Long-		2nd L-		-Long		-Long-	Long	Long	71
10			2nd L			Nath		Nath	-*Bl-	-Nath Alex	Nath	38
11	-Dull	-Dull-			For-	Dull		Dull		Mer-	-*Dull	32
12			Ros		Ros-				Ros	Ros	Ros	178
13		Moth-		Moth-				-Moth	-Moth-	-Moth	Moth	165
14		Jaq-	Kath		*Kath-	Jaq-	*Jaq-		Kath	Kath	Kath	58
15			Mar		Mar-				Mar	Mar	Mar	36

* indicates mute   - enters after beginning or exits before end of scene

FIGURE 4

A MIDSUMMER NIGHT'S DREAM

(Doubling Chart)

Actor	I, 1	I, 2	II, 1	II, 2	III, 1	III, 2a	III, 2b	IV, 1	IV, 2	V, 1a	V, 1b	No. of Lines
1		Bot			Bot			Bot	-Bot	-Bot / Pyr		271
2	Thes-							-Thes-		Thes		243+28
3			Fairy- / Ob-	-Ob-		Ob-		Ob-			-Ob	225
4	*Phil-		Rob	-Rob	-Rob-	-Rob-	-Rob			Phil-	Rob	207+24
5	-Lys-			-Lys-		-Lys-	Lys	Lys-		-Lys		172
6	-Dem-		-Dem-	-Dem-		-Dem-	-Dem	Dem-		-Dem		141
7	-Ege-	Quin			Quin-			-Ege-	Quin	-Quin / Prol+Bl		133+41
8		Flu	*Pea-	Pea-	Flu- / Pea			Pea-	Flu	-Flu / Thisbe	-Pea	57+
9		Star	*Cob-	*Cob-	Star- / -Cob			Cob-	Star	-Star / Moon	Cob	
10		Snou	*Moth-	*Moth-	Snou- / Moth-			Moth-	Snou	-Snou / Wall+Bl	-Moth	
11		Snug	*Must-	*Must-	*Snug- / Must			Must-	Snug	-Snug / Lion	-Must	
12								*Th at-				
13	-Hel		-Hel	-Hel		-Hel-	-Hel	-Hel-		-*Hel		229
14	-Herm-			-Herm		-Herm-	-Herm	Herm-		-*Herm		165
15	*Th at		-Tit-	Tit	Tit			Tit-			-Tit	143
16	Hip-							-Hip-		Hip		34

* indicates mute   - enters after beginning or exits before end of scene

Reinhardt which was all moonlight and fairies; and critics have delighted in commenting on the contrast between the grotesque materiality of Quince, Bottom, and the four rude mechanicals and the ethereal beauty of Titania and the diminutive fairies. We assume that the fairies are intended to be played by small boys, because we think of fairies as tiny folk; but that is a recent and not a generally held Elizabethan notion.[14]

The clue to Shakespeare's intention and the indication of the effects he wishes to produce are provided by working out the doubling patterns of the play. The only problem again arises from the large number of parts apparently designed for boys. There are four women characters who cannot double—Helena, Hermia, Titania, and Hippolyta (Helena, Hermia, and Titania are on stage together at IV, 1:1; and though Titania exits at 106 while the other two remain, Hippolyta immediately enters at 107, so none of these four parts can be doubled). In addition there are the four fairies attendant on Titania (Pease-blossome, Cobweb, Moth, and Mustard-seede) in II, 1, II, 2, IV, 1, and V, 1*b*. If these parts are not doubled, *A Midsummer Night's Dream* would require a cast of 19: 11 men and 8 boys. But analysis of the text reveals that Shakespeare has carefully constructed his play to keep the two realms, fairyland and Athens, separate from one another. Bottom is the only mortal who is awake and on stage with the fairies; none of the other mortal characters in the play ever sees Oberon, Titania, and their fairy train. The four rude mechanicals (Flute, Starveling, Snout, and Snug) and the four fairies never appear on stage together, and there is always an interval, ranging from 29 to 178 lines, between the exit of the one group and the entrance of the other, which is ample for a costume change. So it is evident that the four fairies are played by the same large lumbering adult actors who take the parts of the four rude mechanicals and that the play can easily be produced by 11 adult and 4 boy actors (see Fig. 4).[15]

14 Katherine M. Briggs, *The Anatomy of Puck* (1959), pp. 13–16, shows that Elizabethans thought of fairies variously—as of human size, as larger than human, or as smaller.

15 Most modern editors divide the play into nine scenes; but the stage is cleared at III, 2:412 and V, 1:377 (so I add III, 2*b* and V, 1*b*), and the action is continuous in II, 2—III, 1 and III, 2*b*—IV, 1 because Titania or the lovers remain asleep on the stage. The First Folio text represents a

Therefore the visual effect that Shakespeare intended to be conveyed by the fairies was not one of literal diminutive beauty; if he had wanted that he could have refashioned his play so that the smaller boy actors could play the fairy parts. Instead he appears to have intended an effect either of bulky grotesquerie, or of something quite different from and more subtle than productions in our time have indicated.

---

later performance with slight changes that may not be Shakespeare's—in V, 1a Egeus is substituted for Philostrata (quite illogically, because in I, 1 Philostrata is Theseus' master of the revels), and the four Pyramus-Thisbe players are ushered in by "Tawyer with a trumpet before them" (Tawyer is a late comer to the company, recorded in 1624 as a musician serving as Heminge's apprentice). This makes impossible the doubling of Egeus and Quince, and requires a cast of 16.

Most modern editors have followed the suggestion of F. G. Fleay (*Life and Work of Shakespeare*, 1886, p. 182) that the Quarto and Folio texts have a "double ending," one for a public performance and the other for private performance at a wedding, and that therefore even the Quarto retains signs of adaptation and revision. But analysis of the casting shows this to be an unnecessary hypothesis. All Shakespeare's early comedies have company finales in which the entire cast assembles on the stage in the final scene; but in this play the necessities of doubling require that the mortals must exit before the fairies can appear. Theseus' final admonition to the lovers and Robin's introductory speech, 28 lines together, provide the interval needed for the two mechanicals who danced the Bergomaske to change into fairy costume and reenter with the other two as the train of Oberon and Titania. Shakespeare keeps the two realms of his play separate to the very end, and makes artistic capital out of the exigencies of his cast.

III

THEATERS AND PRODUCTION

X

F. P. WILSON

Ralph Crane, Scrivener to the King's Players

I

We have been slow to realize the important bibliographical evidence to be gained from a study of the extant manuscripts of Elizabethan and Stuart plays. In the eighteenth and nineteenth centuries most scholars were content with the evidence to be extracted from printed books. Only within the last few years has it been fully recognized that manuscripts may give us authentic knowledge of the kinds of copy handled by the printer and of the accidents which might happen to it. As we have no dramatic manuscripts used as copy by an Elizabethan or Stuart printer, it is the more important that the extant manuscripts should be used to control bibliographical speculations based upon printed texts. In recent years it has also been abundantly shown that a study of the handwritings in these manuscripts is of great importance as a guide to authorship, and it is perhaps in the identification of handwritings that our advance has been most notable. In the play of *Sir Thomas More* (Harleian MS. 7368) the hands of Anthony Munday and Dekker, possibly even of Shakespeare, have so far been identified, and the MS. has not yet yielded up all its secrets. Within the last year or two Dr. W. W. Greg has found conclusive evidence that two of the manuscripts in Egerton 1994—*The Captives* and *Calisto*—are in the handwriting of Thomas Heywood: and Dr. Greg and Mr. C. J. Sisson have shown that a single person—perhaps the "bookholder" of the King's Company—is the scribe of Beaumont and Fletcher's *The Honest Man's Fortune* (MS. Dyce 9), of Beaumont and Fletcher's *Bonduca* (MS. Add. 36758), and of the

The Library, 4th ser., 7 (1926):194–215. Reprinted by permission of the author's executrix and the editors of *The Library*.

theatrical additions to Massinger's *Believe as You List* (MS. Egerton 2828). In an important article on "Prompt Copies, Private Transcripts, and 'The Playhouse Scrivener'" (*The Library*, September, 1925) Dr. Greg suggests that Fletcher and Massinger's *Sir John van Olden Barnavelt* (MS. Add. 18653) and Middleton's *The Witch* (MS. Malone 12) are in the same handwriting. The present article will show that both these plays were "manuscribed" by Ralph Crane, that Crane is also the scribe of Fletcher's *Demetrius and Enanthe* (in the possession of Lord Harlech) and of two manuscripts of Middleton's *A Game at Chess* (Lansdowne 690 and MS. Malone 25), and that by his own showing he was transcribing plays for the King's Players before 1621.[1]

II

The most assiduous lover of the by-ways of seventeenth-century literature might well be ignorant of the existence of Crane. His one published book *The Workes of Mercy* (1621), republished after 1625 as *The Pilgrimes New-yeares-Gift*, is a collection of undistinguished religious verse which can have roused little interest in his own age and has none for ours. But as Crane the scrivener is more interesting than Crane the writer, and is likely to prove more important than has been suspected, it has seemed desirable to supplement the short account of his life given in the *Dictionary of National Biography*. The main sources of our knowledge are the long biographical preface in verse to *The Workes Of Mercy*, the enlarged version of this preface in *The Pilgrimes New-yeares-Gift*, and the dedications to the manuscripts which he presented to his patrons. It is hoped that the discovery of more manuscripts which may lie hidden in private libraries in this country and in America will increase our knowledge of the man and of his work.

Ralph Crane (who always spelt his Christian name "Raph") was born in London: probably in the fifties or sixties, for by

---

[1] A sixth MS. may have to be added to this list. Mr. Frank Marcham states in *The King's Office of the Revels 1610–22* (1925, p. 6) that a MS. of *The Beggar's Bush* written about 1620 is "in a hand somewhat similar to the Bodleian manuscript of Middleton's *Witch*." This is one of the manuscripts sold from the Lambarde Library by Messrs. Hodgson on 19 June 1924 (Lot 528). I have failed to trace the present owner.

1621 he was already an old man. Lodge (born *c.* 1557) hails him as friend, and dedicates *Scillaes Metamorphosis* (1589) to him "and the rest of his most entire well willers, the Gentlemen of the Innes of Court and Chancerie." His father was a freeman of the Merchant Tailors' Company, and in this Society "with good esteeme bore offices of worth."[2] His education past, "Sweet Master Crane," as Lodge calls him, "tride the Aire of diuers noble Counties," and it was perhaps at this period of his life that he became a household servant in the "Honourable House" of "the worthy Deseruer of all true Honors, and noble Louer of Religion and Learning, Mrs Dorothie Osborne."[3]

> *Much variation* I haue had since then
> With one blest Gift, *A Ready Writers Pen.*

First, he was "painfull Clarke" for seven years to Sir Anthony Ashley, Clerk of the Privy Council from 1588 and perhaps earlier. This post enabled him to mark the goodness and the nobility of the peers.

> That (haplesse) *thence* I slipt, (wanting firme hold)
> I only sigh the fate, but leau't vntold.

Next to the Signet Office and the Privy Seal, where he served as an "under-writer" during the Clerkship of Lewin Munck. In 1621 he still possessed "some gentlenesse from thence" to lessen his sorrows. Crane's pen also did service to the "Tribe of Levi" and "writ their Oracles," but above all his laborious hand was employed by "the renown'd and learned Lawyers." He proceeds (*The Workes Of Mercy,* sig. A 6):

> And some imployment hath my vsefull *Pen*
> Had 'mongst those ciuill, well-deseruing *men,*
> That grace the *Stage* with *honour* and *delight,*
> Of whose true honesties I much could write,
> But will comprise't (as in a Caske of Gold)
> Vnder the *Kingly Seruice* they doe hold.

---

[2] If his father was the John Crane twice mentioned in C. M. Clode's *Memorials,* pp. 217 and 544, it does not appear that he was held in so good esteem as his son would lead us to think. He was committed to ward in 1568 for keeping a "foreigner," and in 1608 the Company was still in possession of gilt plate "pawned and forfeyted" by him many years past.

[3] Presumably the grandmother of the famous letter-writer.

So ends the history of his life's "sad Pilgrimage" up to 1621, the evening of his age.[4] It is a mark of his poverty and of his skilful mendicancy that *The Workes Of Mercy* has at least three dedications and as many patrons: Dorothy Osborne (Bodleian copy, Art. 8⁰. D. 15), John, Earl of Bridgewater (Thorpe's Sale Catalogue, 1834, pt. 3, no. 690—perhaps the Britwell copy sold at Sotheby's on 7 February 1922), and his old chief Lewin Munck, Esquire, of Babraham in Cambridgeshire (a copy formerly in the possession of William Cole of Milton, cited by Hunter, *Chorus Vatum*, Add. MS. 24488, fo. 159). But he does not follow the practice of those "Falconers" satirized in Dekker's *Lanthorne and Candle-light*, whose epistles dedicatory varied in nothing but in the titles of their patrons. For each patron he writes an appropriate epistle.[5]

It was perhaps in 1622 that Crane transcribed "A Song in seuerall parts" by Thomas Middleton, which was performed at a feast given by the Lord Mayor, Edward Barkham, to his brethren the aldermen and other guests in the Easter holidays of this year. The manuscript of this "Invention" is now in the Public Record Office (*State Papers, Domestic*, vol. 129, doc. 53). Middleton thought well of Crane's penmanship, for he employed him to transcribe two of his plays.[6]

Crane saw the horrors of the great London plague of 1625 and escaped the infection. But he was not exempted from

> Her Markes of *Penury*, *Expence*, and *Woes*
> Of Debts, *engagements*, all heart-breaking throes;
> But that I still about me beare the signe.

[4] The name is so common that we cannot be sure he was (1) the Ralph Crane to whom was granted on 10 March 1609 the benefit of the recusancy of Bridget Morgan of Heyford, Northamptonshire (*Cal. S. P. Dom.*, 1603–10, p. 497), or (2) the Ralph Crane whose son Ralph was baptized at St. Martin's-in-the-Fields on 14 June 1611.

[5] The one copy of *The Pilgrimes New-yeares-Gift* which I have seen (British Museum, C. 37 d. 7) has no dedication, but it is clear from the preface that one or more were intended.

[6] It is curious that in the Stationers' Register (14 December 1620) *The Workes Of Mercy* is entered as the work of T. M. Whoever may be the author of the poems—and they do not read like Middleton's work—Crane is certainly the author of the autobiographical preface.

At this crisis in his fortunes he began making "private transcripts" of poems and plays for presentation to his patrons, several of which survive to attest the industry of his pen and the beauty of his calligraphy. The first dated manuscript of his now known is his transcript of Fletcher's *Demetrius and Enanthe*, dedicated on 27 December 1625 to Sir "Kelham" Digby (Plate I). An account of his transcripts of plays will be given below. Of his non-dramatic manuscripts three are in the British Museum, two in the Bodleian, and one in the Huntington Library.[7] These six manuscripts, five of which have dedications, are our sole authority for the last years of his life. They are now described in rough chronological order. It will be seen that his taste, or that of his patrons, is for moral and sacred verse, and that the work of many writers is represented.

MS. Rawl. poet. 61 is one of the largest of these transcripts. It contains: (1) "Meditations" upon Job 17:1 and 13 (22 pages) by William Austin, the barrister of Lincoln's Inn whose works were printed posthumously in 1635. (2) "Certaine selected Psalmes of Dauid (in Verse)" (109 pages) by Francis and Christopher Davison, Joseph Bryan, Richard Gipps, and Thomas Carey,[8] most if not all of them members of the Inns of Court. (3) William Austin's "Certaine deuine Hymnes, or Carrolls for Christmas-daie Togeather with diuers deuout and zealous Meditations vpon our Sauiours Passion" (36 pages). This is dated 23 October 1626 and is dedicated to Crane's friend, John Peirs. (4) "A Sumarie; and true Distinction, betweene the Lawe, & ye Ghospel" (8 pages) by Crane himself. (5) "Londons Lamentable Estate, in any great Visitation," a poem of 206 lines (11 pages) on the plague of 1625 by "Ph. M." which appears to have escaped the attention of writers upon Massinger.

Two of Crane's transcripts are made up entirely of Austin's

---

[7] A MS. which I have not seen, formerly in Corser's Library and described by him at some length in *Collectanea Anglo-Poetica* 3:231–36, may be by Crane. It contains a religious poem—"The Most Auntient Historie of God and Man"—by R. C., finished on 29 July 1629. Is this the *"deuine Argument"* which Crane had "vpon the Anvile" in 1625 (see Plate I)? The author appears to have prepared the poem for publication, but a sacred poem of some 12,000 indifferent lines would not readily meet with a publisher. At the Huth Sale in June 1912 this manuscript was sold for ten shillings.

[8] A namesake of the author of "Ask me no more where Jove bestows."

poems. One, formerly in the Heber Library and now in the British Museum (Add. MS. 34752), is dedicated to Lord Baltimore. This MS. is undated, but must have been written after 1624, when George Calvert was raised to the peerage, and before 1632, the year of his death. In the dedication Crane states that Austin's poems came to him "by a bless'd Holy chance" and that this book may be "his last Oblation ere he die." The other (MS. Rawl. D. 301) is dated May 1628 and is dedicated to Lady Anne Cooper, wife of Sir John Cooper and sole daughter and heir to his old master Sir Anthony Ashley, who had died in the previous January. "He was my *Master*, and though my outward Garment speakes not his death, yet my in-ward Loue sighes his departure. . . . And had not too-too many Disasters too-too much weakened my Habilities, a more expressiue and appropriated *Epitaph* had attended his Hearse."

"The Faultie Fauorite," now in the Huntington Library,[9] is a "Theologicall, Vsefull, & Applicable Exposition" in prose upon 2 Kings 7:2. Crane claims nothing therein but the manuscription, but does not give the name of the author. The dedication to John, Earl of Bridgewater is dated January, 1631. Crane mentions this manuscript as an annual tribute, his "yeerely Destinate to some Corner" of the Earl's Library. The calligraphy supports his claim that his pen "is not yet so much decaied, as my Age (to my Ruine) makes Men beleeue."[10]

Harl. 6930, which now contains no dedicatory epistle, has most of the psalms in MS. Rawl. poet. 61: and the contents of Harl. 3357 agree with those of MS. Rawl. poet. 61 with the omission of Crane's work and Ph. M.'s and the inclusion of Randolph's "A diuine Pastorall Eglogue" (ff. 88–91). Harl. 3357 has a dedication to Sir Francis Ashley, brother of Sir Anthony, in which Crane refers to the rarity of the poetical dish he has prepared, "there not being three such any where extant; and not One (vnles surreptitiously gotten) but of my Pen." Ashley is asked to consider this book "(for Age, Affliction, Greif and

[9] I am indebted to Mr. R. B. Haselden, Keeper of the Manuscripts in the Huntington Library, for sending me particulars of this MS. and of the Huntington MS. of *A Game at Chess* and for presenting me with photostats of parts of each of these MSS.

[10] He complains again in *The Pilgrimes New-yeares-Gift* that he is too old to get work: *"now young ones raigne."*

Want tell Me, it will be so) the Vltimum Vale, of Him that hono[rs]. your Name." This MS. is dated December 1632, and Crane's struggles with want and the patron must soon have ended. Did he escape the worst enemy of all, the jail? His will is not preserved at Somerset House, and it is improbable that he found it necessary to make one. No juster epitaph upon this unfortunate man could be found than that which he writes for himself in *The Pilgrimes New-yeares-Gift:*

> Through *City, Countrie, Court, Church, law & stage*
> I haue pass'd thorough in my *Pilgrimage,*
> Yet here I stand *Fortunes Anatomie,*
> A spectacle of *Times Inconstancy.*

III

If Crane had been employed only by the Court, the Church, and the Law, it would not be necessary to exempt him from oblivion. But his statement that his "useful pen" found "some employment" among the King's Players raised the hope that at last it might be possible to give a name to one of those hitherto elusive persons, the "playhouse scriveners." A comparison of *The Witch* (MS. Malone 12) with Crane's poetical manuscripts led to the belief that they were by a single hand, but to be certain it was necessary to get a sight of his one signed dramatic manuscript. My grateful acknowledgments are due to Lord Harlech, the owner of *Demetrius and Enanthe,* for depositing the MS. in the Bodleian, so that I might consult it at my leisure, and for granting permission to reproduce facsimiles of the dedication and of a page of the text (Plates I and II). Bodley's Librarian has kindly allowed me to give illustrations from *The Witch* (Plate III) and *A Game at Chess* (MS. Malone 25—Plate V), and from a MS. of *A Game at Chess* in the British Museum (Lansdowne 690) I am able to show a page of yet another of Crane's dramatic transcripts (Plate IV). For facsimiles of folio 27 and of the upper half of folio 1 of *Barnavelt* (MS. Add. 18653) the reader is referred to Miss W. P. Frijlinck's edition of this play, published in this country by the Oxford University Press. A portion of folio 4*b* (with a marginal note by Buc) is reproduced in *English Literary Autographs 1550–1650* (ed. W. W. Greg), Plate xxx (c).

The editor of *The Library* has been so generous in his allowance of facsimiles that it is hardly necessary to describe and to compare the handwriting in these MSS. The evidence is before the reader. To bring out more clearly the striking similarity between the italic letters I have chosen to reproduce the pages containing the words "Actus Secundus," but indeed the general impression given by any page that these MSS. are in a single hand is overwhelming and is sustained by a detailed analysis. Attention may be called to the remarkable italic "d." The long flourish above the loop is formed with a separate stroke of the pen. It will be seen that the last two letters of "Actus" are made in exactly the same way. The "E" of "Enter" in *The Witch, Barnavelt*, and Lansdowne 690 is not to be found in the scene-divisions of *Demetrius and Enanthe* and MS. Malone 25, but it is used elsewhere in these MSS. The secretary hands are of the same formal type, and contain the same variant forms and the same intermixture of italic letters. See for example the two kinds of capital "S" (e.g. Plate III, l. 12), of "d" (Plate II, l. 8), and of "a" (*ibid.*, l. 17). The secretary hand in *Barnavelt* is less calligraphic, but there is no doubt that it is Crane's.

Barnavelt is in folio, as are all extant playhouse MSS. of this period. The four other MSS. which we are to consider are in quarto: these are private transcripts written throughout in Crane's hand (except the dedicatory leaf in MS. Malone 25) and without erasures.[11] The page-measurements are as follows: *Barnavelt* (57 pages of text), $11\frac{5}{8}$ by $7\frac{1}{2}$ inches; *Demetrius and Enanthe* (128 pages), $7\frac{3}{8}$ by $5\frac{11}{16}$; *The Witch* (97 pages), $7\frac{1}{2}$ by $5\frac{1}{2}$; *A Game at Chess*, Lansdowne 690 (102 pages), $7\frac{1}{16}$ by $5\frac{1}{2}$; *A Game at Chess*, MS. Malone 25 (75 pages), $7\frac{1}{4}$ by $5\frac{3}{4}$. *Barnavelt* has about fifty-five lines, the private transcripts from about twenty-four lines to twenty-seven lines, to the full page.

THE TRAGEDY OF SIR JOHN VAN OLDEN BARNAVELT. As *Barnavelt* is the only one of these MSS. that is a prompt copy, it is not surprising that the hand is here less calligraphic. The date of composition can be assigned with confidence to July and August 1619 and the date of performance to August (Frijlinck, xix). Internal evidence shows it to have been written for the

---

[11] A private transcript might, however, be in folio, as for example *Bonduca* (Add. MS. 36758).

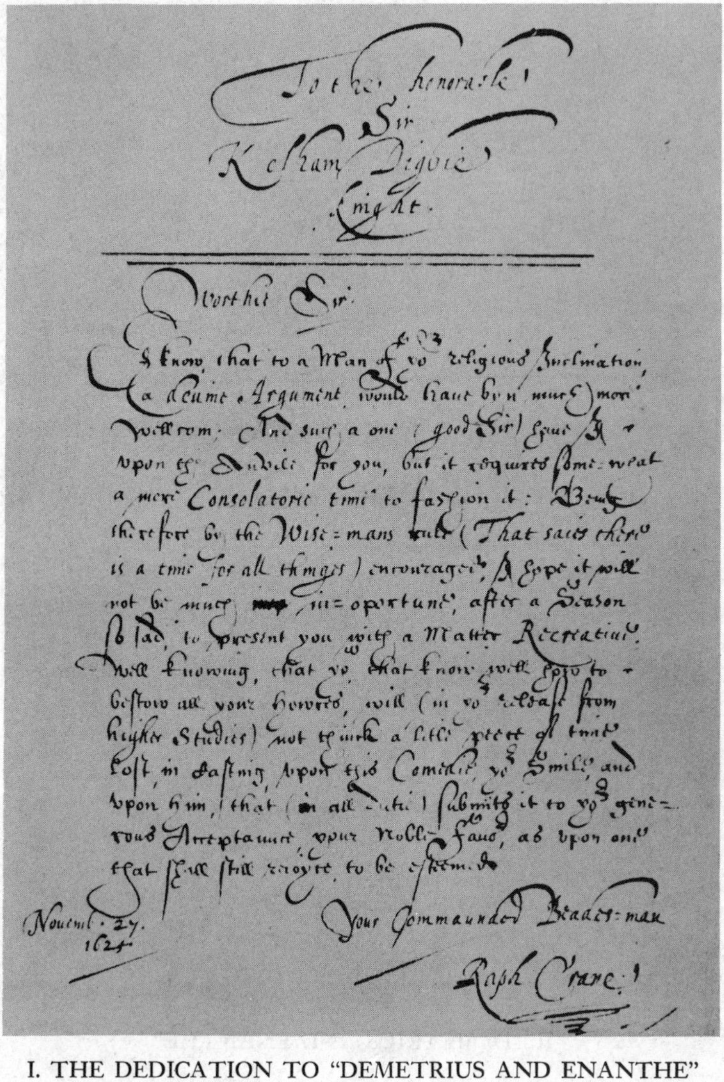

I. THE DEDICATION TO "DEMETRIUS AND ENANTHE"

23.

but still remember, if your fooling with me
make me forget my Trust.
Cel. I haue done: Farwell (Sir)
neuer looke back, you shall not stay, not a minutt.
Dem. I must haue one Farwell more.
Cel. now the Dromes beate:
I dare not stall your stond, not a sound more:
onely this Looke: The Godd preserue, and saue yee. — Exeunt
seuerally

___

Actus Secundus

Scea pria: Enter Antigonus: Carinthus, &
Timon.

Ant. What! haue ye found her out!
Car. we haue beene after her:
Ant. what's that to my, desire!
Car. your Grace must give vs
Time, and a little meanes.
Tim. She is sure a Stranger:
if she were bredd, or knowne here:
Ant. your dull indeauours
should neuer be imploid: How are you certaine
she is a stranger.
Tim. being so young, and handsome,
and not made pryby to your Graces pleasures
for I presume vntill your gracious fauo
                                                        you

II. "DEMETRIUS AND ENANTHE"

Her: in good fashion

Ab. let me but see that, and I'll sup wth you —— she Coniures. And

the Catt and Fiddle: em posterial Ordinarie   Enter a Catt (playing

You had a devill once, in a flea-skin   on a Fiddle, and

                                                  Spiritts (wth Meate)

Her. Oh; I haue him still: come walke with me Sir. — Ext

Firi: how lost, and ready is a Drunckard now to reile to his

Devill. I will I'le even so, and see how his catts, and

I'a be sworne if he be not the father of the brood

with laughing at em. — Exit   Finis Actus sori.

Actus Secundus.

Scā: priā. Entr Antonio, & Gasparo.

Gas. **Good** Sir, whence Springes this Sadnes: trust me Sir,

Yo' looke, not like a Man was Married yesterdaie:

there could come no ill Tidings since last night

to raise that discontent: I was wont to know all

before you had a Wiffe (Sir) you nere found me

without those parts of Manhood, (Trust, & Sarvice)

An. I will not till this this.

Gass. not your true Servant Sir.

An. True: you'll all sweare according to yr Tallent

                                                      this

Actus Secundus.

Scæ^a pri^a Enter ye whit~ Queenes-Pawne (reading) & to
her the Black Bishop's Pawne.

W.Q:P And here agen: It is the Daughters dutie
to obaie her Confessors Commaund, in all things,
without Exciption, or Expostulation.
It is the most gennrall Rule that ere I read of.
Yet when her spirituall Good howe bounelesse Virtue is,
Goodnes, and Grace, itt gently reboundes.
And then it appeeres well, to giue the power
of the Dispensoͬ as virtue & vice shalbe.

Bl.B:P This's hard vppont: I tread the most modest step
that I could vse, to open my Quentes.
What little, or no pains goes to some mens Exploits.
Hah! what haue we here? a sealed Note! what is this!
To the Black Bishops Pawne This: how to me!
strange: Who Subscribes it the Black-King: what would he!
Pawne sufficientlie holie, but Vnmeasurabelie Politique.
We had late Intelligence from our most
industrious Seruant (famous in all Parts of Europe)
our Knight of the Black - house, That you haue at this
                                                      instant

Actus Secundus.

Scæ prima.

The white - Quitnes Pawne (reading) The Black
Bp. Pawne, Then ye Black Quitnes-Pawne
Then ye Black Bishop, & Black Knight

wh.Q.P And see agen: It is th. Daughters Duty
to Obay her Confessors Command in all Things
without Exception, or Expostulation.

Hos hes most gentdlee Rule, that as shee read of.

Out, when his spirit hon boundles Vertue is
Goodnes, and Grace, 'tis gently reconcild
And you it appeard well to have the power
of the Dispense as vuirtuous bibds.

Bl.B.P Shee th. past the generalle Rule, the large Extent
off our Inscription, for Obedience,
and yet with great Clariti of Soule
Hee shee moved on the Lettre

wh.Q.P holy Sir
too long shee have myssd you: oh, your Absence starves mee.
Easter for I much redemption (worthi Sir)

for

King's Players by Fletcher and Massinger. *Barnavelt* is therefore one of those King's plays, perhaps the only one now extant, upon which Crane claims to have employed his useful pen before 1621. Those who maintain that a playhouse copy at this period was usually in the author's autograph may still abide by their opinion, for an exception must clearly be made for plays of multiple authorship. Crane no doubt was presented with the authors' "foul papers," and told to make a fair copy. Anthony Munday had done the same office twenty years or so before in that part of *Sir Thomas More* which is in his handwriting. It is worth noting that Crane boasts of being employed by the King's Players, not by the dramatists employed by the King's Players. There is good evidence that dramatists sent in autograph MSS. to their playhouse. The services of a scribe were called in later, if required, by the playhouse. Heminge and Condell say of Shakespeare: "His mind and hand went together: And what he thought, he vttered with that easinesse, that wee haue scarse receiued from him a blot in his papers." Heminge and Condell are speaking here for the King's Players. Mr. A. W. Pollard has shown how reasonable it is to take them at their word and believe that Shakespeare's Company received from him his autograph manuscripts.

Three distinct hands are to be found in *Barnavelt:* (1) The text of the play is in Crane's handwriting. (2) A member of the company, perhaps the stage-manager, has written marginal reminders to get ready various properties (a bell, pen and ink, a table, a scaffold, &c); and to the stage-directions marking the entrance of minor characters he has added the names or initials of the actors who played them. (3) Sir George Buc, Master of the Revels, has written a warning note on f. 4*b;* where the offence lay only in a word or phrase he has here and there substituted a more politic reading (e.g. at l. 2436 in Miss Frijlinck's edition);[12] and he has marked for cancellation several passages which he found offensive to the state or to morality (see especially ff. 7*b*, 22*b*, 23*a*, 24*a*). When we see how

[12] At l. 2436 the words "cutt of his opposites," which replace "tooke that course that now is practisd on you," are in Buc's handwriting. Of the other interlineations in this MS. (e.g. at ll. 36, 51, 206, 281, 587, 588, 803, 804, 2445) some may be in Buc's handwriting, some in Crane's, some in another hand or hands.

slight is the reason for some of Buc's objections, we begin to wonder how much of him lies embedded in Shakespeare and still more how much of Shakespeare was scored out by his active pen. Was he, for example, in part responsible for the drastic cutting of *Macbeth*? A play which presented the murder of a Scottish king might well make the Revels Office nervous. This creative censor may again be seen at work in one or two lines of *The Second Maiden's Tragedy*.

It was possible to omit some of the passages cancelled by Buc without affecting the sense, but others it was necessary to rewrite. Three lines written vertically in the right margin replace six cancelled lines on folio 7*b*, a short leaf written on one side only replaces the original eighth leaf, and five lines, also written down the page and themselves afterward cancelled, replace thirty-nine lines on folios 23*a* and 23*b*.[13] It is interesting that all these substitutions appear to be in Crane's handwriting. From *The Workes Of Mercy* we get the impression that he was not a regular employee of the King's Players, but rather a casual laborer whose services as a professional scrivener were called in when occasion demanded. To call him a stage-manager or the Company's "book-keeper" would certainly be to go beyond the evidence. But it is clear from *Barnavelt* that he was in close touch with the players and was asked to make alterations which are often quite slight and which sometimes, as for example in the substitution of "Grotius" for "Vandermitten" at the heading of Act 1, Scene 1, and elsewhere, seem to be dictated by the actors rather than the censor.

DEMETRIUS AND ENANTHE. The MS. of *Demetrius and Enanthe* was first printed by Dyce in 1830,[14] and independent collations are given in the Cambridge *Beaumont and Fletcher*. We still await an accurate transcript. In the Folio of 1647 the

13 The MS. has two other short leaves inserted between ff. 14 and 15 and ff. 27 and 28, written on the recto only, the one with 20 lines, the other with 32 lines. These are not due to the censor's alterations, but to an afterthought of the author or a mistake of the transcriber.

14 It was then in the possession of Wm. W. E. Wynne, Esquire, of Peniarth, whose family was connected with that of Digby. In 1837 it was given to W. Ormsby Gore, Esquire, the grandfather of Lord Harlech. See a note on a preliminary leaf, printed in the Cambridge *Beaumont and Fletcher*, 2:508.

play is called *The Humorous Lieutenant,* but the title in the MS. is as much to be preferred to that in the Folio as *Benedick and Beatrice* might be to *The Humorous Constable.* Dyce prints in italics the many lines in the MS. that are lacking in the Folio. "By whom they were originally omitted—whether by the players or the editors—it is in vain to inquire. If by a strange and happy chance we were to discover Shakespeare's own manuscript copies of some of his finest pieces, we should perhaps find that similar 'sins of omission' were to be charged on the persons who first consigned those dramas to the press." Nowadays we should be inclined to acquit the editors and to bring our indictment against the actors, the Revels Office, and occasionally the dramatist himself. And our view is in part corroborated by the testimony of the stationer, Humphrey Moseley, in his epistle to the Readers of the First Folio of Beaumont and Fletcher. "When these *Comedies* and *Tragedies* were presented on the Stage, the Actours omitted some *Scenes* and Passages (with the *Authour's* consent) as occasion led them; and when private friends desir'd a Copy, they then (and justly too) transcribed what they *Acted.*" But when Moseley adds: "But now you have both All that was *Acted,* and all that was not; even the perfect full Originalls without the least muti-lation," we know that in at least one instance he is claiming too much.

It is instructive to note that rather more than a dozen broken lines in the Folio text can be patched up from the MS., and that the Folio, which contains some lines not in the MS., completes some half-dozen lines that are broken in the MS. There are scores of verbal differences throughout. For example, the MS. rejects such oaths as "Lord," "Death," "What a Devil," "plague take him," "God ha' mercy," and even "I protest" and "by this hand," though it admits such expressions as "Faith," "by heaven," "for heaven-sake," perhaps on the ground that these are asseverations, not oaths (*pace* Sir Henry Herbert).[15] Crane may have been transcribing from a MS. in which the oaths were

[15] Cf. Herbert's Office-Book, 9 January 163¾ (Variorum *Shakespeare,* 1821, 3:235); "The kinge is pleasd to take *faith, death, slight,* for assevera-tions, and no oaths, to which I doe humbly submit as my masters judg-ment; but under favour conceive them to be oaths, and enter them here, to declare my opinion and submission."

curtailed in accordance with 3 Jac. I, c. 21. Or he may have made these changes himself to suit his own taste or the "religious Inclination" of Sir Kenelm Digby.

Demetrius and Enanthe is an unusually interesting example of a private transcript because it is dated. Dr. Greg in the article already cited suggests that "until the study of dramatic manuscripts has reached a more advanced position than at present, it would be exceedingly rash to assume that [the practice of selling transcripts of plays to private amateurs] obtained before about 1630." The date "about 1630" which Dr. Greg was so rightly cautious in suggesting may now be pushed back to "about 1625."

This transcript raises another interesting point. *Demetrius and Enanthe* is one of Fletcher's liveliest comedies. It has all the ingredients of a popular success—love and battle, farce and the supernatural, an inflated hero and a sprightly heroine. Pepys indeed at his second visit thought it a silly play, but his contemporaries disagreed with him. "After the Restoration *The Humorous Lieutenant* enjoyed much popularity: it was the first play that was acted, and that for twelve nights successively, at the opening of the theater in Drury Lane, April 8, 1663. Langbaine says that he had 'often seen it acted with applause.' "[16] There is no reason to suppose that it did not meet with the like success before the Restoration. That there should exist private transcripts of *The Witch* which nobody wanted to act and of *A Game at Chess* which nobody was allowed to act is not surprising. But it is curious that so notable a get-penny as *Demetrius and Enanthe* should have been allowed to stray outside the playhouse, and should have existed in a private transcript twenty-two years before it got into print. It looks as if the King's Players no longer needed to hoard their MSS. jealously as in the old bad days of piracy. Since 1607 most plays were licensed for publication by the Master of the Revels, and the influence of the King's Men with the Revels, with the Stationers' Company, and if the necessity arose with the Lord Chamberlain, was sufficient to prevent all but the most unscrupulous publishers from publishing their plays without permission.

[16] R. Warwick Bond in the Variorum *Beaumont and Fletcher*, 2:460. Cf. also Dryden's *Essays* (ed. W. P. Ker), 1:166.

This MS. is perhaps the most beautiful example of Crane's calligraphy that we have. In 128 pages of text there is hardly an erasure, and the pen never falters. Moseley tells us that when Gentlemen desired but a copy of any of Beaumont and Fletcher's plays, the meanest piece cost them more than four times the price of his Folio. Crane deserved this and more for his pains.

THE WITCH. *The Witch* is perhaps the worst of Middleton's plays, but it has long been famous for its Shakespearian interest. MS. Malone 12[17] is the only authority for the text, yet no attempt has been made to print the MS. as it stands since Isaac Reed's *editio princeps* of 1778. Neither the play nor the transcript can be dated exactly. The transcript was ordered from Crane by the author himself, and contains Middleton's dedicatory epistle: "To the truely-worthie and generously-affected *Thomas Holmes*, Esquier." It was at Holmes's desire that "This (ignorantly-ill-fated) Labour" was dragged from the "imprisond-Obscuritie" in which she had long lain, and it was "not without much difficultie" that the author recovered the play into his hands. The title informs us that the play was "long since Acted by his Maties. Seruants at the Black-Friers." As the King's Men began to act at the Blackfriars in 1609, the transcript may have been made at any time between about 1620 and the year of Middleton's death, 1627.

A GAME AT CHESS. This play was acted at the Globe for nine days in August 1624 before crowded audiences, but its political and personal allusions brought the actors and the Master of the Revels into conflict with the Privy Council, the play was banned, and the playhouse copy confiscated.[18] The following note in Malone's handwriting is prefixed to one of his editions of this play (now Malone 247): " 'A new play called *A Game at Chesse*, written by Middleton,' was licensed by Sir Henry Herbert, June 12. 1624. So his Office-Book MS."

[17] "Bought at the sale of Mr. Steevens's books, May 20th. 1800, at the enormous price of £7 10. 0. E.M." A note by Steevens states that the MS. was in the collection of Benjamin Griffin, the actor, and passed into the hands of Lockyer Davis, bookseller in Holborn, who sold it to Major Pearson. Steevens bought it at the Major's auction for £2 14*s*. One hundred copies were printed off by Reed as presents to his friends.

[18] Cf. Middleton's *Works* (ed. Bullen), 1:lxxix–lxxx.

This extract from Herbert's Office-Book, hitherto unprinted, is not repeated in the Variorum *Shakespeare* of 1821 and is not included in J. Quincy Adams's edition of Herbert's *Dramatic Records*. It is clear that Fleay is wrong in identifying this play with the unlicensed *The Spanish Viceroy* (*A Chronicle History of the London Stage*, p. 268), but it is not so clear whose backing induced the cautious Herbert to license so fierce and obvious an attack upon Spain and Gondomar. It is a measure of the excitement which the play aroused that at least four printed editions are extant and at least four manuscripts.[19]

In *Demetrius and Enanthe* we have a transcript presented to his patron by a professional scrivener hopeful of being rewarded for his pains. *The Witch* and the Malone MS. of *A Game at Chess* are transcripts ordered by the author himself and presented by him to his admirers. In the British Museum MS. of *A Game at Chess*, which now contains no dedication, we have perhaps a transcript, like those mentioned by Moseley, ordered by a private amateur for his own pleasure. The title of Lansdowne 690, which is surrounded with corkscrew scrolls in ink like those on the title-pages of *Demetrius and Enanthe* and MS. Malone 25, reads as follows: "1624. |A Game att Chesse| By Tho. Middleton." The date is that of composition and first performance, not necessarily of transcription as Bullen supposed. A note in Douce's handwriting on a preliminary blank leaf states that this MS. "is far more correct than the printed copies." Collations of some (but not all) of the variant readings are given by Dyce and Bullen.

The Bodleian MS. of *A Game at Chess* (MS. Malone 25) has not been consulted by any editor of Middleton. Bullen, who knew of the existence of this MS., hunted high and low for it, but in 1887 was unable to discover the possessor of it. It was sold by C. J. Stewart, the London bookseller, about 1860–70, perhaps to the Bodleian.[20] I am indebted to Mr. R. C. Bald,

[19] A third is at Trinity College, Cambridge, a fourth (formerly in the Bridgewater Library) is in the Huntington Library. The Huntington MS. is in two different hands, neither of them Crane's. One of these hands is that of the scribe of the Trinity MS.: Mr. R. C. Bald identifies it with Middleton's.

[20] Cf. *A Summary Catalogue of Western Manuscripts*, no. 30623. The pressmark is misleading, for the MS. was never in Malone's Library. Ma-

Clare College, Cambridge, for calling my attention to this MS. It is good news that he is preparing a full account of the manuscripts and printed texts of this interesting play.

Middleton's dedication to Thomas Holmes in *The Witch* is in Crane's handwriting. As the dedication in MS. Malone 25 is the only page of this MS. not in Crane's hand, the presumption is that it is autograph.

> To the Worthilie-Accomplish'd, Mr: William Hammond.
> This, which nor Stage nor Stationers Stall can showe,
> (The Common Eye maye wish for, but ner'e knowe)
> Comes in it's best Loue with the New-yeare forth,
> As a fit Present to the Hand of Worth.
>   'A Seruant to youre
>   Vertues,
>   T. M.[21]

The suggestion that we have in William Hammond the "W. H." of Shakespeare's sonnets is the catchpenny puff of C. J. Stewart.[22] There are several printed editions of this play, one dated 1625, the others undated. The dedication implies that the play was still unprinted, so that the New Year must be that of 1625. After this year Middleton could have presented Hammond with a printed copy.

Stewart's claim that MS. Malone 25 is "the original draught of the work" cannot be maintained. It is a shortened version of the play given in the printed editions and in the other MSS. On a rough calculation some 760 lines or parts of lines are omitted

---

lone's own MSS. stop at MS. Malone 24. On a preliminary leaf is the signature "John Pepys," probably the brother of the Lord Chief Justice, Richard Pepys. For some evidence of John Pepys's misspent youth see Tanner MS. 167, fols. 72–73—"Articles ministred in Causes ecclesiasticall against John Pepes now or late of Cetenham in the County of Cambridge Gent" about the year 1630.

[21] It is interesting that Middleton signs with his initials. Fleay argues that *The Blacke Booke* and *Father Hubburds Tales* are not Middleton's because their dedicatory epistles are signed "T. M." But apart from this dedication, there is plenty of evidence to disprove Fleay's statement that Middleton "always put his name in full to all publications authorized by himself" (*A Biographical Chronicle*, 2:89).

[22] See a cutting from Stewart's printed advertisement bound up in MS. Malone 25.

from the text given in Bullen's edition.[23] The abridgement betrays by its broken and hypermetrical lines that it is later than the fuller version.

IV

A brief description has been given of each of Crane's dramatic manuscripts. It is proposed now to consider some general characteristics of his work.

1. A publisher who came by one of Crane's transcripts might reasonably expect from the printer an accurate text, free from literal errors, unless indeed it be argued that the best manuscript is always handed to the worst compositor.

2. All Crane's transcripts are carefully divided into acts and scenes. Act-divisions are common in the printed and MS. plays of this period, and have been attributed to the musical intervals observed between the acts at the private theaters. But full divisions into both acts and scenes are perhaps not common in the manuscripts of King's plays at this time. *The Honest Man's Fortune* and *Bonduca*, both in the hand of a contemporary scribe who also worked for the King's Players (see above, pp. 137–38), are divided into acts but not into scenes, and the full divisions which Massinger has marked in *Believe as You List* are deleted by the same scribe. Since the publication of Mr. Pollard's *Shakespeare Folios and Quartos* (1909) it has been well known that the following plays in the First Folio of Shakespeare are divided into acts and scenes: the first four comedies (*The Tempest, The Two Gentlemen, The Merry Wives, Measure for Measure*), *As You Like It*, and the two last comedies (*Twelfth-Night, The Winter's Tale*); all the history plays except *Henry V* and *Henry VI*; and four of the last six tragedies (*Macbeth, King Lear, Othello, Cymbeline*). It has been usual to suppose that these full divisions are due to the care of the editors who prepared the Folio for the press, and it is certainly curious that of the seven fully divided plays in the fourteen comedies four should be placed at the beginning and two at the end. On the other hand, why should *As You Like It* be so treated and not

[23] Some 71 lines are omitted from Act I, 290 from Act II, 212 from Act III, 107 from Act IV, and 80 from Act V. The Induction and Epilogue are given in full; the Prologue is omitted. Bullen is in error in stating that the Prologue is omitted in Lansdowne 690.

the five comedies which precede it or the two which follow it? Or why *Macbeth* and not the six tragedies which precede it and the one which follows it? It is reasonable to suppose that some of the available manuscripts were already divided into acts and scenes before they were revised (if they were revised) for the press.[24]

3. Those stage-directions in *Barnavelt* which are in Crane's handwriting give little information apart from mere statements of exits and entrances. Only in one place—V, 1. "2 Chaires"— do they suggest a playhouse origin: for we must dismiss "within," "above," and even "A Bar brought in"[25] and "a Scaffold put out" as non-committal. The practical directions are added by the stage-manager. In Crane's other transcripts the directions never smack of the theater. Occasionally they are descriptive, and have a literary flavor. For example, in *Demetrius and Enanthe*, IV, 3: "Enter a Magitian wth a Bowle in his hand. He seemes to Coniure: sweete Musique is heard, and an Antick of litle Fayeries enter, & dance about ye Bowle, and fling in things, & Ex^t." Again, in *A Game at Chess* (Lansdowne 690), IV, 3: "Enter ye Black Q^s. Pawne (wth a Tapo^r in her hand) and Conducts the White Q^s. Pawne (in her Night Attire) into one Chamber: And then Conuaies the Black B^s. Pawne (in his Night habit) into an other Chamber: So putts out the Light, and followes him." It is significant that the private transcripts contain no such direction as "2. Chaires." A skilled scrivener like Crane would not be likely to allow so theatrical a signpost to appear in a private transcript. We cannot, however, regard it as significant that *Demetrius and Enanthe, A Game at Chess,* and to a less extent *The Witch* contain directions more full and more literary than those in *Barnavelt*. The explanation is rather that these plays afford more opportunity for descriptive directions. *A Game at Chess* has a dumb show, *Demetrius and Enanthe* a magician and an antick of fairies, *The Witch* witches and black magic. The descriptions of these spectacles are part of the book of the play and may well have appeared in playhouse MSS. as

---

[24] Two of the fully divided plays (*Richard II, 1 Henry IV*) are reprinted from corrected copies of earlier editions: the others are printed from MSS.

[25] I cannot agree with Miss Frijlinck that these four words are in another hand.

well as in these private transcripts, though they were sometimes
perhaps deleted as unnecessary by the book-holder. The directions in *The Second Maiden's Tragedy* (Lansdowne 807), a
playhouse manuscript in a scrivener's hand not unlike Crane's,
are much more elaborate than in any of Crane's transcripts.
The Tempest, which of all the plays in the First Folio of Shakespeare is richest in descriptive directions, may well have been
printed from a playhouse manuscript. We must attribute these
literary directions to the dramatist, rather than to a scribe, or
the playhouse, or an editor.

The stage-directions in MS. Malone 25 stand by themselves,
and I cannot match them in any other MS. Descriptive directions, like "Noice within," "Musique," "he appeeres Black underneath," appear at the appropriate places, but statements of
entrances are massed together at the head of each scene. Thus
the direction at the head of Act I, Scene 1 is: "The white-
Queenes, & yᵉ Black-Queenes Pawnes. Then yᵉ Black Bishop's
Pawne: Then yᵉ whi: Bishop's Pawne & yᵉ Bl. Knights Pawne,
Then yᵉ Black-knight, Then yᵉ wh. Kings Pawne." The Black
Bishop's Pawn enters at line 26, the White Bishop's Pawn at
line 141, the Black Knight's Pawn at line 147, the Black Knight
at line 175, and the White King's Pawn at line 241; but these
entrances are indicated only at the head of the scene. In the
First Folio of Shakespeare the entrances in two plays—*The
Two Gentlemen of Verona* and its successor in the Folio, *The
Merry Wives*—are massed together at the head of each scene[26]
and not marked at the appropriate places (except for "Enter
Fairies" in *The Merry Wives*, V, 5:34). Unlike MS. Malone 25
these plays contain no descriptive directions. Mr. J. Dover
Wilson and Mr. R. Crompton Rhodes have independently advanced the theory that the texts of these two Shakespearian
plays were assembled from the piecemeal parts of the actors
with the help of the theatrical "plots." The stage-directions, if
we compare them with the dramatic plots and the player's part
of Orlando printed by Dr. Greg in *Henslowe Papers*, do not
forbid us to apply this theory to MS. Malone 25: and the fact

[26] Most scenes in *The Winter's Tale* are so treated, but often the entrances are also noted at the points of entry. This play contains a few descriptive directions of which the most famous is "Exit pursued by a
Beare."

that the playhouse copy was confiscated by the authorities is an argument in its favor. On the other hand, the printed texts and the Lansdowne and Trinity MSS., in which the notation of entrances is normal,[27] certainly represent the original version of the play. If the textual evidence shows that MS. Malone 25 is based on any of these, we may have to explain the anomaly by assuming some causal connection between the abridgement of a text and the massing of entrances. Anyhow it is curious that Crane did not mark the entrances in the usual manner. Even if he was transcribing from the players' parts, the task was not beyond his capacity. And Mr. William Hammond would then have found his manuscript easier reading.

V

It would have been pleasant to end this article with evidence so conclusive as to establish beyond cavil which printed texts were set up from Crane's transcripts. But to do this we must know what it may never be possible to know: how far he departed from his originals, how far his practice differed from that of contemporary scriveners, and how much to allow for the normalizing habits of the printer. A detailed examination of Crane's manuscripts, however, of the handwriting, of the spelling, of the punctuation, might well yield more interesting results than those outlined above. The work of a man who was scrivener to the King's Players in 1619 and perhaps earlier, and was still making transcripts of their plays in 1625, is clearly worth investigation. For the possibility is established that among the manuscripts from which the Jaggards printed the First Folio one or more may have been in his handwriting.

[27] I have not seen the Bridgewater-Huntington MS. From the four pages of which I have photostats it looks as if the entrances are marked in the usual way.

[NOTE. I regret that until my article was in print I did not know of the note on Crane published by the late Professor Thornton S. Graves of the University of North Carolina in *Studies in Philology*, vol. 21 (April, 1924). Professor Graves quoted extracts from the preface to *The Workes Of Mercy*, but he was too far removed from the necessary materials to do more.]

XI

LOUIS B. WRIGHT

Stage Duelling in the Elizabethan Theater

The consuming passion of the Elizabethans for spectacles of prize-fighting, fencing, bear-baiting, and combats of various sorts is familiar to all students of the period. So great was the love of combat that stage plays met the demand for spectacles of this sort by furnishing elaborate duels and fencing scenes. Advantage was taken of serious crises in the action of plays to make these encounters spectacles well worth watching for their own sakes. Indeed, one fact that is not sufficiently emphasized in discussions of the Elizabethan taste for dramas of blood is the fact that these dramas furnished exciting duels for which contemporary spectators had an inordinate fondness. If a play could furnish a skilful fencing match or a prize-fight, that play was certain of one scene which would please the majority. Combats, frequently exaggerated out of all proportion to the necessity of the action, served a dual purpose of furnishing a scene of vaudeville to please the multitude and of furthering the action of the play at the same time. It is the purpose here to point out uses of stage combats to furnish duelling spectacles in the course of play performances on the Elizabethan stage.

Elizabethan stage fencing demanded skilled swordsmen, and players prided themselves on their technique.[1] The stages of the theaters were used at times for fencing matches; Chambers cites an instance at the Swan which resulted fatally.[2] Stage duels were fought with great earnestness, and playgoers judged the

From *The Modern Language Review*, 22 (1927):265–75. Reprinted by permission of the author, of the Modern Humanities Research Association, and of the editors of *The Modern Language Review*.

[1] T. S. Graves, "The Stage Sword and Dagger," *South Atlantic Quarterly*, 20 (1921):201–12.

[2] E. K. Chambers, *The Elizabethan Stage* (Oxford, 1923), 2:413.

contests critically. Actors were among the most earnest dev-otees of fencing. With them skill in fencing was both a pro-fessional asset and a matter of personal pride. A celebrated fencing school was conducted in the Blackfriars by Rocco Bonetti, the famous Italian fencing master, and his successors, Ieronimo and Vincenzio. Rocco leased the school from John Lyly in 1584;[3] it was there that Shakespeare is believed to have learned the art of fencing; at any rate, other actors of the period learned swordsmanship in this school, and Rocco's fencing jar-gon is frequently found in the plays of contemporary drama-tists; Shakespeare is supposed to refer to him in *Romeo and Juliet* in speaking of a "very butcher of a silk button."[4]

"Skill of weapon" is mentioned as one of the characteristics of an actor by John de la Casa in his *Rich Cabinet Furnished with Varietie of Descriptions*.[5] Players seem to have been lovers of swords. Speaking of three foils, one of the actors in Middle-ton's *A Faire Quarrel* says:[6] "There's three sorts of men that would thank you for 'em, either cutlers, fencers, or players." In discussing the coming of the actors, Hamlet says that the one who plays the part of the adventurous knight shall "use his foil and target."[7] Players lost few opportunities of displaying their swordsmanship.

The playhouses when not being used for stage plays were frequently given over to exhibitions of fencing and other feats of skill or agility. In discussing the prevalence of such perform-ances, Ordish calls attention to the fact that this use of the thea-ters helped to increase the demand for similar displays in regular

---

[3] C. W. Wallace, *The Evolution of the English Drama up to Shake-speare* (Berlin, 1912), pp. 187–88.

[4] Fencing jargon, for example, occurs in *Every Man in His Humour*, Act IV, Sc. 5. Matthew practises fencing; Bobadil explains the terms and boasts of his skill: "I would teach these nineteen special rules, as your punto, your reverso, your stoccato, your imbroccato, your passado, your montano; till they could all play very near, or altogether as well as my-self," etc. Cf. also a passage in Dekker's *Wonder of a Kingdome*, Act I, Sc. 1, in which Vanni boasts of his skill and enumerates various fencing terms.

[5] W. C. Hazlitt, *The English Drama and Stage*, Roxburghe Library (London, 1869), p. 230.

[6] Act II, Sc. 2.   [7] Act II, Sc. 2.

stage plays.[8] The Red Bull was noted as a place for the playing of prizes, and both it and the Fortune were often let to prize-fighters, tumblers, rope-dancers, etc., especially during Lent.[9] Henslowe records in his diary that "Jemes cranwigge" had played a challenge in his house and he should have had twenty shillings for it.[10] Greg supposes that Cranwigge was probably a fencer or tumbler. An extract from Dekker's prose tract, *A Knights Coniuring*, indicates that fencers used playhouses when the actors were present, perhaps between the acts of plays. He says of the devil:[11]

> At sword and buckler, little Davy was nobody to him, and as for rapier and dagger, the Germane may be his iourneyman. Mary, the question is, in which of the playhouses he would have performed his prize, if it had growne to blowes, and whether the money being gathered, hee would haue cozende the fencers or the fencers him, because Hell beeing under euerie one of their stages, the players (if they had owed him a spight) might with a fake trap-dore haue slipt him down, and there haue kept him as a laughing stock to all their yawning spectators.

This passage at least indicates that the fencing devil would have had a choice of playhouses.

Dramatists must have realized that many spectators came to see displays of fencing and thrilling fights regardless of any consideration for dramatic structure. Many expressions of resentment at the tyranny of public taste may be found in contemporary plays; dramatists sometimes warned audiences that they need not expect the usual fare of stage fights and clown play. Such an expression is given by the prologue to *Hannibal and Scipio:*

> Nor need you Ladies feare the horrid sight:
> And the more horrid noise of target fight
> By the blue-coated Stage-keepers.

[8] T. F. Ordish, *Early London Theatres* (London, 1899), pp. 48–49.

[9] J. Q. Adams, *Dramatic Records of Sir Henry Herbert*, Cornell University Studies (New Haven, 1917), p. 48.

[10] W. W. Greg, *Henslowe's Diary* (London, 1904), 1:98.

[11] T. Dekker, *A Knights Coniuring*, Percy Society, 5:16.

The author or authors of *Henry VIII* likewise give notice in the prologue that foolery and fighting will be absent from the performance:

> . . . . . . Only they
> That come to hear a merry bawdy play,
> A noise of targets, or to see a fellow
> In a long motley coat guarded with yellow
> Will be deceived; . . . . . .

Jibes at the crude taste of early theater-goers who sought target fights, jigs, and clownery, followed by a promise of just such target fights, occur in the prologue to Davenant's *The Unfortunate Lovers* (1638):

> Good easy judging souls, with what delight
> They would expect a jig, or target fight,
> A furious tale of Troy, which they ne'er thought
> Was weakly written, so 'twere strongly fought.

Elizabethan stage plays had a long established precedent for the insertion of combats. Contests of strength and skill furnished much of the dramatic interest in the Robin Hood plays. In the fragment of *Robin Hood and the Knight*, containing only forty lines, there are five distinct contests: a shooting match, a stone throwing match, a wrestling match, a fight in which Robin kills the Knight, and a battle with the Sheriff's men.[12] The play is merely a framework for the contests. In the religious drama and later plays, more or less extraneous contests were brought in, and the accentuation of combats naturally occurring fed the popular appetite for such spectacles.

The wrestling match between Trowle and the shepherds in the Chester mystery play, *The Adoration of the Shepherds*, was considerably emphasized.[13] The encounter between Jacob and the angel in the Towneley *Jacob* was an actual wrestling match.[14] The morality, *The Trial of Treasure*, presents a similar wrestling match between Just and Lust.[15] A regular boxing

---

[12] J. M. Manly, *Specimens of Pre-Shakespearean Drama* (Boston, 1897), 1:279–81.

[13] Lines 237–40.   [14] Line 84.

[15] J. S. Farmer, *Six Anonymous Plays*, 3d ser. (London, 1906), pp. 209–10.

match occurs in *Horestes* between the non-essential low characters, Haultersycke and Hempstringe, who are directed to "fyght at bofites with fystes."[16] The same play has a battle scene which is exaggerated for the sake of the spectacle it affords; the direction specifies that the "army" engaged in the battle must "let it be longe, eare you can win ye Citie"; later the combatants are directed to "Stryke vp your drum and fyght a good whil."[17]

Thus before the regular drama of the Elizabethan period had developed, plays were establishing a taste for contests of strength and skill of weapon in dramatic performances which was to result in the elaborate duels on the full-grown Elizabethan stage.

An illustration of the use of duels to provide sensational matter in blood drama is furnished by *Jeronimo*. The fights which occur near the end of the last act are earnestly fought duels. In the first duel, the contestants, Andrea and Balthezar, enter at opposite doors and call attention to their swordsmanship:

> *Bal.* I'll top thy head for that ambitious word.
> *And.* You cannot, prince: see a revengeful sword
> Waves o'er my head.
> *Bal.* Another over mine;
> Let them both meet, in crimson tinctures shine.
> (*They fight; and Andrea hath Balthezar down.*)

The "Portogals" enter, relieve Balthezar, and kill Andrea. Immediately following, another duel takes place between Balthezar and Horatio, with Jeronimo watching and applauding his son. The stage directions are: "They fight, and breathe afresh." In the intermission, the duellists comment on the fight:

> *Bal.* So young and valorous! This arm ne'er met
> So strong a courage in so green a set.
> *Hor.* If thou be'st valiant, cease these idle words,
> And let revenge hang on our glittering swords,
> With this proud prince, the haughty Balthezar.
> (*Horatio has Prince Balthezar down; then enter Lorenzo and seizes his weapons.*)

The duel between Mathias and Lodowick in Act II, Sc. 2 of *The Jew of Malta* was prolonged, thus giving them a chance to

[16] Lines 286–88.   [17] Lines 725–68.

display their swordsmanship, as the words of Barabas, who watches from a balcony, indicate:

> *Bar.* O! bravely fought; and yet not thrust home.
> Now, Lodowick! now, Mathias! So—(*Both fall*).
> So now they have showed themselves to be tall fellows.

Greene's plays furnish several well-staged duels. The duel between Lambert and Serlsby in *Friar Bacon and Friar Bungay*, Act IV, Sc. 3, is fought with rapiers and daggers. After a few preliminaries, Lambert says: "But draw thy rapier, for we'll have a bout." Their sons, who are watching the fight, comment:

> *First Schol.* Ah, well thrust.
> *Second Schol.* But mark the ward.
> (*Lambert and Serlsby fight and stab each other.*)

Orlando Furioso is larded with duels. So great is the emphasis on extraneous spectacle in this play that Greg believes that the version preserved is one designed to appeal to provincial audiences.[18] At every opportunity, Orlando pleases the spectators by his ability in swordsmanship. In Act III, Sc. 2, he kills Brandimart after a sword fight; in Act V, Sc. 1, he vanquishes the mighty Sacripant in single combat; but the climax of Orlando's duelling comes in his encounters with members of the Twelve Peers of France who are seeking to avenge his wrongs. Hearing Oliver call Angelica "strumpet," Orlando challenges him and all the others. Turpin suggests to Oliver that they "chastise the groom":

> *Orl.* Hear you, sir? You that so peremptorily bade him fight,
> Prepare your weapons, for your turn is next:
> 'Tis not one champion can discourage me.
> Come, are ye ready?
> (*He fights first with one, and then with the other, and overcomes them both.*)

Ogier, seeing the discomfiture of his colleagues, challenges Orlando:

> *Og.* Sirrah, prepare you:
> For angry Nemesis sits on my sword to be revenged.
> (*They fight a good while and then breathe.*)

---

[18] W. W. Greg, *Two Elizabethan Stage Abridgements: The Battle of Alcazar and Orlando Furioso*, Oxford, 1923, p. 294.

Ogier exclaims that his opponent is either Orlando or the devil, and Orlando reveals his identity.

A series of quarterstaff fights varies the usual offering of sword fights in *George a Greene, the Pinner of Wakefield.* George fights at every provocation; a good part of the last portion of the play consists in these bouts in which Robin Hood and the Shoemaker of Bradford play a conspicuous part. The effect in this play is that of a series of separate encounters rather than any dramatic climax. So greedy were Elizabethans for feats of strength or skill on the stage that no incongruity was felt when the author of *Nobody and Somebody* inserted a wrestling match between persons of high birth to settle a serious dispute.[19] Better motivation, however, is the only difference between this wrestling match and the encounter between Charles and Orlando in *As You Like It*.[20] Both were trials of strength and elaborate spectacles designed to please for their own sakes.

Thomas Heywood, always ready to outdo his contemporaries in variety-show entertainment, improves on the usual stage fight by letting a pike-tossing exhibition follow one duel and precede several others in *Four Prentices of London.* The first fight comes fairly early in the play between Charles and Godfrey. Hard on this combat, the other pair of brothers, Guy and Eustace, prepare for a duel with rapier and pike. Before fighting, they toss their pikes and comment on the various exercises through which they go:[21]

> *Eust.* Thou wouldst instruct thy master at this play.
> Think'st thou this Rye-strew can ore-rule my arme?
> Thus do I beare him when I vse to march:
> Thus can I fling him vp, and catch him thus:
> Then thus, to try the sinewes of my arme.
> *(They toss their pikes.)*
> *Guy.* But thou should'st charge him thus, advance him thus,
> Thus should'st thou take him, when thou seest from farre
> The violent horses runne to breake our rankes.
> *Eust.* All that is nothing, I can toss him thus.

[19] Richard Simpson, *The School of Shakespeare* (New York, 1878), 1:336. The contest is between Peridure and Vigenius.

[20] Act I, Sc. 2.

[21] Thomas Heywood, *Dramatic Works,* London, 1874, II, p. 203.

> *Guy.* I thus: tis easier sport then the Baloone.
> *Eust.* We trifle time, this shall thy rage withstand.
> *Guy.* With this, our Hoast shall peirce thy Soueraignes Land.
>   (*They fight. Robert and Palatine cast their Warders
>   betweene them, and part them.*)

In the course of this play there are seven single combats, all of which furnish extraneous spectacle. The pike-tossing scene evidently was famous in its day, for the Citizen in *The Knight of the Burning Pestle* advises the Boy to "read the Play of the *Four Prentices of London,* where they toss their Pikes so."[22] Later Webster uses pike-tossing in *The White Devil* in a scene in which young Giovanni gives an exhibition of his manly prowess.[23]

Not all exhibitions of fencing that delighted Elizabethan audiences were so patently inserted for entertainment as were the combats in the *Four Prentices of London.* Some fights were perfectly motivated yet served a purpose of furnishing a spectacle as well. Such a fight is that between Mercutio and Tybalt in *Romeo and Juliet,* for which Mercutio had earlier prepared the spectators by describing Tybalt's skill as a fencer.[24] Without doubt, the fight between Hotspur and the Prince in *I Henry IV* was a thrilling spectacle.[25] The sword fight between Montsurry and Bussy D'Ambois in *Bussy D'Ambois* was spirited.[26] It is significant that Shakespeare makes the dénouement in Hamlet a fencing match with rapier and dagger.[27] As part of the means of expanding the fourth act of *Troilus and Cressida* a duel is staged between Hector and Ajax.[28] The fight between Marcius (later called Coriolanus) and Aufidius in *Coriolanus* is a spectacle contributing little to the play except characterization.[29] Shakespeare and his contemporaries made capital of combats whenever possible.

Jonson, usually scornful of popular demands, departs from his avowed practice of carefully constructing his plays in *The Case Is Altered* and furnishes an extraneous bout with cudgels

[22] Act IV, Sc. 1.   [23] Act II, Sc. 1.

[24] The fight occurs in Act III, Sc. 1; Mercutio's remarks, Act II, Sc. 4.

[25] Act V, Sc. 4.

[26] Act V, Sc. 4.   [28] Act IV, Sc. 5.

[27] Act V, Sc. 2.   [29] Act I, Sc. 8.

LOUIS B. WRIGHT

between Martino and Onion in Act II, Sc. 4. The opening direction is, "*Mart. and Onion play a bout at cudgels*," and Onion exclaims:

> Ha! well play'd, fall over to my leg now: so, to your guard again; excellent! to my head now; make home your blow; spare not me, make it home, good, good again! (Mart. *breaks his head*.)

This contest seems to have been inserted purely for the sake of the spectacle it afforded.

In place of the usual quarterstaff fight in plays where Robin Hood and his men participate in the action, there is a duel with swords between John and Scathlock in *The Downfall of Robert Earl of Huntingdon.*[30] The fight is long drawn out in order to give an exhibition of fencing. Probably the actors who took the parts of the two contestants were skilled in sword fencing and not in quarterstaff bouts.

The stage directions in *Look About You* indicate that the fight between Richard and Gloster is drawn out for the sake of the spectacle.[31] The first direction is, "*Fight and part once or twice*"; four lines later is, "*Fight again and breathe*"; and the last direction in the episode is, "*They breathe, offer again.*" The combat takes up two pages in the text of the play and seems exaggerated beyond any dramatic necessity.

Heywood provides for two spectacular duels between Brutus and the ravisher to close *The Rape of Lucrece* with the proper flourish demanded by an audience at the Red Bull, where the play was first produced. The first fight is with sword and target, "*Alarum, a fierce fight with sword and target, then after a pause and breathe.*" After the antagonists make their boasts again, this direction follows: "*Alarum, fight with single swords, and being deadly wounded and panting for breth, making a strook at each together with their gantlets they fall.*" If the action of the play demanded such a fight, there could be certainly no use in fighting two duels with two sorts of weapons.

An orgy of fighting beyond all dramatic needs occurs in *The Tryall of Chevalry;* the last two acts are little more than a series of combats. Act V contains seven stage directions for fights, single combats and general engagements, and nine "alarums." No wonder some dramatists complained about the craving for

[30] Act V, Sc. 1.   [31] Sc. 29.

164

noise and target fighting. The fight between Syphax and Massinissa in Marston's *Sophonisba* is an elaborate spectacle accompanied by noise of cornets and clash of arms from the surrounding attendants.[32] In *The Dumb Knight*, Act I, Sc. 1, an elaborate tournament is held on the stage. The directions indicate the type of spectacle:

> *The cornets sound; and enter at one end of the stage a Herald, two Pages, one with pole-axes, the other with hand axes, the Duke of Epire and Alphonso, the combatants, etc.*

Similar directions are given for the entrance of the opponents, the King of Cyprus and Philocles; they stage a long drawn out combat, the chief purpose of which is merely that of show. A similar tournament occurs near the end of the play.[33] Chapman makes great capital of the climactic duel between Clermont and Montsurry in *The Revenge of Bussy D'Ambois*. These contestants too must breathe awhile and fight again.[34] Elizabethans demanded such realistic fights that the playwrights had to make shifts to let their actors have breathing spells between blows.

Acknowledgment of the skill of an actor at fencing occurs in the course of a stage fight in *A Woman Is a Weathercock*. Captain Pouts remarks to Strange, his opponent:[35]

> 'Zoons! can you ward so well? I think you are
> One of the noble science of defence.

A similar statement of an actor's skill at fencing occurs in a spectacular fencing match between Moll and Laxton in *The Roaring Girl*. During the fight, Laxton exclaims: "Heart, I think I fight with a familiar, or the ghost of a fencer."[36] Stage fencing beyond dramatic necessity occurs in Webster's *White Devil*, Act IV, Sc. 5, where the plot to kill Brachiano by means of a poisoned helmet comes to a climax in a fight. The directions are: "*Charges and shouts. They fight at barriers, first single pairs, then three to three.*" All of this fighting is brought into the play merely to give Brachiano an opportunity to clap

---

[32] Act V, Sc. 2.   [33] Act V, Sc. 1.

[34] Act V, Sc. 5. There are two interruptions in the fight to give the actors a breathing spell. In the first, Montsurry asks for time to get his "breath a while," and in the second, other players interrupt the fight.

[35] Act IV, Sc. 2.   [36] Act III, Sc. 1.

on a poisoned helmet! The fighting between Palamon and Arcite in *Two Noble Kinsmen* seems to have been exaggerated to give the players a chance to show their skill.[37]

Comment by actors to call attention to skilful fencing in the course of a stage duel was fairly frequent. In *A Faire Quarrel* the fight between the Colonel and Captain Ager is made a regular fencing match which their friends watch and comment upon their technique:[38]

> First Fr. of Cap. An absolute punto, hey?
> Sec. Fr. of Cap. 'Twas a passado, sir.
> . . . .
> Sec. Fr. of Cap. That's a punto, etc.

Similar comment by actor-spectators occurs in the thoroughly essential duel in Massinger's *Unnatural Combat*, but even this fight was not overlooked as an opportunity for spectacle.[39] Not only was fencing the accomplishment of every gentleman of the period, but actual duelling was a popular fashion of the day, so much so that Fletcher satirizes it in *The Little French Lawyer*, especially in the duel scene.[40] Playwrights took care that actors might not slight the combat scenes by providing significant stage directions, as in Webster's *The Devil's Law Case* where the direction is, "*The combat continued to a good length, when enter Leonora and the Capuchin.*"[41]

University plays, as well as plays designed for the public stages, made use of variety entertainments. Fencing is one of the attractions in *Fuimus Troes: The True Trojans*, produced at Oxford in 1625; a fencing match precedes a stage duel in Act III, Sc. 7. The directions for the fencing match are: "*Androgeus and Tenantius play at foils, then Hirildas and Eulinus play.*" After fencing with foils, they take swords and fight.

The chief interest of the play in *Dicke of Devonshire* centers in the skill of weapon displayed by Dick Pike, about whose fencing the action of the play is built. In Act II, Sc. 4, Pike fights a duel with Don John and disarms him. The closing scene of Act IV ends with a series of bouts between him and

[37] Act III, Sc. 6.

[38] Act III, Sc. 1.

[39] Act II, Sc. 1.

[40] Act II, Sc. 1.

[41] Act V, Sc. 6.

Spaniards whom a Spanish judge has sentenced him to fight, one by one. When asked if he dare fight, Pike replies:

> ....can a prisoner
> Glory in playing the Fencer?
> . . . .
> Ile try if I have strength in this chayned arme
> To breake a rapier.

From the context it seems that the hero first fights with a pike against the Spaniards armed with rapiers, for when permitted his choice of weapons after the first combat, he says: "A Quarterstaffe,—this, were the head off." The head is knocked off, and Pike fights three men with his quarterstaff, killing one and disarming the others. One of the Spaniards exclaims: "Hell take thy Quaterstaffe!" Pike is honored by the Spanish duke for his fine display, and the scene, obviously one of sheer spectacle, ends.

The fencing lesson was sometimes used as a pretext for offering spectacles of swordmanship in stage plays. Such an example occurs in Shirley's *Love's Cruelty*. Act II begins with a fencing match between Hippolito and his fencing instructor. There seems to be no dramatic reason for the exhibition, not even that of characterization, as it serves to advance the play in no way. The scene opens in Hippolito's lodgings with the entry of Hippolito and a fencer:

Hip. Come on, sir. (*Practises with his sword.*)
Fen. Pretty well, I protest, la, keep your guard now, sir.
Hip. What do you think on't? I shall never hit your subtle body.
                        (*Makes a thrust at him.*)
Fen. A very dexterous proffer; bring it home; ever while you
      live, bring your weapon home.
Hip. Again, sir.
Fen. But you do not hit me the neat school-way; I won't give a
      rush to be killed out of the school-way; you must falsify
      thus. (*They fence.*)
Hip. How now, man?
Fen. Pretty well, let us breathe.

Shirley is fond of stage fights; in a later play, *The Imposture*, he makes a fake duel, really a fencing match, the machinery by which Volterino and Hortensio seek to discover which one

Florelia loves.[42] As vital to the play as the duel scene is in Act IV, Sc. 3 of *The Cardinal,* it is overemphasized for the sake of the exhibition of fencing.

The popularity of Heywood's *Age* plays, particularly of *The Iron Age,* depended in part on their appeal to the Red Bull audiences' love of spectacular fights. *The Iron Age* is a series of fights among the Greek and Trojan heroes that must have been responsible for Davenant's jibe at target fights in a "furious tale of Troy."[43] One stage direction from the battle between Hector and Ajax is sufficient to show why the rowdy audiences of the Red Bull liked dramatized classical story:[44]

> *Alarum, in this combate both hauing lost their swords and Shields. Hector takes up a great peece of a Rocke, and casts at Ajax; who teares a young Tree vp by the rootes, and assailes Hector, at which they are parted by both armes.*

Sometimes dramatists were put to strange shifts to explain away skilful fencing matches demanded by the spectators when such exhibitions of skill were distinctly out of character. In Fletcher's *The Elder Brother,* Charles, the scholarly brother, is supposed to know no swordcraft, yet he engages in a duel with his younger brother, a skilled swordsman, and wins. Fletcher makes Eustace, the younger, explain that Charles had learned to fence "from the book."[45]

Attention has already been called to the frank confession of Davenant that the fencing match in Act IV, Sc. 1 of *The Unfortunate Lovers* (1638) is a concession to popular taste. The fight takes place between Galleoto and Altophiel and is so long drawn out that five interruptions are necessary to allow the fencers to get their breath.[46] A similar duel occurs in Suckling's *The Goblins.* The play opens with a lively scene of fighting between Samorat and Philatel. There are several pauses; one direction says: *"Fight again; Samorat takes away Philatel's*

---

[42] Act IV, Sc. 3.

[43] Prologue to *The Unfortunate Lovers.*

[44] Pt. I, Act II, Sc. 1.   [45] Act V, Sc. 1.

[46] Stage directions show that the fight was expanded for effect: *"They fight awhile and part,"—"Fight again and sever,"* etc. Between fights, the two fencers call attention to their skill and also mention their scanty breath that requires the brief rest periods.

sword, and takes breath, then gives it him." This fighting, and other amusements provided, are mentioned in the epilogue as necessary to please all the spectators. A duel very much like the one in *The Goblins* is employed by Suckling in Act V, Sc. 1, of *Brennoralt*. Other examples of this type of stage fight might be cited,[47] but the fact that dramatists took advantage of plot situations to furnish spectacular entertainment is unquestionable and needs no further evidence.

By emphasizing scenes of fencing, the players had an opportunity of turning to account their skill as fencers and of displaying a technique of which they were often vain. The theater-goers throughout the Elizabethan period greedily demanded physical contests of strength and skill. With both players and public eager for stage contests, dramatists could not omit such spectacles, even though in many cases the exhibitions were extraneous, or, at best, much over-emphasized. Thus theatrical demands were responsible for a type of variety-show entertainment which strains or violates the principles of dramatic structure.

[47] E.g. the duel in Act II, Sc. 1 of *Fortune by Land and Sea*, and the fight in Act II, Sc. 1 of *The Custom of the Country*. One scene in Brome's *The Antipodes*, Act IV, Sc. 5, has in it a boxing bout between two courtiers, one of whom receives a "Box o' th' eare," precipitating a fight in which the stage direction is, *"They buffet."*

XII

CHARLES J. SISSON

Introduction to *Believe as you List*

The manuscript of Massinger's *Believe as you List* is in the British Museum, where it is classed as MS. Egerton 2828, and receives the full honors due to an almost perfect autograph play by a dramatist of the first importance in the great age of the English drama. It bears the autograph license of the Master of the Revels, it is corrected and prepared for acting by a stage-adapter, and shows all the processes through which the copy passed on its way from the author to the prompter. It is an invaluable document to the historian of the stage as well as of the drama.

The manuscript has had as many vicissitudes as its tragic hero Antiochus, though its history has come to a happier ending than his. It fell upon evil days in the early nineteenth century, and declined to the degradation of a rubbish heap, whence it was rescued with one leaf torn away. Carefully repaired and bound, it now shares with *Sir Thomas More* the dignity of a show-case in the British Museum.

The play is first mentioned by Sir Henry Herbert, Master of the Revels, in his Office Book. "This day being the 11 of Janu. 1630, I did refuse to allow of a play of Messinger's, because itt did contain dangerous matter, as the deposing of Sebastian king of Portugal, by Philip the [Second,] and ther being a peace sworen twixte the kings of England and Spayne" (*Variorum*, 3:229–31). Herbert does not give the name of the play, but the most cursory examination of this manuscript shows that Herbert is referring to the first draft of *Believe as you List*. The play was revised by Massinger, who substituted the story of Antiochus for that of Sebastian, and it was again submitted to Herbert, in the form of the present manuscript.

From *Believe as you List By Philip Massinger 1631*, Malone Society Reprints (Oxford, 1927). Reprinted by permission of the author and of the Malone Society.

It had possibly already been prepared for acting by a stage-adapter, and the parts assigned and learned. Herbert licensed it unconditionally on 6 May 1631. "This Play, called Beleiue as you liste, may bee acted. this 6. of May. 1631. Henry Herbert." His Office Book, however, gives the date of licensing as 7 May. Malone's note (*Variorum*, 1821, 3:230), reads "Believe as you list, May 7, 1631. Acted by the king's company. This play is lost." Massinger's copy was prepared for the King's company, and formed part of their stock of plays, as is evident also from the names of the actors Taylor, Lowin, Benfeild, and others entered in the manuscript by the stage-adapter.

The play is next mentioned in the Stationers' Register on 9 September 1653. "M^r. Mosely. Entred also for his Copies the severall Playes following," 41 plays, including 10 entries of plays "by Phill: Massinger," all with alternative titles which seem to represent different plays in reality. Among these entries is "The Iudge, or Beleiue as yo^u list." There is no semblance of a Judge in *Believe as you List*, and *The Judge* was licensed separately by Herbert (*Variorum*, 3:230, note: "The Judge, June 6, 1627. Acted by the king's company. This play is lost"). A second list of plays is found in an entry in the Register dated 29 June 1660: "Mr Hum: Moseley. Entred for his Copies (vnder the hand of Mr Thrale Warden) the severall Plays following." There are 26 entries of plays, including 11 by Phillip Massinger," and among these is "Believe as you list. a Tragedy" (altered from "a Comedy"). *The Judge* does not appear in this list.

The majority of plays thus entered to Moseley were not printed by him, as a matter of fact. Whatever the reason for these entries, and for the frequently inexplicable alternative titles given, the future history of this manuscript, as of other plays entered, argues that it did not actually pass into Moseley's hands. It ceased to be known in bibliographical history until it was mentioned in *The British Theatre* (Dublin, 1750, p. 42), a compilation for which W. R. Chetwood was responsible.

> Mr. *Massenger*, I believe, was Author of several other Dramatic Pieces, one I have seen in Manuscript, which I am assured was acted, by the proper Quotations &c. The Title runs thus,
>
> *Beleeve as you List.* Written by Mr. *Massenger*, With the following Licence,

THIS Play, called *Believe as you List,* may be acted this 6th of
May, 1631.   HENRY HERBERT.
This was my Lord *Herbert,* in the Reign of *Charles* I.

An identical entry occurs in *A List of Dramatic Authors
and their Works,* appended in 1756 to the fourth edition of the
Apology of Colley Cibber, who has hitherto been quoted as
the authority for this mention of the manuscript (vol. 2, pp.
202–3). It will be noted that here the distinction is observed
between the spelling of the title on the titlepage and in the
license, and that the words "A Tragedy" on the titlepage as it
at present stands are not quoted. The writing, in fact, suggests
to me that they were added subsequently by some later possessor. There is no reason for doubting Chetwood's statement
(except as regards Lord Herbert), apart from this confirmation.

The manuscript, we may presume, had passed into the possession of the Drury Lane Theatre, at which Chetwood was employed as prompter from 1722 or 1723 to 1741, when he left
London to go to the Smock Alley Theatre at Dublin. At the
Restoration the plays belonging to the old King's company, for
which *Believe as you List* was written, had been allotted by the
Lord Chamberlain to Killigrew, except for certain plays given
to Davenant. Our play is not mentioned in the lists (printed in
A. Nicoll, *A History of the Restoration Drama,* pp. 314–16),
no doubt as being disused, and Killigrew took it with him to
Drury Lane as the property of the new King's company.

The next mention of the manuscript is to be found in Warburton's famous list, in MS. Lansdowne 807, where it figures
along with 57 other items, including many by Massinger. Of
these number 35 is "The Judge A C. by Phill. Massenger," and
number 38 is "Belive as yo^u. list C. by Phill. Massinger." Both
of these are on the recto side of the slip containing the list. It
will be observed that Warburton's version of the title is a new
variation and corresponds neither to the manuscript, nor to the
license, nor to the Stationers' Register, and that he describes
both plays as "C(omedies)." There is no good reason for
thinking that Warburton was ever in actual possession of the
manuscript of *Believe as you List,* or that Betsy was responsible
for tearing out folio 5. The Warburton legend has long since
been dealt with by Dr. Greg, and the premonitory skepticism

of Halliwell-Phillipps in 1857, expressed in a note (printed below) on the fly-leaf of this manuscript, was fully justified.

The manuscript remains unknown to authentic history until 1844, though in the meantime a writer in the *Monthly Mirror* (September, 1808, p. 177), recalling the remark in Cibber's *Apology*, in the course of his comments on Gifford's edition of Massinger, suggests that the manuscript "may yet be in existence, and if so, could perhaps be traced by Mr Gifford." T. Crofton Croker, the first editor of the play, reports in the Preface to his edition (Percy Society Publications, vol. 27, 1849, p. vi) that Gifford failed to trace it, and adds "I have heard him (1819) more than once lament the circumstance, and doubt its existence." On 26 April 1844, however, Samuel Beltz wrote to Croker enclosing the manuscript itself with his letter, followed by a second letter dated 6 June, both printed by Croker in his Preface. Beltz states that the manuscript was found in a "vast mass of rubbish" belonging to his late brother George, which he inspected before it was destroyed, and from which he selected certain papers, including this. He suggests that it came to his brother after having been in the possession of Garrick, though he can only infer this. The inference is reasonable enough, though he does not give his grounds. George Beltz was an executor to the estate of Garrick's widow, who had purchased from a nephew, the Rev. Carrington Garrick, his interest under Garrick's will in his famous library, which she augmented considerably. Garrick's old printed plays had been bequeathed to the British Museum, at his death in 1779, by a special clause in his will. We may fairly assume that Garrick had the manuscript from the archives of Drury Lane, adding it to his collection, and that it passed at the death of his widow to her executor, possibly being overlooked in the disposal of her effects. Garrick's widow died in 1822, and the remainder of his collection of books was then sold by auction and dispersed in 1823. The Sale Catalogue in the British Museum, which gives the history of the library in a prefatory note, mentions no manuscript play. A manuscript like *Believe as you List* in an unbound and dilapidated condition would be quite likely to be thrown aside among other papers of less value. Samuel Beltz writes that George "was entirely unconscious of its existence," as perhaps he was. Samuel had not sufficient patience to read the play through, but he thought it might be acceptable to an editor of the poet, and in any case he begged Croker to put it among his other curiosities. The history of the manuscript is thus clear from Massinger and the old King's company at the Globe in 1631, through Killigrew and the new King's company, Chetwood, and Garrick, all at Drury Lane, to Croker in 1844. The gaps in its history, oddly enough, begin with more recent years. Croker was a member of the Council of the Percy Society, which decided to request him to edit the play for the Society. He completed the work at the very end of 1848, and it appeared early in 1849, with Croker's apologies for his delay. The manuscript appears to have passed thereafter into the possession of Halliwell, who was then Secretary of the Society. How, I do not know. It does not appear in any of his lists of acquisitions. Nor is there any trace of it in Croker's will, or in the Sale Catalogues (in the British Museum) of Croker's library, after his death in 1854. But there is an inscription by Halliwell on a fly-leaf of the manuscript which runs thus:

> This is one of the few play-house copies of any English plays before the Suppression of Theatres known to exist, & the present is a peculiarly interesting one, being a play of Massinger's long supposed to be lost, not included in any edition of his works, & known only by name until M^r. Croker resuscitated it for the Percy Society. It is the original copy licensed by Sir Henry Herbert, & I strongly suspect has some corrections in Massinger's own autograph. This is one of the plays said to have been made into pye-bottoms by Warburton's servant, a story in which I have no faith whatever. I gave the present MS. to Mr Corser, April, 1857, in exchange for a fragment of sixteen leaves of the first edition of Shakespeare's Lucrece.
>
> J. O. Halliwell.

When Cunningham re-edited Massinger in 1870 he was unable to trace the manuscript, and took Croker's edition as the basis of his text for this play. In the same year, however, it reappeared, in the sale-room this time. The fifth portion of books belonging to the Rev. T. Corser was sold at Sotheby's, 11 to 15 July, and this manuscript (lot 366) was bought by "James" for £17, as appears from the Sale Catalogue in the British Museum. Sir Edward Maunde Thompson seems to have made pencil notes on another copy of the Catalogue, in the Manuscript

Department, and one note "£15" suggests that the authorities had thoughts of purchasing it then. Sir Edward's notes show especial interest in the names of actors appearing in the stage-adapter's directions.

There can be little doubt that the purchaser was Edward Woolford James, a book-collector of Greenwich. The manuscript does not appear, however, at the sale of some of his books in 1873 at Puttick's, nor can I find any trace of it at his death at Folkestone in 1897. It was again sold at Sotheby's on 27 November 1900, being lot 191 in the sale of books belonging to the late Henry Newnham Davis, when it was bought by Quaritch for the British Museum for £69, out of the Farnborough Fund. It is curious that the price should have gone up so steeply, as it was still not realized that the manuscript was autograph. The Sale Catalogue (in the British Museum) repeats Croker's view, "the title . . . said to be in Massinger's autograph." But Sir George Warner had surely grasped the truth (and the dealers may have suspected it), when he was responsible for its acquisition by the Museum.

The manuscript forms a thin small folio volume, bound in half morocco, of which the leaves measure $12\frac{3}{8} \times 7\frac{1}{2}$ inches. The title is written in a large formal Italian hand on the back of a folded sheet of vellum containing an indenture dated 7 October 1595, between Nicholas Fuller, probably the distinguished Reader in Gray's Inn, and Thomas Jones and Judith his wife. Fuller grants a lease of a tenement in Romsey Court (formerly part of the property in London of Romsey Abbey in Huntingdonshire, see P. R. O. *Rentals and Surveys,* Portfolio 11/36), in St. Giles without Cripplegate, for thirty years at a rental of ten shillings yearly. The document therefore ceased to be valid in 1625, and would be available as a wrapper for the manuscript play in 1631. The folios are at present numbered 1 to 29. Folio 1 is a modern fly-leaf, with Halliwell's note, folios 2 and 3 the folded vellum indenture, originally the wrapper, and folios 4 to 29 the prompt-copy of the play. Massinger's text covers folios 4 to 27. Folio 28 contains on the verso the Prologue, and folio 29 on the recto the Epilogue and on the verso memoranda by the adapter concerning properties.

A tankard watermark appears in folios 4, 7, 9, 10, 13, 15, 16, 18, 21, 22, 24, and 26. Massinger's text was therefore written upon twelve sheets, and these are numbered consecutively by him in the top left-hand corners of the first page of each 1 to 12. In folio 29 a fleur-de-lis watermark indicates that the Prologue and Epilogue were added upon a separate sheet of different paper, probably at the theater. The fragment remaining of folio 5 has been mended with modern paper with a horn watermark. I have not been able to date this paper and consequently cannot fix the date of mounting and binding. But it was bound before it was sold in 1870, as the Sale Catalogue shows. The vellum wrapper in which the play was originally stitched seems to have been refolded, and an inch of the right leaf turned in, at the time of binding. The stabs of the original stitching are now visible an inch from the inner margin of the right leaf.

The manuscript is on the whole in good preservation, and has come well through the ordeal of the rubbish heap. The only serious loss is that of folio 5, almost entirely torn away. But the top and bottom edges of most leaves are frayed or torn more or less severely. The ink has also faded in many places. Certainly something has been lost since Croker edited it in 1848, but not much, and apart from folio 5 there is little that careful reading cannot establish with fair certainty. It is regrettable that the lost folio 5 contained the clue to Herbert's only censorial interference with the revised text. The manuscript has on the whole been carefully mended and bound, with unimportant exceptions.

Four different hands belonging to three writers may be distinguished, apart from Halliwell's Note, and the words "A Tragedy" on the titlepage, and the "what" in line 511, which are probably modern.

The most important hand is that of the writer of the text of the play, which is undoubtedly that of its author, Massinger, as Sir George Warner first pointed out (*The Athenaeum*, 19 January 1901, pp. 90–91). Nothing but inveterate prejudice in favor of transcription, and a complete neglect of the available material, could obscure this patent fact. The Foljambe copy of the first quarto of *The Duke of Millan*, with an autograph signed poem by Massinger attached and with autograph corrections in the text, had been brought into prominence by Gifford, and came into the possession of Dyce. It is now in the

South Kensington Museum. Gifford had, however, acclaimed this discovery as proving that the hand of Massinger was the same as that of *The Parliament of Love,* a manuscript now in the same collection, an identity which he was anxious to accept in order to rebut the evidence, in the Stationers' Register, of Rowley's authorship of this play (Gifford's *Massinger* [1813], 1:iii; 2:312). The assertion, incomprehensible as it is to those who compare the two hands at South Kensington, was not questioned, and Gifford took some pains to warn off other readers from the manuscript (2:237). I note that the late Professor Cruickshank, writing as recently as 1924, in *The Library* (vol. 5; 179), appears to imply acceptance of Gifford's perverse identification (cf. his *Massinger*, p. 198). In fact, no one until lately considered the question of the writing seriously. Halliwell no doubt took for granted the invariable intermediary of a transcriber, and his ascription to Massinger's hand of certain corrections, I can hardly imagine which, was pure guesswork. So was Croker's view, and the Sale Catalogue statement in 1900, that the titlepage was in Massinger's hand. Yet the well-known letter to Henslowe among the Dulwich Papers, with a postscript written and signed by Massinger, was copied and printed by Collier, and might easily have been seen by Halliwell. The identity of the two hands is unmistakable. There are also clear examples of author's corrections, or alterations in the course of composition, e.g. at lines 392, 790–98, 1038–39, and elsewhere. There are, it is true, numerous instances of errors or slips due to copying, e.g. at lines 387–88, 629, 809, and *passim,* but these are explained when we understand the history of the complete re-handling of the play and of the transcription of the greater part of it with different *dramatis personae* by the author himself, to meet the demands of the censorship, a revision first conjectured by Cunningham in 1870.

Massinger's hand is of a mixed type, the use of English or Italian forms being dictated by no system that I can discover, though it is evident that the English forms came more naturally to him. Three peculiarities seem to be strikingly evident in his writing. The letters tend to be written separately. They tend to be disproportionately sized and irregularly aligned, thus giving a general impression of awkwardness and untidiness. Different forms of the same letter are often found with no apparent reason in one word. It would lead too far to enumerate the minor peculiarities which go with these to create the general impression and picture of his writing, but it is remarkably individual. I use the letter M. to indicate both the author and his hand. M. uses a dull brown ink here, which has a yellowish tinge when faint or thin, and approaches blackbrown when it is more concentrated or clotted. The color appears to darken generally as the play progresses.

M.'s spelling is characteristic of the age but sometimes peculiar, e.g., *accompe* 432, *alleage* 423, *bouyde* (= *buoyed*) 124, *buisnesse* 594, *cought* 1543 (cf. *tought* 444), *course* (= *coarse*) 1989, *currall* (= *coral*) 405, *cyndars* 2097, *ghest* (= *guest*) 1720 and 2843, *guiftes* 2469, *pacyence* 34, *plauges* (= *plagues*) 2829, *prodegie* 912, *rivoletts* 44, *sclanders* 963, *seaventeene* 791, *statsemen* 1502 and 1542, *syx* 1327, *thowgh* (*passim*) and *thowh* 1948, *tite* (= *tight*) 1805, *towgh* (= *tough*) 282, *tyr'd* (= *tired*) 658, *whoelye* 1487, *woemen* 1436, *wowlde* 418 (cf. *showlde passim*), *wrot* 2418. Signs of French influence are perhaps to be observed in *champaigne* 796, *counterfaite* 646, *compagnions* 2125, *interressed* 1141, *retraite* 1078. He takes thought concerning the spelling of *noose*, which he changes to *nooze* 1543, and *perfe(ct)*, which he changes to *perfit* 2513 (cf. 342, 1051). But *sude*, for *sute* (= *suit*) 306, is left uncorrected. M. invariably inserts a *c* in such words as *thancke, sincke*, &c. He tends to prefer *w* to *u* in words like *showlde*. The forms *mee, bee, els, bene, of* (= *off*), *noe, soe, theis, yf, hym*, and *his*, are invariable. A *v* is very frequently used medially, as in *ever, exevnt, trivmph*, whether for consonant or vowel: *gieven* occurs 2612, but *gieue, gieuinge, gieuen*, and *giun* show his normal usage. *Lentulus* and *Antiochus* are spelled with *u*, while *Flaminivs* and *Sempronivs* have *v* after the vowel. The doubling of *o* is rare, but occurs, as in *affoord* 1939, 2821. The tailed *j* is used in present participles after *i*, as in *crijnge* 2272, *denijnge* 1723, *varijnge* 1205. The widest variety of form is shown in his past participles, as in *denid* 1842, *denide* 1967, *repli'd* 2306, *tri'ed* 2430, *depo'sd* 2330, *pas'de* 2713, *Hono'rd* 2525, *honor'd* 2553. And the utmost caprice appears in *wer't* 476, *were't* 2763, *wer'et* 2170, *weret* 2761, *wast* 2762, all being the second person singular of the past tense of the verb *to be*.

M.'s punctuation is spasmodic and light. Colons are rare, and semi-colons come in patches. The most characteristic feature is the frequent separation by a comma of two limbs of one phrase, as in *two, and twentye yeares* 530, *our longe, and tædious travaile* 674. While the speech of Berecinthius, lines 390–409, is carefully punctuated, with rhetorical effect, an essential rhetorical stop is omitted in line 478, and an essential grammatical stop in line 511. In the latter instance the omission led to a misunderstanding of the passage by some reader, who attempted to amend the passage, quite unnecessarily; for the writing of the emendation *what* appears to be modern. The speech of Amilcar, lines 801–13, may exemplify M.'s frequent carelessness in punctuation. At least one aside is not indicated either in punctuation or in stage-direction, lines 702–3. Parentheses are frequently used, but not for this purpose. The manuscript has a great number of marks of the pen which appear to be accidental, and it is not always easy to distinguish intentional punctuation marks. The problem is complicated by a number of distinct punctuation marks which appear to be in modern ink. These are not printed in the present text, but their presence is signalled in the notes. Most of them appear in Croker's edition, and presumably were inserted either by Croker or by some earlier reader.

The second hand, for which I use the letter A., is that of the stage-adapter, who added stage-directions, names of actors, and other indications necessary to make the copy serve for prompt use. He also made a few corrections in the text, wrote the titlepage, and appended memoranda of properties required on the back of the last leaf of the manuscript. A. uses a rounded Italianized hand in large letters, and in a greyish-black ink. It has this resemblance to Massinger's that it is obviously that of a man using a hand which does not come freely or naturally to him. It is here printed in thick italic in two sizes, to correspond to the varying sizes of his directions and corrections, though these are naturally not always as clearly distinguished in the original as they necessarily are in print.

The third hand is to be found in certain alterations in the text, especially in an insertion at line 2022, which is in a hand mainly English with some Italian admixture. The peculiarities of formation and linking of letters, and the tone of the ink, to be found here, are found again in the Prologue and Epilogue, which show also, in an exaggerated form, the tendency to flourish the same letters. On a first inspection I was inclined to distinguish this somewhat elaborate and ornate hand from hand A., even allowing for normal differences between the English and Italian hands of the same writer. Sir George Warner singled out this hand as individual. The ink seemed to be brighter and blacker. The deletion of *Sebastian* and the addition of *Antiochus* in line 634 seemed to be in a different hand and ink from those of the interlined *King* and the caret mark. It seemed as if one person had corrected the name and another, the writer of this third hand, had added *King* and set the meter right. On the other hand, it did not seem reasonable that at line 2022 one person should write the prefix *Sempro:* and another should be called in to write the lines of dialogue following. A search through some of the available dramatic manuscript material of the period settled all doubts. Dyce MS. 9 in the South Kensington Museum contains a prompt-copy of a play by Beaumont and Fletcher, originally acted in 1613, revived and transcribed in 1624, and sent to Herbert to be re-licensed. This, *The Honest Man's Fortune*, is written in hand A. and in this third hand. The stage-directions and prefixes are in hand A., and the text in the other hand. But in the first three lines of the text the word *Orleans* occurs twice in hand A. It is evident therefore that the stage-adapter and transcriber here used his flowing, rather dashing, English hand for dialogue, and his ungainly, but distinct, Italian hand for stage-directions and speakers' names, and not unnaturally also for proper names in dialogue too. This explains the small problems of lines 634 and 2022, and establishes the identity of the writer of hand A. with the writer of this third English hand, which I may therefore designate A*. The scribe of *The Honest Man's Fortune* writes the name *Jhon* elaborately after his *ffinis*, but it is not certain that this was meant to be his own, and I have been unable to identify further the adapter of *Believe as you List*. Another example of his hand is to be found in the British Museum manuscript, Addit. 36758, which contains his transcript, for a private patron probably, of *Bonduca*. This hand is printed here in thick roman type.

The fourth hand used in the manuscript is that of Sir Henry Herbert, in whose autograph the license is written and signed,

in a red-brown ink. The word *buried* in the left margin opposite line 174 is in this hand also. The angles, formation, and
linking of *ed* in *buried* and in *acted* in the license are the same,
and all other letters are paralleled too.

The censor's strictures upon *Believe as you List* in its original
form evidently entailed a complete revision, of which the clearest traces remain in the manuscript, with its deleted and altered
relics of names proper to the first draft, e.g. *Hermit* 32, *German* 536 (cf. 538–39), *Dom Sebastian* 634, 2662, *Sebastian* 1127,
Venice 1173, *Sampayo* 2199. The play originally dealt with the
adventures of Sebastian King of Portugal ("the late, & sad
example" hinted at in the Prologue, l. 5), who led an army
into Africa and was there believed to have perished in 1578 at
the battle of Alcacer-el-Kebir in Morocco. Two years later
Philip II of Spain annexed Portugal. Various pretenders arose,
claiming to be the lost king and finding support among the
discontented Portuguese. Of these the most notable appeared
at Venice in 1598. He seems to have persuaded the Republic to
admit his pretentions, but was driven thence on the complaint
of the Spanish ambassador. After a checkered career in various
countries he was finally executed by Philip III in 1603. He
seems to have been a Calabrian named Marco Tullio. His
adventures were accompanied by a great deal of publicity and
propaganda by his supporters and by the avid journalism of the
time both in the press and on the stage. Various sources were
available from which Massinger could draw his material. In
April and May, 1601, Henslowe paid Chettle and Dekker £6
for a play, *King Sebastian of Portugal* (Henslowe's Diary, ed.
Greg, 1:136, 137; 2:217), now lost, as is also the ballad on the
same subject entered in the Stationers' Register on 12 April
1601. Massinger certainly used P. V. P. Cayet's *Chronologie
Septenaire* 1605, and Munday's compilation from Spanish
sources through a French translation, entitled *The Strangest
Adventure containing a discourse concerning the success of the
King of Portugal, Dom Sebastian* 1601. These he supplemented
by other pamphlets, *The True History of Dom Sebastian* 1602,
and *A Continuation of the lamentable Aduentures of Don
Sebastian* 1603. It is to be noted that Massinger, like Munday in
1601 and Cayet in 1605, leaves his hero in the air and the story
unfinished, though he was executed in 1603, a fact that was

apparently unknown to Cayet in 1605. Circumstances had changed considerably between 1601 and 1631. The Spanish Alliance, however unpopular, became an accomplished fact and an established policy under James I, and after an interval of fresh war peace had again been declared in 1630, Charles I giving way upon the question of the Palatinate. Now, the story of Sebastian accused Spain of usurpation and tyranny, and might be interpreted to accuse Charles of pusillanimity in his refusal to succor Frederick of Bohemia, husband of his sister Elizabeth, against Spain and the Emperor. The survival of the word *Batavian* (1279) lends color to this view. Such a play would be intolerable to Charles on both counts. On revision the play was transformed into a story of a Syrian king reported to have been overthrown by Rome in Achaia and to have fallen in the battle.

The new hero is the Seleucid king known to history as Antiochus the Great, whose conquests in Asia rivalled those of Alexander. Titus Quinctius Flaminius, consul in 198 B.C., defeated Philip of Macedon, ally of Antiochus, at the battle of Cynoscephalae in this year, while Antiochus was completing his conquests in Asia Minor. In 192 the Aetolian confederacy invited him to ally himself with them against Rome, and he sailed with an army to Greece, where Hannibal, then an exile from Carthage, joined him. He was defeated at Thermopylae in 191 by the consul Acilius Glabrio, and fled to Asia. In 190 the Romans, under Scipio Africanus, invaded Asia and crushed him at Magnesia. In the revolts of his vassals that followed his defeat by the Romans Antiochus was believed to have perished in Luristan, in 187, though varying accounts of his death are given.

It is evident that, of the "bookes tost and turnde to make it up" (Prologue 15–16) by Massinger, Raleigh's *History of the World* was the chief, though he consulted Plutarch, and possibly also Livy, Diodorus, and Justin, all of whom were available in English as well as in the original. The events related in these histories are skilfully adapted to enable Antiochus to be substituted for Sebastian as far as possible. Plutarch's story of the betrayal of Hannibal to the Romans by Prusias, king of Bithynia, is transferred to Antiochus with this intent. There is no authority for his supposed escape from death, his sojourn in India, his return and his persecution by the Romans. But this was an essential part of the story of Sebastian and Spain. In the play Antiochus therefore reappears after twenty years spent in a desert, and seeks recognition and help first from his old ally Carthage, then in Bithynia, and finally after persecution by the Roman ambassador to Carthage comes into the power of a great Roman official who, with his wife, was formerly closely associated with him. Thus Carthage corresponds to Venice, Bithynia to Florence, Marcellus and Cornelia to the Duke and Duchess of Medina Sidonia, the Stoic to the Hermit, and Berecinthius to Sampayo, as the story is told in the various accounts of Sebastian. The hero is represented as a genuine king and a persecuted martyr.

The revision was carried out by Massinger himself, as is obvious, and the manuscript shows the clearest examples both of such errors as arise in a transcript of existing copy, and such corrections as occur in free original composition, as the notes to the passages point out. These two types of correction will serve to indicate which parts of the play were taken over verbatim, and which were written as substitutes for deleted parts of the first draft. For example, the part of Berecinthius seems to have been newly composed in the main. Massinger has apparently endeavored to save himself trouble as much as possible. For instance, the proper names chosen are such as may serve as the metrical equivalent of the disused names, Antiochus for Sebastian, Carthage for Venice, and even Demetrius Castor, the chirurgeon, for Sebastian Nero. I do not think that Massinger was responsible for the Prologue and Epilogue, which point out fairly clearly to the audience that the play is a disguise for another and more recent set of characters. The original title is not given by Herbert in his note. Presumably it resembled that of Chettle's and Dekker's play, and the present title can only be fitted to the piece as revised. On the question whether Massinger was responsible for the new title, one may follow the advice of the title itself. It is quoted in the Prologue, but there is no hint of it in the text. As to the Prologue and Epilogue, however, it is unreasonable to suggest that Massinger could write the text of the play in his own hand, neatly enough to serve for a prompt-copy, and that he wrote the Prologue and Epilogue so illegibly as to demand transcription on a separate sheet to be appended to the text for prompt purposes. They were evidently not attached to the play when it went to Herbert, or surely they would have been preserved in Massinger's hand, if by Massinger, and would have preceded the license. Most of the prologues and epilogues in the 1647 folio of Beaumont and Fletcher are clearly by other and later hands. A.'s spelling, however, closely follows Massinger's, with the slight exception of *Grecian* for *Græcian*. But the other manuscripts containing his transcripts do not enable us to complete the inductive process. There is not enough evidence, perhaps, for a dogmatic pronouncement.

Apart from this general revision, carried out at Herbert's orders, there is little trace in this second version of censorial intervention. The one certain instance is the deletion of lines 173, 175, 176, or parts of them, indicated by underlining the beginnings of each line and by crosses in the margin, with the insertion of the word *buried*, written in the margin, and linked to line 174 by a marginal line. Unfortunately most of the leaf is torn out, and it is impossible to reconstruct the alteration. It is clear, however, from this and from examples in other manuscripts, that the censor could be helpful as well as critical, and was prepared on occasion to mend what he had marred. It is difficult to attribute any other deletions to the censor. Lines 1358–62 appear to have been deleted in M.'s ink. Yet they were apparently deleted after the stage-adapter had inserted the directions appropriate to this passage, and the deletion would mar the precision of those directions. I can only suggest that the directions were entered before the play went to Herbert for his license, and that Massinger, in a final review, deleted this passage on account of its references to the deity, even though it were the heathen "Ioue," a subject upon which Herbert was extremely squeamish. This view is strengthened by the fact that all objectionable relics of the first draft have been corrected by the adapter, and this must certainly have been done before the play went to Herbert, else they would have been deleted by him. The deletion by M. in lines 1445–46 may be justified on dramatic grounds, as improving the effect of lines 1450–51. And the deletions by M. in lines 2179 and 2182, though the first ruins the meter of a line, are explicable enough without reference to the censor.

It appears to be probable, therefore, that the stage-adapter was charged with the duty of general supervision of the play as it was submitted by Massinger, as well as the especial function of preparing it for the stage, and that his work was done upon the copy before it was finally dispatched to the censor. Further evidence of this may be found in at least three specific corrections in the text, in hand A*, apart from the removal and correction of relics of the first draft. In line 1493, in M.'s original *managine*, the final *e* is corrected to *g*, written over it by the adapter. In line 1618 he inserts the word *be*, omitted by M. at the end of the line. In line 548 he alters a speech of the First Merchant in order to make it more explicit, with no respect for meter. And in line 2335, M.'s rhetorical affirmative "it is not sufficient" is unnecessarily altered to the interrogative "is it not sufficient," by the same hand. These last alterations are most significant, for they present the adapter in the light of a close and meticulous reader and editor, if necessary, of the text. (A. left it to the present editor, however, to observe M.'s error in l. 2011.) Nevertheless, his principal function was to furnish the play with the indications necessary to translate it into the medium of the stage. Nor was this a light task. Editorial work was involved here also. Massinger omitted speakers' names on occasion, which A. had to supply, *Iaylor:* 1989, *Sempron:* 2023, *Antio:* 2081. And in preparing the text for use as a prompt-copy, other errors of the poet became evident, probably before rehearsals began, possibly after a preliminary reading. M. confuses Demetrius with Calistus in Act II, Sc. 1, and in the stage-direction at line 618, and the speakers' names at lines 704 and 709, A. alters *Calistus* to *Demetrius*. Later on, theatrical economy leads A. to retain Titus only out of the two characters Demetrius and Titus who figure in M.'s play towards the end, when there was no need for Flaminius to have two confidential policemen at his disposal. Indeed, in the somewhat confusing activities of these persons the name of the actor Baxter, to whom these parts were allotted by A., forms the real unity. It is interesting to observe that the characters Calistus and Demetrius are presented in Act I by Baxter and Pattrick, and in Act II by Hobbes and Balls, a third actor, "Rowland," taking over the part of Demetrius in Act III (l. 1185). Such minor parts were evidently very slightly individualized, or this could not have been done. And this fact explains why Titus could as it were swallow up Demetrius and Calistus, when Baxter is again deputed to be the officer attending upon Flaminius. The partial casting of the play, therefore, shown in A.'s stage-directions, points to one direction in which the poet is seen to be less of a practical man of the theater than A.

A full cast of the play should not be expected from the stage-directions of the adapter. We may look there only for such indications as are necessary to supplement a formal casting of the principal parts, and to meet subsequent emergencies in connection with minor parts of less individuality, e.g. the Merchants, Officers, and Guards. For instance, at line 732 *Rowland: w^m. Mago: Nick:* are the officers attending the Carthaginian Senators, and not the Senators themselves, despite the odd coincidence of the historical Senator of Carthage named Mago (an error into which Collier fell in casting the play, here and elsewhere, *Shakespeare Society Papers*, vol. 4 [1849], pp. 138–39). The principal exception to this apparent rule is the note of *m^r Rob:* (Robinson) after *Lentulus:* upon his first entrance at line 1223. But the part of Lentulus was comparatively small, and A.'s memorandum of properties required (p. 98) shows "A letter. for Mr Robinson." At line 1224 A. is simply reminding himself that Robinson is Lentulus and wants the letter provided when he enters. The mention of actors playing important parts arises from the natural tendency of the prompter to think of the persons by their own names and not by their temporary and fictitious names. The greater part of the cast of the play may be made out with the help of A.'s directions and of his memorandum of properties on folio 29^b, and is shown in the list of characters appended to this introduction (pp. 193–94), with the source of information indicated in each case.

A.'s directions show in other ways a different point of view from that of the man of letters writing a play. Massinger, for instance, sees his play as proportioned into five divisions called Acts, each made up of several sub-divisions called Scenes. But the stage-adapter pays no attention to Scenes, and for the most part A. deletes M.'s references to them. Thus he deletes M.'s *Actus secundi, scæna secunda.* and writes in the margin *Ent:–*, prefixed to the names of the persons following in M.'s direction upon the deleted words (l. 732). So also *Actus secundi, scæna prima.* is deleted in favor of *Act: 2. Ent:——* (l. 575). A. is concerned mainly with the entrances of the characters, and similar alterations are made in subsequent Acts. There can be no question, moreover, that he conceives of the Acts mainly as intervals or pauses in the play. Cotgrave uses Act as synonymous with pause "in a Comedy or Tragedy." And in *A Midsummer-Night's Dream* between Acts II and III "They sleep all the Act." This surely furnishes the clue to the word *Long* inserted by A. alongside his marginal notes of *Act: 2* and *Act: 4* (ll. 575, 1791). The first appears to have been written before the words *Act: 2*, the second after the words *Act: 4*, but both by A. It seems reasonable to interpret this as referring to the duration of the Act or pause, as showing that the words *long (pause)* were in A.'s mind the first thought on one occasion, and the word *Act* an afterthought. There is the clearest confirmation of this interpretation in the direction "Act long" at the end of Act IV of Part I of Heywood's *The Fair Maid of the West* (1631, sig. H 3), and at a later date in "I ordered the Drummer to beat a long Act" (*The Greenwich Strowlers*, in *Covent Garden Drollery*, 1672). Thus the performance of this play involved four intervals, of which two were of some duration, probably with musical interludes. *Harry: Willson: & Boy* (ll. 1968–70) were evidently available for songs with accompaniment of a lute. I am reasonably confident that at line 575 the mark following the word *Long* might well be read as the figure "1." So that the direction *Act: 2:* is synonymous in A.'s mind with "Pause 1." It will be observed that A. gives no direction at the begining of the play in place of M.'s heading *Actus primi scæna prima*, which is evidently indifferent to him. It is true, however, that in the memorandum of properties A. uses Act in the sense of a division of the play.

The precise positions of the entrances are again instructive, as marked by M. and A., respectively. M. marks the entrance of a character opposite the first line of his ensuing speech. A. deletes these directions, and replaces them with directions for entrance three or four lines higher up, at the precise moment when the character is due to enter at the back of the stage, giving him time to come to the front before his first line. A. is careful to mark the exact cue by a heavy dash. There is a great difference between such precision of technique and the unpractical directions of M., though M. corrects one such direction himself at line 1982, for more obvious reasons. It will also be observed that A. makes notes in the margin which remind him to give due warning to actors in anticipation of their later appearance. The preparation for the ascent of Antiochus by a trap-door at line 1936 (probably) is begun at line 1825, and Antiochus is called already at line 1877. (No further proof is needed that there was no interval before M.'s Act IV, Sc. 2, which begins at l. 1915.) Similarly preparations of properties and actors for Act II, Sc. 2, are made at lines 654 and 661. *M*^r *Hobs:* we may presume, was "calld vp" from the front of the house, where this veteran actor probably had other duties, to take the part of Calistus in this play which made such heavy calls upon even a large company. The six chairs here required are evidently for the four Senators of Carthage, Flaminius, and Antiochus, and were doubtless brought on by the officers of the Senate, as the two chairs provided at line 1793, probably by Sempronius, for Metellus and Flaminius. M., it will be observed, makes no reference to chairs in either case. Where he mentions properties, his directions are altered by A. M. writes vaguely at line 1118 *the recordes brought in.* A. deputes "Rowland," officer to the Senate, to do so, and at line 982 provides the book necessary, *the great booke: of Accompte,* possibly the actual account book of the company (compare ll. 1968, 2022, and 2025). At line 1915 M.'s *with a poniard & halter.* is an afterthought. The literary and unpractical nature of M.'s directions is perhaps best shown at line 1987, as compared with A.'s direction at line 1986. In general, it is evident that M. was inexperienced in the technicalities of the stage, and that he could hardly have ever been an actor himself, as indeed he never was.

Finally, one alteration in the text carried out by A. is peculiarly interesting as showing his close attention to the actual needs of the stage. The copy as given in by M. would be very inconvenient for prompt-use at the foot of folio 20^a and the top of folio 20^b. Preparations for music and a song are made on folio 20^a at line 1968, and the lute strikes up between lines 2021 and 2022 (not, as M. had it, at line 2025). The song follows during the speech of Sempronius that immediately follows, and continues after this speech. But in M.'s copy this speech came overleaf, on folio 20^b. A. therefore wrote this short speech in at the foot of folio 20^a, and deleted it overleaf.

He thus had all the passage concerning the song and music on one page and could attend to this delicate business without turning the page. Once this speech was spoken, and the song under way, he was at leisure to turn over to the place where the dialogue began again after the song was finished.

An important inference to be drawn from this discussion of A.'s activities is that a dramatist's copy was evidently anything but sacred to the stage-adapter, and that this must be taken into account in considering the history of all dramatic texts, including those of Shakespeare (cf. *The Review of English Studies*, 1 [October, 1925]:421 *et sqq.*).

Herbert's entry in his Office Book dated 11 January 1630/1, and the Licence appended to this prompt-copy, show that the play was originally completed about the end of 1630 and was rewritten between 11 January and 6 May 1631.

The play was first edited from this manuscript by T. Crofton Croker for the Percy Society between April 1844, when he received it from Beltz, and 30 December 1848, the date of the Preface to his edition. It was published at the beginning of January 1849, as appears from Collier's article referred to below. Croker had the help of F. W. Fairholt, the editor of Lyly's *Dramatic Works* in 1858, for folios 4ᵃ and 4ᵇ at least, and acknowledges his help on page 5 of his Preface. Sir George Warner, in his *Athenaeum* article, describes his editing as "strangely careless and unintelligent." Strange as are some of Croker's readings, those with which Fairholt's "industry and perseverance" furnished him are perhaps more surprising. I have given in the notes examples of his variations from my readings. The edition was promptly criticized by Collier in Art. xiv, dated 9 January, of the Shakespeare Society *Papers*, vol. 4, 1849 signed "A Member of both Societies" (i.e. Percy and Shakespeare). He suggests that Croker employed an unskilled transcriber, points out certain obvious errors, such as the long-lived reading *Asolrubal* for *Asdrubal* (retained in J. T. Murray, *English Dramatic Companies*, 1910), *ower* for *order*, *conjure* for *censure*, but also proposes false readings of his own, *fortune* in place of *conjure* (= *censure*), *denies* for *deines*, and gives a list of actors with their parts which is incorrect. Croker immediately replied in a pamphlet, *Remarks on an article inserted in the Papers of the Shakespeare Society* (*1849*), including a list of errata said to have been previously prepared and sent to

Lord Ellesmere, and defending certain readings challenged, e.g. *lonely* for *lovely*, *inglinge* for *iuglinge*, with as much confidence as Collier's own "clear as the sun." Both of them should inspire a salutary caution in the pronouncements of later editors. It is not likely that there was much that was visible to Croker in the manuscript and invisible to a reader today. Where he gives fuller readings than the manuscript would now warrant, one cannot be sure that his imagination was not called upon to redress the outrages of time. But Croker had several merits as an editor, above all this, that he had the definite intention to print the play exactly and literally as it stood in the manuscript. Having followed the spelling, but compromised on the punctuation up to page 32 of his edition, he thereafter followed the punctuation also of the original, in spite of the protests of his conscientious and recalcitrant printer Richards. The Malone Society owes him this praise and recognition.

If goodwill possibly led Croker, in the desire not to lose one drop of his author's blood, to transfuse a few drops of his own silently, the next editor, Cunningham, boldly undertook to fill up out of his own head some of the gaps left in Croker's transcription. In his revision of Gifford's *Massinger*, in 1870, he gives himself generally a free hand, and *Believe as you List*, which he added to Gifford's edition, is temerariously handled. He did not consult the manuscript, which he was unable to trace, though one can hardly think that his search was serious. The following is a fair example of his inventiveness, as compared with that of Croker and Fairholt. Where these read (lines 62–63):

> Old [   ]sper with his fierce beames nour[ishing]e in vaine
> Their olives and . . . . .

Cunningham reads, with engaging irresponsibility:

> Old [He]sper with his fierce beams [scorc]hing in vain
> Their [wives, their sisters, and their tender daughters]

I agree that M. probably wrote *wives*, not *olives*. But I am sure that no editor has the right to give either reading in his text. Cunningham had a passion for correcting what he considered faulty verse-lining, and in innumerable instances rearranges the lines, interpolates words, alters words, to force M.'s text into his idea of what meter should be. He is capable of enormities. Where M. wrote (lines 790–92):

> our enemies, our confæderates, and freindes
> founde it as firme as fate. are seaventeene kinges
> our fædaries, ...

Cunningham ventures thus wantonly:

> Our enemies, our confederates and friends,
> And seventeen kings, our feodaries, found it
> As firm as fate. ...

For the rest, he was aware of Collier's strictures and corrections, and adopts most of them. But he hits upon more than one essential correction himself, and reads *the chining of his horse* instead of the false *the chininge of his fork* (line 1321, see N.E.D. s.v. chining), and *censure* for *conjure* (Collier *fortune*) in the Epilogue. Cunningham, I may repeat, was the first to conjecture the identity of this play with that which Herbert refused to license on 11 January 1631.

The play was next printed in the selection from Massinger's plays in the Mermaid Series, edited by Arthur Symons in 1887. The text is eclectic, mainly from Croker, with readings from Collier and Cunningham. S. W. Orson was responsible for the text of this edition, and remarks "as the Manuscript, notwithstanding diligent enquiry, cannot now be found, the true reading in several places is still uncertain." It is a perfunctory piece of work, and unnecessarily bowdlerized.

Believe as you List next appeared (entitled *Believe As Ye List*) in the "Tudor Facsimile Texts," reproduced in collotype from the manuscript under the direction of J. S. Farmer in 1907, with an introduction which reprints Warner's *Athenaeum* article and refers to S. R. Gardiner's discussion of the political aspects of this and other plays in *The Contemporary Review* for August 1876 (cf. New Shakespere Society *Transactions* [1875–76], 11:332, *The Political Element in Massinger*, by the same writer). Farmer gives in facsimile the whole of the manuscript as it now stands except folio 1 with Halliwell's Note, folio 2^b and folio 3 (the wrapper), and folio 28^a which is blank. On the whole the facsimile gives a clear reproduction for ordinary working purposes of the written text. It fails, of course, to permit of reading what is hidden under mending paper, and certain words or letters deleted or overwritten, and of distinguishing inks or watermarks, or minute details of writing.

The most recent edition of the play is that of Professor R. A. Sherman, of Nebraska, in a series edited by Professor F. E. Schelling, "Masterpieces of the English Drama," 1912 *et sqq.* Professor Sherman's selection from Massinger's plays forms Vol. 5 in this series, arranged for college use. He seems to have based his text upon Croker's edition, and follows him in certain errors corrected by Collier or Cunningham, also in omitting part of a perfectly legible speech of Berecinthius (lines 1038–41), alleging corruption in the manuscript, whereas the true reason obviously is to eliminate the only unsavory passage left in the play after the destruction of folio 5. Professor Sherman refers frequently to "the manuscript," but appears only to have infrequently consulted the facsimile. The short introduction immediately prefixed to this play is very inaccurate.

The manuscript was collated by the late Professor Cruickshank in his *Philip Massinger* (1920, pp. 177 *et sqq.*). He falls into several snares, passes over some difficulties, suggests some risky conjectures, but corrects a few of Croker's misreadings.

A further partial collation has appeared since the present text was printed, in an article by S. A. Tannenbaum, *Corrections to the Text of 'Believe as You List,'* in "Publications of the Modern Language Association of America," September 1927. Dr. Tannenbaum here offers corrections of the text of the Mermaid Series edition (which he ascribes to Symons instead of Orson) on the basis of an examination of the facsimile. With this unsatisfactory material, he is led into several errors and conjectures, and is obliged to pass over some cruxes. But a number of misreadings in this perfunctory text, some of which had already been corrected elsewhere, are here set right.

The present text attempts to reproduce the manuscript as it now stands. Where fuller readings are given by Croker they will be found in the notes, as I do not think I should be justified in inserting them in brackets in the text. I have also given in the notes the more interesting variant readings of his edition, many of which bear upon the peculiarities of M.'s writing. The various hands in the manuscript are distinguished typographically as far as possible. In every case of intervention by a hand other than M.'s information will be found in the notes, which refer to M.'s own corrections or deletions, as a rule, only where comment seems desirable either to explain the alteration or to indicate its position in the text or its significance (see note on p. 2 of the text).

LIST OF CHARACTERS AND CAST

in order of appearance.

ANTIOCHUS, King of Lower Asia.

Joseph Taylor. Fol. 29[b], l. 4 (cf. 1106–7); 1831 (cf. 1877–79, 1931).

a Stoic Philosopher.

CHRYSALUS SYRUS GETA } bondmen of Antiochus.

Elyard Swanston. Fol. 29[b], l. 2 (cf. 274–79).[1]

BERECINTHIUS, a Flamen of Cybele.

Thomas Pollard. Fol. 29[b], l. 3 (cf. 301, 343).

first Merchant second Merchant third Merchant } former subjects of Antiochus.

John Honyman 2199.
William Penn 2367, 2825.
Curtis Greville 2367, 2826.

TITUS FLAMINIUS, Roman Envoy to Carthage.

John Lowin. Fol. 29[b], l. 6 (cf. 1185).

CALISTUS

DEMETRIUS } Freemen of Flaminius.

{ (1) Richard Baxter 575.
(2) Thomas Hobbes 829, 1185.
(1) William Pattrick 608.
(2) Francis Balls 830.
(3) "Rowland" (= Rowland Dowle?) 1185. }

AMILCAR, Prince of Carthage.

HANNO ASDRUBAL CARTHALO } Senators of Carthage.

Carthaginian Officers.

{ "Rowland" 732, 830, 1116.
William Mago 732.
"Nick" (= Nicholas Burt?) 732. }

LENTULUS, Roman Envoy to Carthage in place of Flaminius.

Richard Robinson. Fol. 29[b], l. 5 (cf. 1224).

[1] Apparently the writing, with the piece of silver enclosed, was conveyed by Chrysalus to Antiochus, and this action occurred on the lost fol. 5.

TITUS, a spy in the service of Flaminius.

Richard Baxter 1258, 1445 (cf. 1448), 1687, 2199 (= officer, 2214, &c.), 2516, 2556 (= Demetrius).

PRUSIAS, King of Bithynia.
The Queen of Bithynia.
PHILOXENUS, chief counsellor to Prusias.

Attendants on Prusias.

"Rowland" 1362.
William Mago 1362.
Francis Balls 1362.
"Nick" 1362.

a Lady in attendance on the Queen.
Bithynian Guard.
A. METELLUS, Roman Proconsul in Asia.
SEMPRONIUS, a Roman Centurion under Metellus.
a Jailor at Callipolis.
[a Lute Player]
[a Singer] } within.
a Courtesan from Corinth.
a Jailor's assistant.

William Penn 1915.
Henry Wilson 1968.
"Boy" 1970.

"Rowland" 2187
(= "others").

MARCELLUS, Roman Proconsul in Sicily.

Robert Benfeild. Fol. 29^b, l. 7 (cf. 2367, 2390, 2859).

Attendants upon Marcellus.

"Rowland" 2367, 2632, 2721.
Francis Balls 2367.
"Nick" 2367.
Richard Baxter (2632, 2709–13, 2716).

CORNELIA, wife to Marcellus.
a Moorish Woman, servant to Cornelia.
a Roman Captain under Marcellus.

William Pattrick 2588.

Roman Soldiers.

NOTE: There can be little doubt that Demetrius is acted by Balls at l. 830, and not by "Rowland," who is clearly shown at l. 732 as a Carthaginian officer. This character is thus represented, at different stages, by no less

than three actors, and Calistus by two. The confusion in later representations of "officers" is almost insoluble. But it seems clear that after l. 2556
Baxter ceases to be the officer of Flaminius, whether under the name of
Titus (as A. conceives him) or of Demetrius (as M. continues this character eliminated by A.), and becomes an officer of Marcellus at l. 2632. He
receives orders from Marcellus as "servant," l. 2711, is described by Antiochus as servant of Marcellus, l. 2712, and enters in this capacity at l. 2716.
Flaminius is reasonably left servantless in this scene of his disgrace. One
may fairly conjecture that the missing indication at l. 2861 would show
Baxter (or possibly "Rowland") as the Guard who hales him off to prison,
in either case a pretty reversal of function on the part of the actor. These
arrangements are all very significant of the want of individuality in such
minor parts, even considerable speaking parts, as are those of Calistus and
Demetrius. It may be observed that Pattrick and Rowland play Demetrius
when he is to speak, and Balls when he has a silent part. Hobbes acts Calistus, ll. 829 *et sqq.*, a silent part, and continues it, now a speaking part, in
the following scene, ll. 1185 *et sqq.*, when Baxter is required for the long-
continued part of Titus, ll. 1257 *et sqq.*, into which Demetrius seems to be
merged by A.

The principal parts are taken by actors who were well-known members
of the King's company. Among others available for parts, to which A.
gives no clue, were Richard Sharpe, Anthony Smith, John Shanks, George
Vernon, James Horne, and for women's parts John Tomson, Alexander
Goffe, William Triggs, to judge from the casts given in Quartos of plays
written by Massinger for the King's company, dated 1629 and 1630. Little
is known of Baxter and Mago, and nothing of "Rowland," Balls, and
"Nick," or the lute-player "Harry Wilson." I may note here that Richard
Baxter was born in 1593, was a hired man in Queen Anne's company at
the Red Bull from about the time of the opening of that theater in 1605–6,
until he left them, probably in 1623, to join the King's company. Francis
Balls was probably the son of one Richard Balls, musician to the King,
employed also by the King's company at the Blackfriars theater, who died
shortly before 1623. This fact may explain why in one instance (l. 830)
he is called "ffan [= Fran] Balls" and elsewhere "Mr Balls" (ll. 1362, 2367).
In both these cases my information is derived from Chancery records, as
yet unpublished. "Rowland" is probably Rowland Dowle, who figures in
the list of servants of the King's players granted privileges in 1636. "Nick"
was probably Nicholas Burt, who served under Shanks with the King's
men, had a reputation for women's parts, probably joined Beeston's company in 1637, acted Latorch in *The Bloody Brother* at the Cockpit in 1648,
and at the Restoration, as Pepys tells us, rose to the part of Othello at the
same theater, where he was one of the leaders of the new King's company.
"Harry Willson" is probably another member of the family of musicians,
of whom Nicholas Wilson and the "Iacke Wilson" mentioned in the quarto
of *Much Ado about Nothing* (1600) are recorded. He may well have been
the "Mr Wilson a cunning Musition" involved in the performance in the
house of the Bishop of Lincoln on 27 September 1631 (J. T. Murray,
English Dramatic Companies, 2:148–50).

XIII

RICHARD HOSLEY

The Discovery-Space in Shakespeare's Globe

This paper[1] proposes the theory that the tiring-house of the First Globe was essentially similar to that of the Swan as pictured in the De Witt drawing of 1596. Thus the Globe tiring-house would have been equipped with two (or three) double-hung stage-doors. (Probably there were three rather than two doors, but since the problem of discoveries is essentially the same in the one case as the other we may leave the question temporarily undetermined.) Each door (since as wide as high) would have been some 7 feet or 8 feet wide and (since hinged on the outside) would have opened upon the stage. When fully opened, either door (or a presumptive third door) would have discovered a considerable space within the tiring-house; and this space might have been discovered by drawing aside curtains instead of opening a door if we accept the expedient of fitting up hangings in front of the open doorway. Such a "discovery-space" (behind an open doorway in the tiring-house façade) must be distinguished in what follows from that other kind of discovery-space known as the "inner-stage."

I

The Elizabethan "inner-stage," as commonly reconstructed, may be defined as a curtain-covered recess in the tiring-house wall, measuring some 7 feet or 8 feet in depth and 20 feet or

From *Shakespeare Survey*, 12 (1959): 35–46. Reprinted by permission of the author, the editor of *Shakespeare Survey*, and the Cambridge University Press.

[1] Read (in preliminary form) at the Eighth International Shakespeare Conference at Stratford-upon-Avon, 2 September 1957. The underlying research was completed while the writer held a fellowship of the John Simon Guggenheim Memorial Foundation.

more in width, and persistently used for actions localized in "interior" scenes (since these occasionally require such properties as beds, tables, chairs, and the like).

The first thing that strikes us about this "inner-stage" is that the term itself apparently never occurs in Elizabethan documents. Moreover, there does not seem to have been a generally employed alternative term. Perhaps the closest we can come to it is the periphrastic *"middle of the place behind the Stage"* in which a *"brazen Head"* is to be set in Greene's *Alphonsus King of Aragon* (*c.* 1587). Without question this is important evidence for the Elizabethan discovery-space. However, the term is not quite the same as *inner-stage* (in fact it is quite different), nor does it necessarily imply the sort of playing-area usually understood by that term. For example, it may well designate the space behind a middle door in the tiring-house wall. Again, the term *study*, occasionally used in Elizabethan stage-directions calling for discoveries, designates a discovery-space only when a study is required by the fiction of the play in question. In other fictional situations the discovery-space is referred to as a *shop*, a *tent*, a *cabin*, a *tomb*, a *closet*, a *porch*, a *counting-house*, and so on.

Next we may recall that the concept of an "inner-stage," though occasionally regarded as a fact, is no more than a theory by which a number of investigators since the early nineteenth century have sought to explain the "internal" evidence of discoveries in Elizabethan dramatic texts. That evidence is capable of alternative explanation. And so is the "external" evidence of contemporary pictures showing tiring-house curtains. For example, the "curtains" in the *Roxana* vignette may well be hangings fitted up along a tiring-house wall. In fact there is no unambiguous evidence whatsoever for an Elizabethan "inner-stage."

Finally we may note a theory that the proscenium arch "evolved" through gradual enlargement of a proto-alcove we have come to know as the "inner-stage." But this theory may not be invoked to support that of an "inner-stage" without lapse into circular argument. In any case it is probable that the proscenium arch, as its name implies, originated through enclosure of the stage itself—the *proscænium*. This is the theory proposed by Richard Southern in *The Open Stage* (1953).

With these considerations in mind we may approach the question whether there was an "inner-stage" in Shakespeare's Globe (always understanding by this term the elaborate recessed playing-area referred to above). Since there is no relevant external evidence, we must depend on the internal evidence of the plays. Here let us confine our attention to a group of plays designed for performance presumably at the Globe and in no other theater. These are the thirty extant plays first performed by the Chamberlain-King's Men between the spring of 1599, when the Globe was built, and the autumn of 1608, when the King's Men may have begun using the Blackfriars as well as the Globe.

A scene-by-scene examination suggests that twenty-one of these thirty plays were produced without a single discovery or "concealment" (deliberate closing of a discovery-space so as to hide a player or property from view of the audience): *As You Like It, Every Man out of his Humour, Henry V, Julius Caesar*, and *A Warning for Fair Women* (1599); *Alarum for London, Hamlet* and *Twelfth Night* (1600); *All's Well That Ends Well* (1602); *The London Prodigal* and *Sejanus* (1603); *The Fair Maid of Bristow, Measure for Measure*, and *Othello* (1604); *King Lear* (1605); *Macbeth* and *A Yorkshire Tragedy* (1606); *Antony and Cleopatra* and *The Miseries of Enforced Marriage* (1607); *Coriolanus* and *Timon of Athens* (1608). (The dates are approximate, and the other nine plays in the group are listed on pp. 209–11 below.)

If the reader will tentatively accept this proposition, we may follow one of its implications to a conclusion. Twenty of these twenty-one plays have actions localized in interior scenes. (The exception is *Alarum for London*.) Yet over two-thirds of these interior actions were demonstrably produced without discovery or concealment. It follows that there was not an "inner-stage" at the Globe, for if there had been it would presumably have been used in these twenty plays.

That the twenty plays here referred to were produced without discovery or concealment is suggested by absence from the substantive texts of any stage-direction or dialogue calling for or implying the opening or closing of curtains or other discovering agency. In the past, proponents of the "inner-stage" theory have met this difficulty by recourse to two assumptions.

The first is that Elizabethan dramatic texts are largely deficient in directions for staging. It is true that a few texts are without stage-directions and that others occasionally lack an important direction, either because the text in question was printed from a manuscript to which the direction had not been added or from which it had been excised, or because the direction was omitted in the course of printing. But by and large Elizabethan dramatic texts are well-furnished with stage-directions. Not, generally, with such as are sometimes supplied in present-day texts "in order to help the reader visualise the action": *After she leaves the room, X throws himself down in a chair; he lights a cigarette and sits puffing abstractedly as—the curtain falls.*" But, generally, with such as will account for the salient needs of Elizabethan production: *"A bed thrust out," "Enter X above," "X arises in the midst of the stage," "Enter X at one door, Y at another," "X draws a curtain discovering Y,"* and so on. Since it cannot be demonstrated, the assumption that evidence is largely missing from our texts cannot be refuted; but for the same reason it may be rejected with impunity.

The other assumption is more important. It is that the unqualified term *Enter* in Elizabethan stage-directions can mean "is discovered," a sense not recorded by the *Oxford English Dictionary* and not current in the modern theater. (Occasionally the term *Enter* does seem to have borne the sense "is discovered," when qualified in the direction by allusion to a discovery-space, as in Marlowe's *Doctor Faustus*, *"Enter Faustus in his Study"*; or in dialogue by the requirement of discovery, as in Fletcher's *Sea Voyage*, *"Sure this Curtaine will reveale. Enter Albert."*) In the nature of things this assumption (like the one concerning evidence) is not capable of demonstration; hence in the nature of things it also may be rejected. Throughout Elizabethan drama the unqualified term *Enter* seems to have retained the full force of its Latin original (*introire, intrare*) in implying the idea of motion: "To go or come into . . . ; to pass within the boundaries of . . ." (*O.E.D.*). The unqualified term *Exit* seems also to have retained its original meaning (*exire*) suggestive of motion.

(I do not press the interpretation that the unqualified terms *Enter* and *Exit* generally meant no more than "comes on stage" and "goes off stage," for this is a conclusion of the present argument, and in any case we are here concerned only with an assumption occasionally invoked to explain the absence of a certain class of evidence. But in passing I would point out that once these terms are accepted at face value we may suppose that practically all "entrances" and "exits" in Elizabethan drama were walk-ons and walk-offs.)

The argument against an "inner-stage" at the Globe is based not only on absence of evidence for discovery or concealment in these twenty-one plays. There is also occasional evidence in stage-directions that the players walked on stage at the beginning of actions localized in interior scenes; and if so the actions in question did not begin with discoveries. "Walk-on directions" (as they may be called) have occasionally been noticed by editors and other commentators, but they have not, apparently, been noticed systematically and their significance has been largely ignored by investigators of the "inner-stage" persuasion. They are of several kinds, the following list including all examples noted at the beginning of interior actions in the twenty plays under discussion. Scene-locations in inverted commas are by Kittredge or Gifford, otherwise by the present writer.

One kind of walk-on direction involves reference to doors:

(1) *Henry V*, V, 2 (F): "*Enter at one doore, King Henry, Exeter, Bedford, Warwicke, and other Lords. At another, Queene Isabel, the King, the Duke of Bourgougne, and other French*" ("The French King's Palace").

(2) *Antony and Cleopatra*, III, 2: "*Enter Agrippa at one doore, Enobarbus at another*" ("Caesar's house").

(3) *Timon of Athens*, I, 1: "*Enter Poet, Painter, Jeweller, Merchant, and Mercer, at severall doores*" ("Timon's house").

(4) *Ibid.*, III, 6: "*Enter diverse Friends at severall doores*" ("A banqueting hall in Timon's house").

Another kind calls for bringing on stage a "sleeping," "injured," "dead," or otherwise non-ambulatory player:

(5) *A Warning for Fair Women*, sc. 19 (sig. G4 in Q): "*Enter John Beane brought in a Chaire, and master Barnes, and master James*" (a room).

A third kind calls for bringing properties on stage:

(6) *Coriolanus*, II, 2: "*Enter two Officers, to lay Cushions, as it were, in the Capitoll*" ("The Capitol").

(7) *Timon of Athens*, I, 2: *"A great Banquet serv'd in"* ("A room of state in Timon's house").

A fourth kind calls for a player to enter and immediately seat himself (instead of being discovered seated):

(8) *A Warning for Fair Women*, sc. 21 (H3v): *"Enter some to prepare the judgement seat to the Lord Maior, Lo. Justice, and the foure Lords, and one Clearke, and a Shiriff, who being set, commaund Browne to be brought forth"* (a court of justice).

(9) *Othello*, I, 3 (Q): *"Enter Duke and Senators, set at a Table with lights and Attendants"* ("A council chamber").

(10) *Coriolanus*, I, 3: *"Enter Volumnia and Virgilia, mother and wife to Martius: They set them downe on two lowe stooles and sowe"* ("A room in the house of Marcius").

And a fifth kind of walk-on direction involves qualification of the verb *Enter* by a participle or adverb expressing the idea of motion:

(11) *A Warning for Fair Women*, sc. 25 (K 1): *"Enter Anne Sanders and her keeper following her"* (inside a prison).

(12) *Every Man out of his Humour*, IV, 1 (Q): *"Enter Fungoso, Fallace following him"* ("A Room in Deliro's House").

(13) *Ibid.*, IV, 2: *"Enter Deliro, with Macilente, speaking as they passe over the Stage"* ("Another Room in the same").

(14) *Ibid.*, V, 6: *"Enter Deliro, Fungoso, Drawer following them"* ("A Room at the Mitre").

Evidence of dialogue for walk-ons and walk-offs seems also to have been imperfectly appreciated. There is, to be sure, a useful essay by Warren D. Smith on "entrance-announcements," or the sort of remark one player makes to another in order to identify a third who is appearing on stage—"Here comes so-and-so." ("The Elizabethan Stage and Shakespeare's Entrance Announcements," *Shakespeare Quarterly*, vol. 4 [1953].) Generally entrance-announcements shed no light on whether a given action began with a walk-on, for of necessity they almost always occur in the midst of an action, when players are already on stage.

In plays with "Presenters" remaining on stage, however, entrance-announcements can be very instructive. One of our twenty Globe plays is of this type, *Every Man out of his Humour* (Q). Apart from choral commentaries by the Grex, this play has eighteen individual actions, of which fifteen are localized in interior scenes. References by the Grex to entering players suggest that eleven of these fifteen interior actions began with a walk-on instead of a discovery:

(1) II, 2 in Q (4–6 in F): "So sir, but when appeares Macilente againe? *Enter Macilente, Deliro, . . .* here he comes, and with him Signior Deliro a merchant" ("A Room in Deliro's House").

(2) III, 1 (1–6): "Stay, what new Mute is this that walkes so suspiciously? *Enter Cavalier Shift*" ("The Middle Aisle of St Paul's").

(3) III, 3 (9): "Here comes Macilente and Signior Briske freshly suted, . . . *Enter Macilente, Briske*" ("An Apartment at the Court").

(4) IV, 1 (1–2): "See who presents himselfe here? . . . *Enter Fungoso, Fallace following him*" ("A Room in Deliro's House").

(5) IV, 2: "*Enter Deliro, with Macilente, speaking as they passe over the Stage*" ("Another Room in the same"). No entrance-announcement is possible since the action is not preceded by a choral commentary; however, the action begins with a walk-on direction.

(6) IV, 3 (3–6): "Stay, here comes the Knight Adventurer. . . . I, and his Scrivener with him. *Enter Puntarvolo, Notarie, with Serving-men*" ("Puntarvolo's Lodgings").

(7) IV, 4 (7): "Behold here hee comes, very Worshipfully attended, and with good variety. *Enter Fungoso with Taylor, Shoe-maker, and Haberdasher*" ("A Room in Deliro's House").

(8) IV, 5 (8): "O here they come from seal'd and deliver'd. *Enter Puntarvolo, Fastidius Briske, serving men with the Dog*" ("Puntarvolo's Lodgings").

(9) V, 1: "Here come the Gallants, . . . *Enter Puntarvolo, Fastidius Briske, Fungoso, and the Dog*" ("The Palace Stairs").

(10) V, 2: "Here they come, . . . *Enter Puntarvolo, Saviolina, Fastidius Briske, Fungoso*" ("An Apartment in the Palace").

(11) V, 3: "*Enter Shift*" ("The Palace Stairs"). No entrance-announcement is possible since the action is not preceded by a choral commentary.

(12) V, 4 (4–7): "I, here he comes: . . . *Enter Carlo*" ("A Room at the Mitre").

(13) V, 5 (8): "*Enter Macilente and Deliro*" ("A Room in Deliro's House"). No entrance-announcement.

(14) V, 6 (9): "here comes the Pawne and his Redeemer.

Enter Deliro, Fungoso, Drawer following them" ("A Room at the Mitre").

(15) V, 7 (10–11): "*Enter Briske and Fallace*" ("The Counter"). No entrance-announcement is possible since the action is not preceded by a choral commentary.

One of the three exterior actions also begins with an entrance-announcement.

More generally informative than entrance-announcements are what may be called "walk-off cues," by which is meant such tags of closing dialogue as "Come with me," "I'll follow you," "Let's in to dinner," and so on. The reader will of course have noticed these dramaturgical aids to the player in gracefully getting himself and his fellows off stage without benefit of blackout or curtain-drop. Walk-off cues crop up in Greek tragedy, Roman comedy, and medieval drama, and they occur throughout Elizabethan drama with a frequency that is surprising when one first begins systematically to notice them. They do not usually occur in soliloquies, for when a person alone decides to leave a place he need not communicate his intention to anyone, and a single player does not have a traffic problem in walking off stage. But when two or more players are on an "open" stage the careful dramatist usually gives them one or more walk-off cues. The device seems to have two theatrical functions. First it prepares the audience for the players' imminent departure from view, and in this respect the walk-off cue is also (in a sense) "realistic," for when two people leave a place they must usually come to some sort of verbal agreement about their leave-taking. The other function is to regulate the exit of two or more players at a single door: if one of the players is to precede the other off stage (for occasionally players go off two or three abreast), the order of their going must be clearly implied by the script in order to avoid hesitation or collision. Especially interesting examples are those in which one player, a person of rank, orders a second to precede him and a third to follow him off stage.

The device of the walk-off cue may conveniently be illustrated from *Macbeth*, *A Warning for Fair Women*, and *The Miseries of Enforced Marriage*.

In *Macbeth* there are twenty-nine individual actions, of which fourteen are localized in interior scenes. Dialogue suggests that twelve of these interior actions ended with a walk-off rather than a concealment:

(1) I, 4: "Let's after him, Whose care is gone before, to bid us welcome: . . . *Exeunt*" ("The Palace").

(2) I, 5: "*Exeunt*" ("Macbeth's Castle"). No walk-off cue (two players exit).

(3) I, 7: "Away, . . . *Exeunt*" ("Macbeth's Castle").

(4) II, 2: Retyre we to our Chamber: . . . *Exeunt*" ("Macbeth's Castle").

(5) II, 3: "Therefore to Horse, And let us not be daintie of leave-taking, But shift away: . . . *Exeunt*" ("Macbeth's Castle").

(6) III, 1: "Ile call upon you straight: abide within, . . . *Exeunt*" ("The Palace").

(7) III, 2: "So prythee goe with me. *Exeunt*" ("The Palace").

(8) III, 4: "Come, wee'l to sleepe: . . . *Exeunt*" ("Hall in the Palace").

(9) III, 6: "*Exeunt*" ("The Palace"). No walk-off cue (2 players exit).

(10) IV, 1: "Come bring me where they are. *Exeunt*" ("A cavern").

(11) IV, 2: "Run away I pray you. *Exit crying Murther*" ("Macduff's Castle").

(12) V, 1: "Looke after her, . . . So goodnight, . . . Good night good Doctor. *Exeunt*" ("Macbeth's Castle").

(13) V, 3: "Bring it after me: . . . *Exeunt*" ("A room in the Castle").

(14) V, 5: "Arme, Arme, and out, . . . *Exeunt*" ("Within the Castle").

Twelve of the fifteen exterior actions also end with a walk-off cue.

In *A Warning for Fair Women* there are twenty-six individual actions, five involving Presenters and thus unlocalized, twenty-one constituting the fiction proper. Of these twenty-one actions, eleven are localized in interior scenes. Dialogue suggests that each of these interior actions ended with a walk-off rather than a concealment:

(1) Sc. 4 (B3v in Q): "come Roger let us go, . . . *Exeunt*" (a room).

(2) Sc. 5 (C1v): "Ile folow you" (a room). No exit-direction.

(3) Sc. 12 (F2v): "Ile up into the Presence. . . . *Exeunt*" (a buttery).

(4) Sc. 13 (F3): "go thou and watch For master Brownes arrival from the Court, . . . In the meane space I will go after her" (probably a room). No exit-direction.

(5) Sc. 15 (G1): "come my lords, lets in, . . . *Exeunt omnes*" (a court of justice).

(6) Sc. 16 (G2): "farewel Nan, . . . God be with you, good Captaine. . . . Farewel, gentle Hodge" (probably a room). No exit-direction.

(7) Sc. 18 (G3v): "Come master Maior, . . . farewell good neighbor Brown. . . . *Exeunt*" (a room).

(8) Sc. 19 (G4): "Come, Ile go along with you. *Exeunt*" (a room).

(9) Sc. 20 (H2): "Farewel George Browne, . . . *exeunt om.*" ("*at the Court*," Q).

(10) Sc. 21 (H3v): "Jailer, away with them. . . . *Exeunt*" (a court of justice).

(11) Sc. 25 (K1): "The time is come sweete hearts, and we must part, That way go you, this way my heavie heart. *Exeunt*" (within a prison).

Eight of the ten exterior actions and one of the five unlocalized actions also end with a walk-off cue.

In *The Miseries of Enforced Marriage* there are thirteen individual actions, of which six are localized in interior scenes. Dialogue implies that each of these interior actions ended with a walk-off rather than a concealment:

(1) Sc. 2 (sig. B2 in Q): "come get you in: . . . *Exeunt*" (a room).

(2) Sc. 5 (D3v): "Why then lets come and take up a new roome, . . . *Exeunt*" (a room).

(3) Sc. 6 (E2): "Well then, I will go tel him newes of his of-springs. *Exit*" (a room).

(4) Sc. 7 (E4): "weele first to the surgeons. . . . *Exeunt*" (probably a room).

(5) Sc. 12 (H3v): "Ile stay his journey, least I meet a hanging. *Exeunt*" (a room).

(6) Sc. 13 (K1v): "And in your eies so lovingly being wed, We hope your hands will bring us to our bed. FINIS" (a room). No exit-direction.

Five of the seven exterior actions also end with a walk-off cue.

The incidence of walk-off cues in the interior actions of

these three plays is exceptionally high. Nevertheless walk-off cues occur in over two-thirds of all interior actions in the twenty plays under discussion. (The incidence is approximately the same in exterior actions, and also in actions of each kind in the ten plays not under discussion.) Limitation of space forbids printing further examples, but the phenomenon may easily be verified in a text of the reader's choice.

To sum up the argument from our twenty Globe plays: walk-on directions, entrance-announcements, and walk-off cues, in view of the absence of any evidence for discovery or concealment, suggest that, in over two-thirds of the interior actions of these plays, the players were not discovered or concealed within a discovery-space but rather walked on and off stage. In general the actions of these plays (excepting those of *Sejanus* which begin with character-lists in the neo-classical style) begin and end with stage-directions employing the term *Enter* or *Exit*. Hence we have evidence that the unqualified terms *Enter* and *Exit* generally meant no more than "comes on stage" and "goes off stage."

II

Let us return to our chief source of information about the Elizabethan stage, the Swan drawing. This does not show curtains. But absence of curtains does not mean that discoveries were not effected at the Swan, even as we see it in the De Witt sketch. We must recognize that a discovery can be effected without curtains in a tiring-house whose doors open out upon the stage. The Swan doors evidently did open out, and being also some 7 feet or 8 feet wide they would have disclosed a space adequate to the needs of most Elizabethan discoveries. A few examples may suffice to illustrate the convention of discovery by opening a door:

(1) Anon., *Arden of Feversham*, V, 1: "*Then they lay the body in the Countinghouse. . . . Then they open the counting-house doore, and looke uppon Arden. Ales.* See Susan where thy quandam Maister lies" (*c.* 1592, theater unknown). One player reclining; also a concealment.

(2) Dekker, *The Shoemakers' Holiday*, III, 4: "*Enter Jane in a Semsters shop working, and Hamond muffled at another doore, he stands aloofe. Ham.* Yonders the shop, and there my faire love sits" (1599, Rose). One player seated.

(3) Chapman, Jonson, and Marston, *Eastward Ho*, I, 1: *"En-ter Maister Touch-stone, and Quick-silver at severall dores, ...
At the middle dore, Enter Golding discovering a Gold-smiths shoppe, and walking short turns before it"* (1605, Blackfriars). One player standing.

(4) Anon., *The Second Maiden's Tragedy*, line 1926 in the Malone Society Reprint: *"On a sodayne in a kinde of Noyse like a Wynde, the dores clattering, the Toombstone flies open, and a great light appeares in the midst of the Toombe; His Lady as went owt, standing just before hym all in white, Stuck with Jewells and a great crucifex on her brest"* (1611, Blackfriars or First Globe). One player standing.

(5) Fletcher, *The Island Princess*, II, 5: Armusia, in search of the imprisoned King, forces open a door: *"The King discover'd"* (1619–21, Blackfriars or Second Globe). One player.

(6) Fletcher and W. Rowley, *The Maid in the Mill*, V, 2: The King forces the lock of a "closet" in which Otrante has incarcerated Florimel: *"Florimell discovered"* (1623, Blackfriars or Second Globe). One player.

(7) Massinger, *The Renegado*, III, 6: Asambeg, going to re-lease the imprisoned Paulina, *"opens a doore, Paulina discovered comes forth"* (1624, Cockpit). One player standing.

(8) Massinger, *The Guardian*, III, 6: *"Enter Severino (throw-ing open the doors violently) having a knife"* (1633, Blackfriars). One player standing.

The possibility of discovery by opening a door necessarily modifies our interpretation of numerous Elizabethan discoveries. Nevertheless, we know from contemporary stage-directions that many discoveries were effected by opening curtains of some sort, and we know also, from a letter by John Chamberlain describing a hoax perpetrated by Richard Vennar in 1602, that the Swan was capable of being fitted out with "curtains" and "hangings." (See T. S. Graves, "A Note on the Swan Theatre," *Modern Philology*, vol. 9 [1911–12].) It will be remembered that Vennar had promised an expensive entertainment called *England's Joy*, to be performed by "certain gentle-men and gentlewomen of account." The response was enthusiastic but there was no play; and Vennar absconded, only to be apprehended almost immediately and bound over "in five pound to appear at the sessions." "In the meane time [writes Chamberlain] the common people, when they saw themselves deluded, revenged themselves upon the hangings, curtaines, chaires, stooles, walles, and whatsoever came in theire way, very outragiously, and made great spoile; there was great store of goode companie, and many noblemen."

Presumably some of the "hangings" here referred to were stage-hangings concealing trestles or posts beneath the open stage. But how might "curtains" or "hangings" have been fitted to the tiring-house that we see in the Swan drawing? One method would have been to set up a curtained booth against the tiring-house façade, as suggested by George F. Reynolds in *The Staging of Elizabethan Plays at the Red Bull Theater* (1940) and by C. Walter Hodges in *The Globe Restored* (1953). Another method would have been to fit hangings along the front of the tiring-house, thus hiding one or both of the stage-doors and possibly the whole length of the tiring-house façade. That some such arrangement was occasionally resorted to is shown by the *Wits* frontispiece (1662), which depicts a player entering from behind an arras apparently concealing a door.

Furthermore, essentially the same arrangement may well be pictured in the *Roxana* vignette (1632). (And also in the *Messalina* vignette, 1640, but since this may have been influenced by the earlier picture we may not, in this respect, regard the two illustrations as independent sources of information). The curtains or hangings in the *Roxana* vignette are usually interpreted as concealing the opening of an "inner-stage." Possibly they do, but if so it is curious that the picture fails to show the stage-doors we should then have to imagine on either side of the presumptive "inner-stage." Doors may, of course, have been omitted from the sides of the picture as a result of cropping (though even in this case the hangings might still conceal only a middle door in the tiring-house wall). On the other hand, it is possible that no doors are shown in the *Roxana* vignette because the curtains are hangings which conceal them.

The general interpretation is supported by Florio's definition (1598) of the word *scena* in the classical sense of tiring-house: "a skaffold, a pavillion, or fore part of a theater where players make them readie, being trimmed with hangings, out of which they enter upon the stage."

Accordingly I would suggest that hangings were occasionally fitted up along the façade of the Swan tiring-house in front of its open stage-doors, the leaves of each door having been swung open through 180° and lying flat against the tiring-house façade. (Alternatively, the hangings might have been fitted up in front of one door only, or behind one or both of the doors.) Thus the players, in the rigid situation of a permanent tiring-house, would have re-created the flexible situation of the curtained booth which they presumably used as a temporary tiring-house in performances away from a regular theater.

In addition to making possible a variable stylistic *décor*, the arrangement of hangings in front of open stage-doors would have had three practical advantages. First, it would have eliminated much opening and closing of doors by enabling the players to enter and exit by slipping through openings in the hangings. Second, the arrangement would have made readily available an "arras" behind which an eavesdropping player might "hide," either completely disappearing or remaining partly within view of the audience as desired. And third, the arrangement would have permitted discovery of a space of indeterminate depth some 7 feet or 8 feet wide by means of drawing aside or looping up the hangings in front of one of the open stage-doors, the hangings being manipulated by attendant players or by stage-keepers. (On stage-keepers see Leslie Hotson, "False Faces on Shakespeare's Stage," *The Times Literary Supplement*, 16 May 1952.) If masking were considered necessary, a curtain backing might also have been fitted up a few feet behind the doorway.

III

Let us now consider evidence for the Globe discovery-space. Discoveries are required in nine of our thirty Globe plays:

(1) *The Merry Wives of Windsor* (1600), I, 4 (F): "goe into this Closset [Q: *He steps into the Counting-house*]: ... dere is some Simples in my Closset, ... O Diable, Diable: vat is in my Closset?" One player (Simple) "goes into" the discovery-space; a concealment. He is then discovered (possibly by door).

(2) *Satiromastix* (1601), I, 2: "*Horrace sitting in a study behinde a Curtaine, a candle by him burning, bookes lying confusedly.*" One player seated, a table; by curtain.

(3) *Thomas Lord Cromwell* (1602), II, 1–2: "*Cromwell in his*

study with bagges of money before him casting of account."
One player seated, a table.

(4) *Ibid.*, III, 2: "Go take thy place Hodge, . . . *Hodge sits
in the study, and Cromwell calles in the States.* . . . Goe draw the
curtaines, let us see the Earle, O he is writing." A player (Hodge,
who will impersonate the Earl of Bedford) "goes" and sits "in"
the discovery-space; a concealment. He is then discovered seated
at a table; by curtains.

(5) *Ibid.*, IV, 5: "*Enter Gardiner in his studie, and his man.*"
One player (possibly two).

(6) *Troilus and Cressida* (1602), III, 3 (F): "*Enter Achilles
and Patroclus in their Tent. Ulis.* Achilles stands i'th entrance
of his Tent." Two players standing.

(7) *The Merry Devil of Edmonton* (1603), Induction: "*Draw
the curtaines.* . . . Behold him heere laide on his restless couch,
. . . And by him stands that Necromanticke chaire, In which he
makes his direfull invocations, . . . And in meane time repose
thee in that chayre. . . . *Sit downe.* . . . Enough, come out." One
player (Peter Fabel) discovered reclining on a day-bed, a chair;
by curtains. Another player (Coreb) sits in the discovery-space
and then "comes out."

(8) *Volpone* (1605), I, 1–5 (F): "next, my gold: Open the
shrine, that I may see my saint. Haile the worlds soule, and
mine." Property only (Volpone's gold), presumably upon a
table.

(9) *The Revenger's Tragedy* (1606), I, 4: "*Enter the discontented Lord Antonio, whose wife the Duchesses yongest Sonne
ravisht; he Discovering the body of her dead to certaine Lords:*
. . . A prayer Booke the pillow to her cheeke." One player reclining; also a concealment.

(10, 11) *The Devil's Charter* (1607), Induction: "*Enter, At
one doore betwixt two other Cardinals, Roderigo in his purple
habit close in conference with them, one of which hee guideth
to a Tent, where a Table is furnished with divers bagges of
money, which that Cardinall beareth away: and to another Tent
the other Cardinall, where hee delivereth him a great quantity
of rich Plate.*" (10) Properties only (bags of money), upon a
table. (11) Property only (rich plate), presumably upon a table.
This direction is part of the evidence for three doors in the
Globe tiring-house.

(12) *Ibid.*, I, 4: "*Alexander in his study with bookes, coffers,
his triple Crowne upon a cushion before him.*" One player seated, a table.

(13) *Ibid.*, IV, 1: "*Alexander in his studie beholding a Magi-*

call glasse with other observations. . . . Let me looke forth. *Alex-*
ander commeth upon the Stage out of his study with a booke
in his hand. . . . *Exit Alexander into the studie.*" One player
seated, a table. He "comes out of" the discovery-space "upon"
the stage.

(14) *Ibid.*, IV, 4: "bring forth her ransome hither. *Barbarossa*
[on stage] *bringeth from Caesars Tent hir two boyes.* . . . *Exeunt*
with the boyes. . . . Behold thy children living in my Tent. *He*
discovereth his Tent where her two sonnes were at Cardes."
Two players seated, a table.

(15) *Ibid.*, IV, 5: "*Enter Alexander out of his studie.* . . . *Exit*
Alexander into his study. . . . *Bernardo knocketh at the study.*
Alex. What newes man? . . . *Alexander upon the stage in his cas-*
sock and nightcap with a box under each arme." One player,
who subsequently comes "upon" the stage.

(16) *Ibid.*, V, 6: "*Alexander unbraced betwixt two Cardinalls*
in his study looking upon a booke, whilst a groome draweth
the Curtaine. . . . *They place him in a chayre upon the stage, a*
groome setteth a Table before him." Three players, one seated
in a chair; by curtain. The seated player is then carried on stage
and a table is set before him.

(17) *Ibid.*: "*Alexander draweth the Curtaine of his studie*
where hee discovereth the divill sitting in his pontificals." One
player seated; by curtain. This and the preceding discovery
occur during the same action and apparently in the same discovery-space.

(18) *Pericles* (1608), V, 1: "May wee not see him? . . . Behold
him." One player (Pericles) seated or reclining (since "asleep");
he is then presumably carried on stage.

These discoveries have three noteworthy characteristics.
First, they are few and infrequent, twenty-one of the thirty
Globe plays requiring none and seven of the remaining nine
only one each. (*The Devil's Charter* is exceptional in Elizabethan drama in requiring so many as eight.)

Second, the Globe discoveries are essentially "shows," or dis-
closures, of a player or object invested with some special interest or significance. (Alternatively they might be described
as *tableaux vivants* and still-lifes.) Furniture is involved only in
so far as the discovered player requires something to sit or lie
upon so that he may be shown effectively (a stool, chair, bench,
or day-bed); or in so far as something is required in order to
show him at a characteristic activity (a table for his book,

standish, candle, triple crown, magical glass, bags of money, or game of cards); or in so far as the discovered object must rest upon something in order to be properly visible (a table for Volpone's gold or Roderigo's money-bags). Unless a "show" is to be presented, necessary furniture is always carried on stage; and unless a non-ambulatory player is to be specially "shown" (and even, occasionally, when he is, for example, Discovery number 16), he also is carried on stage. Thus properties or non-ambulatory players are carried on in seven of the nine plays requiring discoveries. In *Merry Wives* (F) a buckbasket is twice carried on stage (III, 3; IV, 2). In *Satiromastix* a banquet is "set out" (IV, 1), a chair (the King's "State") is "set" under a canopy (V, 2), and Cælestine "enters" in a chair (*ibid.*). In *Thomas Lord Cromwell* servants "bring out" a banquet (III, 3). In *Volpone* (F) the supposedly impotent protagonist is "brought in" (IV, 4–6) and Corbaccio is carried on stage (V, 1–2). In *The Revenger's Tragedy* a furnished table is "brought forth" (V, 3). In *The Devil's Charter* Lucretia "brings in" a chair *"which she planteth upon the Stage"* (I, 5), two Pages "enter" with a table (IV, 3), a cupboard of plate is "brought in" (V, 4), a spread table "enters" (*ibid.*), and Alexander (having just been discovered) is "placed" on stage in a chair, whereupon a table is "set" before him (V, 6). In *Pericles* Thaisa is carried on stage in a chest (III, 2).

A corollary may be developed. A "setting" at the Globe (when there was one) was usually created by one or more properties placed on stage within full view of the audience by "servants" or stage-keepers. (Compare the Swan drawing, where a bench at the front of the stage apparently creates as much of a setting as necessary for the action depicted.) It is true that a Globe setting was also occasionally created by discovered furniture, which must therefore have been placed within the discovery-space before this was opened to the sight of the audience. In such cases, however, the discovery-space was used not in order to conceal preparation of the setting but in order to permit the sudden display of a player who (if so much as a single property were discovered with him) would automatically be seen in a setting of one sort or other. Discoveries in the Globe plays are primarily shows of persons or things themselves inherently interesting. They are never (as in the proscenium-arch theater) conveniences for the sake of arranging furniture out of sight of the audience.

Third, the Globe discoveries do not involve any appreciable movement within the discovery-space, the discovered player in one instance being "dead" and remaining within the discovery-space (9) and in all others being discovered as it were *en tableau* and subsequently leaving the discovery-space for the stage, as is indicated either by a direction to that effect (13, 15, 16) or by evidence in dialogue or stage-direction that he later walked or was carried off stage. (Since they could not involve movement, the three discoveries of objects are not considered here.) It may be further pointed out that our texts afford no sign of closing the discovery-space after a discovery, presumably because it was automatically and unobtrusively closed when the attention of the audience was no longer directed to the "show" (8) or when the discovered player had left it or the stage. (The latter explanation is confirmed by 17, which occurs during the same action as 16 and apparently in the same discovery-space, the initially-discovered player leaving the discovery-space and then returning to it in order himself to discover another player.) There are only three formal "concealments" (1, 4, 9).

We may now inquire into the physical conditions of the Globe discovery-space. It is perhaps inexact to speak of a single discovery-space at the Globe, for an action in *The Devil's Charter* requiring discoveries (10, 11) in two separate places suggests that there were (or could be) at least two. For convenience, however, and because "multiple" discoveries are rare in Elizabethan drama, we may continue to speak of a single discovery-space. (On multiple discoveries compare Dekker and Middleton's *Roaring Girl*, a Fortune play of *c.* 1610: "*The three shops open in a ranke.*") Our evidence tells us three things about the Globe discovery-space. First, it was equipped with a curtain or curtains (2, 4, 7, 16, 17). Second, it was off stage, or outside and somehow distinct from the main playing-area, for in one action the discovered player is directed to come on stage out of it (13), and in two others he walks or is carried from discovery-space to stage (15, 16). (Compare also 1, 4, 7, and 15, in which players "go into" or "come out of" the discovery-space.) And third, it need not have been deeper than 4 feet or wider than 7 feet, for no discovery is of more than three players (twelve out of a possible fifteen are of only one) or of more or larger properties than a table and two seats (14) or a day-bed and chair (7).

These conditions would have been fulfilled if the Globe discovery-space was behind an open doorway in the tiring-house wall (usually, we may suppose, the middle doorway of three) essentially similar to the doorways in the Swan drawing and fitted with hangings as in the *Wits* frontispiece or the *Roxana* vignette, for such a discovery-space would have been (1) curtained, (2) off stage, and (3) indeterminately deep and some 7 feet or 8 feet wide. The theory is suggested by the fact that Elizabethan discoveries were occasionally effected by opening a door, it accounts for discoveries in two (or three) separate places since the other two doorways might easily have been used simultaneously in the same capacity, and it harmonizes with the fact that Globe discoveries were few and infrequent "shows" or *tableaux* not involving appreciable movement within the discovery-space.

Finally the theory accords with the fact that certain Globe plays apparently produced without discovery nevertheless allude to "curtains," "hangings," or an "arras." In *A Warning for Fair Women*, Tragedy the Presenter says to the audience: "But now we come unto the dismall act, And in these sable Curtaines shut we up, The Comicke entrance to our direful play" (C4v). In *Every Man out of his Humour* (Q) Fungoso has the following walk-off cue: "Is this the way? good truth here be fine hangings. *Exeunt Puntarvolo, Briske, Fungoso*" (V, 1). And in *Hamlet* Polonius hides behind "the Arras" (Q1). Then, having been stabbed through the arras ("dead for a Ducate"), he apparently falls forward upon the stage, for Hamlet later drags him off: the Folio text reads *"Exit Hamlet tugging in Polonius"* (III, 4). This evidence suggests that the curtains or hangings at the Globe were not intended primarily to effect discoveries. They *might* effect discoveries; but discovery was not their chief *raison d'être*.

XIV

WILLIAM A. ARMSTRONG

The Audience of the Elizabethan
Private Theaters

Though the history of regular performances at the Elizabethan private theaters extends from 1575 to 1642, the evidence concerning the audiences who frequented them is limited and fragmentary and has attracted far less attention than that concerning the patrons of the public theaters. In *Shakespeare and the Rival Traditions* (New York, 1952), Alfred Harbage has surveyed some of the evidence about private-theater audiences relative to the period between 1575 and 1616. The purpose of this article is to examine what can be gleaned from contemporary plays, poems, and pamphlets about the social standing of these audiences, about where they sat and what they paid for their seats, and about the virtues, faults, and foibles which they displayed during the period between 1575 and 1642.

The geography of the private theaters is of some significance, since their situation had an important bearing upon the types of spectator whom they attracted. Whereas the public theaters stood at various points on the periphery of London, the private theaters enjoyed the benefits of relatively central situations. St. Paul's was close to the center of Elizabethan London and it was there that Sebastian Westcott began in 1575 to stage plays in the Almonry House, a small building behind Convocation House. This private theater at Paul's was intermittently used until 1609. In 1576 Richard Farrant opened a theater in the old priory buildings of Blackfriars. This was the first Blackfriars Theater and was intermittently used until 1584. The second and more famous Blackfriars Theater was another set of premises in the same area which James Burbage converted

From *The Review of English Studies*, n.s., 10 (1959): 234–49. Reprinted by permission of the author, the editors of *The Review of English Studies*, and the Clarendon Press, Oxford.

into a playhouse in 1596. It was used by juvenile companies until 1608, and afterwards became the indoor theater used in winter by the leading adult company, the King's Men, until 1642. About 1605 a fourth private theater was established when Michael Drayton and Thomas Woodford leased a building in Fleet Street which had been part of the monastery of White-friars, and converted the old refectory into a theater which was still in use in 1621. A fifth private theater was Porter's Hall, situated in the Blackfriars district. It was opened in 1615, but suppressed soon afterwards. Much more important was the Cockpit or Phoenix, a private theater in the northern part of Drury Lane, which was opened in 1617. The last of the Eliza-bethan private theaters was the Salisbury Court, a converted barn close to Salisbury House in the Whitefriars area, which was opened in 1629. The Cockpit and the Salisbury Court were used until the closing of the theaters in 1642. As this brief sur-vey shows, the private-theater movement began near the center of London, then extended westwards. The two Blackfriars theaters and Porter's Hall were within a few minutes' walk of St. Paul's. The two theaters in the Whitefriars area, the White-friars and Salisbury Court, were within fifteen minutes' walk of St. Paul's. The Cockpit was farther westwards, but it was, nevertheless, more conveniently situated for fashionable play-goers than the Fortune and the Red Bull, the two public thea-ters most accessible to patrons travelling from the center of London.

The choice of central and west-of-center situations for the private theaters was no doubt partly due to the social character of the surrounding districts. St. Paul's was the hub of social and commercial activities in the daily life of the capital. The middle aisle of Paul's was a fashionable rendezvous for news and gossip both in the mornings and in the afternoons. In his *Historical Memoires on the Reigns of Queen Elizabeth and King James* (London, 1658), Francis Osborn records that

> It was then the fashion of those times and did so continue till these . . . for the principall Gentry, Lords, Courtiers, and men of all professions not merely Mechanick, to meet in *Pauls Church* by eleven, and walk in the middle Ile till twelve, and after dinner from three, to six, during which time some dis-coursed of Businesse, others of Newes [pp. 64–65].

Lawyers met their clients in the church, book-sellers set up their stalls in the churchyard, and prostitutes frequented both areas, particularly "the lower end of the Middle Ile."[1] The nearby Blackfriars district contained a number of aristocratic residences, notably those of Lord Hunsdon (who became Lord Chamberlain in 1597), Lord Cobham, Lady Russell, and Sir Thomas Bendish.[2] The Whitefriars district a little farther west also boasted aristocratic inhabitants. In addition, it contained the quarter known as Alsatia, which housed a motley community of debtors, bankrupts, criminals, and prostitutes, attracted thither by the old privilege of sanctuary which still protected persons liable to be arrested. Some patrons of the Whitefriars Theater, as we shall see, were drawn from this community. Only a short distance to the north and the west of Whitefriars were the very different communities of judges, lawyers, serjeants, and students of law who lodged in the Inns of Court. In Fleet Street were Clifford's Inn, the Inner Temple, and the Middle Temple; in Chancery Lane, off Fleet Street, stood Serjeants' Inn; and just west of Fleet Street, in the liberty of Westminster, were Clement's Inn, New Inn, and Lyon's Inn. Like St. Paul's, the Temple Church was a popular meeting-place for lawyers and their clients. The Cockpit Theater in Drury Lane was close to this large and wealthy legal fraternity, and even closer to a number of large houses inhabited by nobles, gentry, and their dependents, for, according to a contemporary historian, "Drury Lane . . . and the Strand were the places where most of the Gentry lived" at this time.[3] On the south side of the Strand at the end of the sixteenth century stood Northumberland House, York House, Durham House (residence of Sir Walter Ralegh), Russell House, Somerset House (later given to Anne of Denmark by James I), and Essex House (residence of the Earl of Essex). Only a short distance northwest of the Strand was the royal residence, St. James's Palace. The private theaters were thus conveniently close to the dwellings and meeting-places of various classes who had the leisure

---

[1] "J. H." in *The House of Correction* (London, 1619), D2ᵛ.

[2] See C. W. Wallace, *The Children of the Chapel at Blackfriars, 1597–1603* (Lincoln, Nebraska, 1908), pp. 26–27.

[3] Arthur Wilson, *The History of Britain* (London, 1653), p. 146.

and the money to attend performances. The direct evidence concerning the constitution of their audiences shows that they drew the majority of their patrons from these adjacent districts.

In references to spectators at the private theaters, the aristocracy and the gentry are mentioned more frequently than any other social class. For instance, in his prologue to *Epicoene*, acted at Whitefriars in 1609, Ben Jonson promises "Lords, Knights, Squires" that he has delicacies suited to their tastes.[4] The four types of spectator who figure in the Praeludium to Thomas Goffe's *The Careless Shepherdess*, acted at Salisbury Court in the sixteen-thirties, include "Spruce, a courtier," who speaks as one familiar with the theater and its plays.[5] When the players of Blackfriars, the Cockpit, and Salisbury Court published *The Actors' Remonstrance* in 1643 as a protest against the closing of the theaters, they claimed that "the best of the Nobility and Gentry" had been their patrons, and nostalgically recalled the "young Gentlemen that used to feast and frolick with them at Tavernes."[6] An interesting representative of the more serious-minded theatergoer of this class is Sir Humphrey Mildmay, who divided his time between his Essex estates and the social round of London. G. E. Bentley's analysis of Mildmay's diary and account-book from 1632 to 1642 shows that he visited theaters regularly and that he had a marked preference for the private theaters. "It is noticeable," observes Bentley, "that though he does not, as a rule, give the name of the theater he visited, Blackfriars is clearly his favourite. He mentions it fourteen times, the Globe four times, and the Cockpit, or Phoenix in Drury Lane, three times. The plays which he refers to by title indicate that he visited the Blackfriars four times and the Cockpit once when no theatre is named." Bentley also notes that Mildmay's preference for the Blackfriars may

[4] *Epicoene* in *Ben Jonson*, ed. C. H. Herford and Percy Simpson (Oxford, 1925–52), 5:163. This edition of Jonson's works is used throughout and is hereafter referred to as "Herford and Simpson."

[5] *The Careless Shepherdess* (London, 1656), p. 5. The Praeludium to this play may have been written by Richard Brome; see G. E. Bentley, *The Jacobean and Caroline Stage*, vol. 4 (Oxford, 1956), pp. 502–4.

[6] In *The English Drama and Stage under the Tudor and Stuart Princes*, ed. W. C. Hazlitt (London, 1869), pp. 261, 263.

have been partly due to the fact that his town residence was near this theater.[7]

Overlapping the aristocratic class of patrons to some extent, and no less important to the economy of the private theaters, were the lawyers and members of the Inns of Court who lived and worked so close to these playhouses. Indeed, a significant passage in Thomas Nabbes's prologue to *The Bride*, a play acted at the Cockpit in 1638, goes so far as to ascribe poor attendances to the fact that the law courts were in recess:

> *Vacation still: so little custom comes*
> *To buy our Merchandize, and fill our roomes,*
> *It would perswade us but for after hope*
> *Of better takings quite to shut up shop.*[8]

Correspondingly, the diary written by John Greene when he was keeping his terms at Lincoln's Inn shows that he and his fellow-students especially favored the Blackfriars and the Cockpit in their theatergoing. In October 1635, for instance, he records that there were "9 or 10 of Lincoln's Inn" at his sister's wedding, that "we are all ther the two days dinner and supper," and that "we were at a play, some at cockpit, some at Blackfriars." In the February of the same year, he records four visits to the Blackfriars and the Cockpit, and the other plays that he mentions having seen in March, April, and June 1635 can all be allocated to the repertoires of the Blackfriars and the Cockpit.[9] It is likewise significant that one of the four types of playgoer portrayed in the Praeludium to Goffe's *The Careless Shepherdess* at Salisbury Court is "Spark, an Inns of Court gentleman" who claims an up-to-date knowledge of "the Laws of Comedy and Tragedy," Plot, Wit, and "the round language of the Theater" (p. 4). It is not surprising to find that the most detailed contemporary description of a private theater audience —*Certaine Observations at Blackfryers* (1617)—was written by a lawyer, Henry Fitzgeoffrey, "Of Lincolnes-Inn Gent," as he styles himself on his title-page.

[7] G. E. Bentley, *The Jacobean and Caroline Stage*, vol. 2 (Oxford, 1941), pp. 680. This work is hereafter referred to as "G. E. Bentley."

[8] London, 1640, A4ᵛ.

[9] E. M. Symonds, "The Diary of John Greene (1635–57)," *E.H.R.*, vol. 43 (1928), pp. 386–89.

Ladies of the upper classes evidently constituted an influential proportion of the private theater audiences, for their attention and favor are solicited with some frequency in prologues. The prologue to Jonson's Whitefriars comedy, *Epicoene*, contains an assurance that his offerings "Be fit for ladies," and in his prologue to *The Ladies' Privilege*, acted at the Cockpit, Henry Glapthorne includes this respectful appeal:

> *Ladies if you praise not*
> *At least allow his language and his plot*
> *Your own just Priviledge.*[10]

Most of John Fletcher's prologue to his Blackfriars comedy, *Rule a Wife and Have a Wife*, is an arch address to the ladies in his audience, whom he invites to "hold your Fannes close, and then smile at ease" when anything *risqué* happens on the stage.[11] Thomas Nabbes shows a more serious concern for feminine sensibilities in his prologue to *Hannibal and Scipio*, a Cockpit play, in which he promises that "Ladies shall not blush Nor smile under their fannes" at anything in his tragedy.[12] Incidentally, masks as well as fans hid their blushes at times. In *The Staple of News*, Jonson has a description of a young lady attending a play and seeing "a little o' the vanity through her masque."[13]

The country gentleman was an occasional patron of the private theaters, though a somewhat uneasy one, to judge by some references to him. In John Webster's Induction to *The Malcontent*, a Blackfriars play by John Marston, Sly retorts to the Tireman, "We may sit vpon the stage at the priuate house: thou doest not take me for a country gentleman, doest? doest thinke I feare hissing?"[14] Landlord, "a country gentleman," is one of the four types of spectator represented in the Praeludium to Goffe's *The Careless Shepherdess*, but his simple tastes are ridiculed by Spruce, the courtier, and Spark, the Inns of Court man, and he decides to stay at the Salisbury Court only "that I may view the Ladies, and they me" (p. 6). Other patrons can be allocated to a miscellaneous class of persons on the fringe of the gentry. Jonson includes a captain and a gamester

10 London, 1640, A3ᵛ.

11 Oxford, 1640, A2ʳ.

12 London, 1637, A3ᵛ.

13 Herford and Simpson, 6:303.

14 London, 1604, A3ʳ.

in his list of those who failed to appreciate John Fletcher's *The Faithful Shepherdess* at Blackfriars.[15] In his account of the Blackfriars audience, Fitzgeoffrey mentions a loquacious traveller and a boastful soldier, Captain Martio.[16] In his twelfth epigram, Jonson satirizes the fraudulent "Lieutenant Shift," who haunts Whitefriars, goes "to plays, Calls for his stool, and adorns the stage."[17]

References to middle-class patrons of the private theater are significantly scanty. In his prologue to *Epicoene* Jonson addresses women of this class when he says that he is offering something suited to the taste of "city-wires."[18] "City wire" was a term applied at this time to a London woman of the citizen class because she wore a ruff supported by wire, a fashion which distinguished her from the noblewoman. The four women who comment on the play in the Induction and Intermeans of Jonson's *The Staple of News* are portraits of bourgeois spectators of this kind, for though they claim to be gentlewomen they chatter like city wives, comparing Pennyboy to an alderman and the "staple of news" to gossip from the bake-house.[19] Most playgoers from the lower middle class seem to have preferred the public playhouses to the private theaters. At any rate Thrift, the tradesman who figures in the Praeludium to Goffe's *The Careless Shepherdess*, decides that the price of admission to the Salisbury Court is too high and retrieves his money in order to go to the Red Bull or the Fortune (p. 8).

In John Marston's comedy, *Jack Drum's Entertainment*, acted at Paul's, Planet praises the selectness of the audiences at that theater:

> Ifaith I like the audience that frequenteth there
> With much applause: A man shall not be choakte
> With the stench of Garlicke, nor be pasted
> To the barmy Iacket of a Beer-brewer.[20]

[15] *"To the worthy Author"* in *The Faithful Shepherdess* (London, 1634), A2ᵛ.

[16] Henry Fitzgeoffrey, *Satyres and Satyricall Epigrams: With Certaine Observations at Blackfryers* (London, 1617), E7ᵛ, E8ᵛ.

[17] Herford and Simpson, 8:30.

[18] *Ibid.*, 5:163.

[19] *Ibid.*, 6:343, 344.

[20] London, 1601, H3ᵛ.

Despite this remark, however, there is evidence that some members of the working classes attended the private theaters, even though the cheapest seats there cost sixpence and were thus six times dearer than a place in the yard of a public theater. In his list of the Blackfriars critics of *The Faithful Shepherdess*, Jonson includes "the shops Foreman, or some such *brave sparke* That may judge for his *sixe-pence*" (A2ᵛ), and in *The Magnetic Lady*, which he wrote for the same theater, he refers scornfully to the "grounds of your people, that sit in the oblique caves and wedges of your house, your sinfull sixepenny Mechanicks."[21] Jonson also indicates that there were theatergoers from Alsatia; in his prologue to *Epicoene* he offers entertainment to "your men, and daughters of *white-Friars*."[22] By "daughters of *white-Friars*" he probably means the prostitutes of Alsatia. A "Cheapside dame" of the same profession is mentioned in Fitzgeoffrey's description of the Blackfriars audience,[23] and the authors of *The Actors' Remonstrance* make it clear that women of this kind continued to visit the private theaters until they were closed in 1642, for they promise "never to admit into our six-penny rooms those unwholesome inticing harlots that sit there meerely to be taken up by Prentizes or Lawyers Clerks" (p. 265). This remark shows that "Mechanicks" and "the shops Foreman" were not the only members of the working class to visit private theaters. It is certain, however, that such patrons constituted only a small minority of the private theater audience.

Little is known of the auditoria of Paul's, the first Blackfriars, Whitefriars, and Porter's Hall. The small theater at Paul's may have provided only two kinds of accommodation for spectators; benches on the floor of the auditorium and stools on the stage. At the second Blackfriars, the Cockpit, and Salisbury Court, however, there appear to have been seats for spectators in five places: on the stage, in the pit, in the boxes, in the middle gallery, and in the top gallery. The top gallery was partitioned into sections called "rooms" in which seats were available at sixpence each; these, as I have just shown, were occupied by plebeian members of the audience. In *Certain Observations at Blackfriars* (E7ᵛ) Fitzgeoffrey describes Captain Martio as be-

---

[21] Herford and Simpson, 6:509.

[22] *Ibid.*, 5:163. [23] *Observations*, F1ʳ–F1ᵛ.

ing in "the middle Region," which probably means the middle gallery. A seat in a "room" in this gallery cost a shilling. In the Praeludium to *The Careless Shepherdess*, acted at Salisbury Court, Landlord, the country gentleman, remarks that there are "None that be worthy of my company / In any room beneath the twelvepenny" (p. 3), thus indicating that the place he is going to take is above the boxes. The diary and account book of Sir Humphrey Mildmay show that he occasionally occupied a seat in a twelvepenny room at the Cockpit and Blackfriars.[24] A seat in the boxes cost half a crown. This fact is established by a play acted at Blackfriars and the Cockpit, Fletcher's *Wit without Money*, in which an old retainer reminds a prodigal gallant of those "who extold you in the halfe crowne boxes, where you might sit and muster all the beauties. . . ."[25] As this passage indicates, the boxes were the special resort of men and women of fashion. Sometimes the seats in certain boxes were taken *en bloc* for special parties; in Philip Massinger's comedy *The City Madam* Anne makes it one of the conditions of her marriage-bargain with Sir Maurice Lacey to have "The private Box took up at a new Play For me, and my retinue."[26] The boxes were also especially favoured by gentlemen of the Inns of Court. In his epigram *In Rufum* Sir John Davies refers to the Blackfriars theater and notes that "the clamorous frie of Innes of court / Filles vp the priuate roomes of greater prise."[27]

From other passages it can be inferred that a place on a bench in the pit cost eighteen pence and that the total cost of a stool on the stage was two shillings. In an epilogue written for the Blackfriars production of *The City Match*, Jasper Mayne declares that his play was not for those "Who if they speak not ill oth' *Poet*, doubt / They loose by th' Play, nor have their two shillings out," but for those "who did true Hearers sit / Who singly make a box, and fill the Pit"[28]—a remark which separates those who paid two shillings from those who sat in the boxes or the pit, and thus gives warrant for the belief that two shil-

[24] See G. E. Bentley, 2:675, 677.

[25] London, 1639, B2ᵛ.   [26] London, 1658, p. 27.

[27] *The Poems of Sir John Davies*, ed. C. Howard (New York, 1941), p. 35.

[28] Oxford, 1639, S2ᵛ.

lings was the price of a seat on the stage. That there were places in the auditorium priced at eighteen pence is proved by Sir Humphrey Mildmay's records, which show that he paid this amount at Blackfriars on 21 January, and at the Cockpit on 20 March 1633/4.[29] On these occasions he very probably sat in the pit. Damplay, the censorious gallant in Jonson's *The Magnetic Lady*, is probably referring to the prices of seats in the pit and on the stage, respectively, when he talks of giving "eighteene pence, or two shillings" for a seat.[30] Drawing attention to an allusion to "twelvepenny-stool gentlemen" in *The Roaring Girl* by Dekker and Middleton, Alfred Harbage has suggested that the spectator who sat on the stage paid a shilling as entrance-fee and a shilling for the stool which he hired on the stage,[31] but there are several references to sixpence as the amount paid for a stool on the stage. The boy who offers to bring a stool for the supposed gallant on the stage in the Induction to Jonson's *Cynthia's Revels*, a Blackfriars play, asks for "sixe pence."[32] Dekker's description of the gallant at the playhouse in *The Guls Horne-book* applies to both public and private theaters, and includes the following advice: "By sitting on the stage you may (with small cost) purchase the deere acquaintance of the boyes: have a good stoole for sixpence. . . ."[33] In *Jonsonus Virbius*, Ralph Brideoak is evidently referring to gallants who hired stools on the stage for sixpence when he remarks,

> Though the fine *Plush* and *Velvets* of the age
> Did oft for sixpence damne thee from the Stage.[34]

It therefore seems probable that the spectator who sat on the stage of a private theater first paid eighteen pence, the price of admission to the pit, and then sixpence for a stool on the stage. Stools on the stage were much favored by courtiers, wits, dandies, and men-about-town. In England, as C. W. Wallace has

29 G. E. Bentley, 2:675–76.

30 Herford and Simpson, 6:545.

31 *Shakespeare and the Rival Traditions*, p. 45.

32 Herford and Simpson, 4:10.

33 London, 1609, p. 29.

34 Herford and Simpson, 11:467.

shown, the custom of sitting on the stage began at Blackfriars in 1597 or 1598.[35] It was prevalent until 1762, when Garrick abolished it at Drury Lane.

In the Induction to Jonson's *Bartholomew Fair,* which was first acted at a public theater, the Hope, in 1614, the Scrivener declares that "it shall bee lawfull for any man to iudge his six pen'orth, his twelue pen'orth, so to his eighteene pence, 2. shillings, halfe a crowne, to the value of his place: Provided alwaies his place get not aboue his wit."[36] In his note on this passage, Dr. Simpson suggests that these prices were actually charged at the Hope when this comedy was first performed.[37] But as the prices specified by Jonson are precisely those which, as I have tried to demonstrate above, were charged for seats in the private theaters, it would seem that Jonson was proudly informing his public-theater patrons that they could only sit in judgement upon him if they paid higher prices—those of the private theaters.

During the latter half of the sixty-seven years of their history the Elizabethan private theaters evidently attracted more playgoers, since performances in them became more frequent then. Harbage has shown that during the first decade of the seventeenth century performances at Blackfriars and Paul's were being given only once a week; on Saturdays at Blackfriars, probably on Mondays at Paul's (p. 44). The latest piece of evidence that he cites derives from a legal dispute which occurred in 1608. Up to that time the private theaters had been used only by companies of boy actors. Shortly afterwards, however, the King's Men began to perform at Blackfriars, and the Cockpit and Salisbury Court were used mainly by adult professional players throughout their history. One result of this displacement of the boy by the adult actor was an increase in the frequency of performances in private theaters. In the address by John Heming and Henry Condell which prefaces the First Folio of Shakespeare's plays there is a reference to those wits who "sit on the Stage at *Black-friers,* or the *Cock-pit,* to arraigne Playes dailie," which certainly suggests that by 1623 performances at these two private theaters were being given

[35] *Children of the Chapel,* pp. 131–34.

[36] Herford and Simpson, 6:15.

[37] *Ibid.,* 10:174–75.

more frequently than once every seven days. Mildmay's diary and account-book contain irrefutable evidence that performances at Blackfriars were more frequent than once a week in the sixteen-thirties. They show that in 1633/4 he visited this theater on successive days—21 and 22 January—and that in 1635 he saw two performances there within four days—on 25 and 28 April.[38]

The evidence concerning the behaviour of the private theater audiences is limited and biased. Most of it is a satirical commentary on their faults and eccentricities from the point of view of the dramatists who wrote for them. The type of spectator who evoked more comment than any other was the gallant or would-be gallant who occupied a stool on the stage. Surprisingly, the inconvenience of having spectators on the stages of these relatively small theaters is seldom mentioned; the speaker of the Blackfriars prologue to Jonson's *The Devil is an Ass* grumbles because the grandees on the stage "thrust and spurne, / And knocke vs o' the elbowes,"[39] but this is an isolated complaint. The dramatists had two main criticisms of the gallants on the stage: first, that their rich attire and ostentatious mannerisms distracted attention from the play; secondly, that they regarded themselves as supreme arbiters of taste and behaved so disdainfully and hypercritically in the theater that they sometimes ruined the performance. There was clearly much justification for the first of these criticisms because it is supported by the independent testimony of Henry Fitzgeoffrey. In his *Observations at Blackfryers* (F1^v–F2^v) he describes one playhouse dandy who wears a Holland shirt, a French-cut suit, Spanish boots, and Scottish spurs, and another who is so richly dressed that his annual income "Is not of worth to purchase such a *Sute*." Playgoers of this kind, complains Glapthorne, "come but to be seene: Not see or heare the Play,"[40] and in *The Devil is an Ass* Jonson satirizes them in the person of Fitzdottrel, who puts on a cloak worth fifty pounds to visit the playhouse and tells his wife,

> To day I goe to the *Black-fryers Play-house*,
> Sit i' the view, salute all my acquaintance,

[38] G. E. Bentley, 2:675, 677.

[39] Herford and Simpson, 6:163.

[40] *Ladies' Privilege*, A3^v.

> Rise vp betweene the *Acts,* let fall my cloake,
> Publish a handsome man, and a rich suite
> (As that's a speciall end, why we goe thither,
> All that pretend, to stand for't o' the *Stage*)
> The Ladies aske who's that? (For, they doe come
> To see vs, *Loue,* as wee doe to see them).[41]

The playhouse dandy sometimes became the dupe of his own vanity. The authors of *The Actors' Remonstrance* confess to "borrowing money at first sight of punie gallants" and to "praising their swords, belts, and beavers, so to invite them to bestow them upon us . . ." (p. 261).

References to the censoriousness of the gallant on the stage are even more numerous than allusions to the ostentation of his dress and manners. Even the First Folio of Shakespeare had to be protected against his carping; Heming and Condell warn him that "though you be a Magistrate of wit, and sit on the Stage at *Black-Friers,* or the *Cock-pit,* to arraigne Playes dailie, know, these Playes haue had their triall alreadie and stood out all appeales. . . ." A few years earlier Thomas Dekker had ironically informed gallants that "By sitting on the stage, you haue a signd pattent to engrosse the whole commodity of Censure; may lawfully presume to be a Girder," and had shown how they could belittle plays by talking noisily during a performance, or by laughing in the middle of a tragedy, or by rising "with a skrued and discontented face from your stoole" and drawing "what troope you can from the stage after you."[42] Behaviour of the latter kind was a serious matter to the dramatists, for it could effectively damn a play; as George Chapman put it,

> *if our other audience see*
> *You on the stage depart before we and,*
> *Our wits goe with you all, and we are fooles.*[43]

The boldest opponent of the hypercritical gallants was Ben Jonson, who campaigned against them throughout his career as a playwright. In the Induction to *Cynthia's Revels,* for instance, the Third Child parodies the grumbling of the disdain-

---

[41] Herford and Simpson, 6:178.

[42] *Guls Horne-book,* pp. 28, 30, 31.

[43] Prologue to *All Fooles* (London, 1605), A3ᵛ.

ful gallant who finds fault with the smallness of the boy actors, rails at the music and the playwright, and professes to find pleasure only in tobacco.[44] The same type of spectator is satirized again in the Induction and Intermeans of *The Magnetic Lady*, where Damplay exhibits not only the gallant's ignorance of the principles of effective comic writing, but also his habit of assuming that certain characters on the stage must be libellous portraits of living people, and his scorn for all attempts to educate him: "I will censure and be witty, and take my Tobacco, and enjoy my *Magna Charta* of reprehension, as my Predecessors have done before me."[45] Jonson created this character when he was still smarting from the failure of *The New Inn* at Blackfriars in 1629, a failure which he attributed in his dedication to that play to "a hundred fastidious *impertinents*, who were there present the first day" and came only "To see, and to bee seene. To make a generall muster of themselues in their clothes of credit: and possesse the Stage against the Play. To dislike all, but marke nothing. And by their confidence of rising between the Actes, in oblique lines, make *affidauit* to the whole house, of their not vnderstanding one Scene."[46] Here we have a pungent summary of all the main criticisms of the gallant who sat on the stage.

By no means all the gallants who frequented the private theaters were as perverse and hostile as these criticisms would suggest, however. Due allowance must be made for the exaggerations of exasperated playwrights. *The New Inn* is not a good play. And Jonson himself represents in the Induction to *Cynthia's Revels* a "more sober, or better gather'd gallant" who speaks as a "well-wisher to the house" and pleads reasonably for plays with fewer borrowings from old books and "common stages."[47] Another portrait of the same kind of spectator is Probee in *The Magnetic Lady*. Probee, like Damplay, is a man of fashion, but his reactions to the play are very different from his companion's; he deplores the malicious custom of assuming that living people are caricatured in plays and is content "to wait the processe, and events of things, as the *Poet* presents them. . . ."[48] Probee is, no doubt, representative of such fash-

[44] Herford and Simpson, 4:39.

[45] *Ibid.*, 6:564.

[46] *Ibid.*, p. 397.

[47] *Ibid.*, 4:39, 41.

[48] *Ibid.*, 6:544, 578.

ionable playgoers as Thomas Randolph, Thomas Carew, and John Cleveland, all of whom wrote in defense of Jonson after the failure of *The New Inn*. Indeed, claques were not unknown in the private theaters, as may be deduced from Thomas Nabbes's declaration in a Cockpit prologue that

> He hath no faction in a partiall way
> Prepar'd to cry it up, and boast the Play.[49]

Like some of the gallants, some women of fashion were accused of treating the private theater as primarily a place for the exhibition of fine clothes. In the bargaining-scene with Sir Maurice Lacey in Massinger's *The City Madam*, for instance, Anne demands not only a private box at the theater but also

> a fresh habit
> Of a fashion never seen before, to draw
> The gallants' eyes that sit on the stage, upon me.
> (P. 27.)

The most detailed portrayal of the behaviour of feminine spectators occurs in the Induction and Intermeans of Jonson's Blackfriars comedy, *The Staple of News*. Again, allowance must be made for the calculated exaggerations of the satirist. The names of the four women represented—Censure, Tattle, Curiosity, and Mirth—are in themselves a commentary. All four are described as "gossips," and their vapid and inconsequent chatter obviously parodies the loquacity of some of the women in Jonson's audience. Like Massinger's Anne, moreover, they come to the theater "to see, and to be seene." Like one sort of gallant, Censure professes exceptionally high standards of histrionic judgement and assumes that the play contains sly references to living persons when none are intended.[50] The actors' costumes constitute the chief common interest of these gossips. Curiosity watches the performance for incongruities of costume, for "what *King* playes without cuffes? and his *Queene* without glooues? who rides post in stockings? and daunces in bootes?"[51] Tattle, on the other hand, is all for fine dress whether it be appropriate or not: "I cannot abide that nasty fellow, the

[49] *Covent Garden* (London, 1638), A4r.

[50] Herford and Simpson, 6:279, 280, 323–24.

[51] *Ibid.*, p. 280.

Begger," she remarks at the end of the first act, "if hee had beene a *Court-Begger* in good clothes; a *Begger* in veluet, as they say, I could have endur'd him."[52] Censure, despite the high critical standards that she professes, is likewise much influenced by the clothes worn by the actors; at the end of the fourth act, for instance, she protests her love for Master Fitton because "He did weare all he had, from the hat-band to the shooe-tie, so politically. . . ."[53] Jonson's satire here had a basis of fact, for the authors of *The Actors' Remonstrance* number among their former patrons "those Buxsome and Bountifull Lasses that usually were enamoured on the persons of the younger sort of Actors, for the good cloaths they wore upon the stage, believing them really to be the persons they did only represent" (p. 263). This credulity is a contrast to the sophistication of other patrons of the private theaters, and shows that some members of their audiences were no less subject to theatrical delusion than the butcher who during a performance of a play about Greeks and Trojans at the Red Bull so sympathized with Hector that he climbed on to the stage in order to protect him from Achilles and his men.[54]

There is little detailed evidence about the tastes and behaviour of other classes of private-theater patrons. Landlord, the country gentleman in the Praeludium to *The Careless Shepherdess*, delights most of all in clowns and would "have the Fool in every Act" (p. 5). Thrift, the tradesman, agrees with him, but they are told not to expect such outmoded crudities at Salisbury Court and are left dissatisfied. Another old-fashioned preference is criticized by Jonson in his Induction to *Cynthia's Revels*—the playgoer with "more beard then braine" swears "That the old Hieronimo (as it was first acted) was the onely best, and iudiciously pend play of Europe."[55] (A clue to the social class of this playgoer is provided in *Every Man in His Humour*, where Bobadil, the boastful captain, declares that *The Spanish Tragedy* (i.e *Hieronimo*) is far superior to any modern play, and has Mathew read it to him while he is dress-

---

[52] *Ibid.*, p. 302.

[53] *Ibid.*, p. 363.

[54] Edmund Gayton, *Festivious Notes upon Don Quixote* (London, 1654), p. 3.

[55] Herford and Simpson, 4:42.

ing.)⁵⁶ Landlord, Thrift, and Jonson's admirer of *Hieronimo* represent types of theater-goer who went more frequently to the public than to the private theaters because their tastes had been formed by plays written for public playhouses. Though the dramatists of the private theaters seldom praise their audiences, they certainly prided themselves on writing for patrons with tastes more cultivated than those of the audiences of the public theaters. A valuable illustration of this attitude is provided by James Shirley's prologue to *The Doubtful Heir.* Shirley had expected that the King's Men would present this play at Blackfriars in 1640, and his prologue expresses his disappointment that it is being staged at the Globe instead. It also implies a contrast between the patrons of Blackfriars, who can appreciate wit, "language clean," and a logical plot, and the audience of the famous public theater, who take pleasure chiefly in dances, combats, bawdry, clowns, fireworks, and devils:

> *Our Author did not calculate this Play*
> *For this Meridian; the Banckside, he knows*
> *Are far more skilfull at the Ebbes and flows*
> *Of water, than of wit, he does not mean*
> *For the elevation of your poles, this scene.*
> *No shews, no dance, and what you most delight in*
> *Grave understanders, here's no target fighting*
> *Upon the Stage, all work for Cutlers barr'd,*
> *No Bawdery, nor no Ballets; this goes hard;*
> *But language clean, and what affects you not,*
> *Without impossibilities the Plot;*
> *No clown, no squibs, no Devill in't: oh now*
> *You Squirrels that want Nuts, what will you do?*⁵⁷

It would seem that by 1640 the more discriminating playgoers were going to the private theaters. Among them were purists who scorned any kind of stage spectacle. Glapthorne complains of patrons of the Cockpit who say "They only come to heare, not see the Play."⁵⁸ At Blackfriars there were fastidious critics of gesture and deportment. Fitzgeoffrey mentions certain connoisseurs of histrionic style there who condemned the raising of a hat with a flourish as a "hateful *Gesture*" and a low bow as "Affecting Proud Humility" (B7ᵛ).

⁵⁶ *Ibid.*, 3:319.

⁵⁷ London, 1652, A3ʳ. ⁵⁸ *Ladies' Privilege*, A3ᵛ.

A favourite intellectual exercise of patrons of private theaters was to try to find points of resemblance between characters in the play and well-known personalities of London. Scandalous speculation of this kind was not confined to a few spectators like Jonson's Damplay and Censure; it was evidently a common practice. "Application, is now, growne a trade with many," complains Jonson in his dedication to *Volpone*, "and there are, that professe to haue a key for the decyphering of euerything: but let wise and noble persons take heed how they be too credulous. . . ."[59] Similar warnings against malicious personal applications were issued by Webster[60] and Fletcher[61] at Blackfriars and by Nabbes[62] at the Cockpit, but the playwrights were not as innocent as they pretended to be. Jonson's plays, for instance, contain many satirical references to living persons. Damplay is one of his several attempts to ridicule Inigo Jones.[63] In one play alone—*The Devil is an Ass*—there are sarcastic references to such well-known London quacks, astrologers, and almanac-makers as Thomas Bretnor, Edward Gresham, Abraham Savory, Nicholas Fiske, and Simon Foreman.[64] Small wonder, then, that "decyphering" was so popular a practice among playgoers. Examples of it occur in the writings of John Aubrey and Margaret Cavendish, Duchess of Newcastle. According to Aubrey, Subtle in *The Alchemist* represented John Dee; Carlo Buffone in *Every Man out of His Humour* represented Charles Chester, "a perpetuall talker" who likewise had his lips sealed with wax; and Volpone represented a certain Thomas Sutton who had "fed severall with hopes of being his Heire."[65] Margaret Duchess of Newcastle also identifies Subtle in *The Alchemist* with John Dee, Face with Edward Kelly, Doll Com-

[59] Herford and Simpson, 5:18–19.

[60] Induction to John Marston's *The Malcontent* (London, 1604), A3ᵛ–A4ʳ.

[61] Prologue to *The Chances* in F. Beaumont and J. Fletcher's *Comedies and Tragedies* (London, 1647), p. 21.

[62] Prologue to *The Bride* (London, 1640), A4ᵛ.

[63] The association of Damplay with Vitruvius (Herford and Simpson, 5:510) is calculated to identify him with Inigo Jones.

[64] See Herford and Simpson, 6:225–27.

[65] *Brief Lives*, ed. A. Clark (Oxford, 1898), 1:214; 2:184, 246.

mon and the widow with Mrs. Dee and Mrs. Kelly, the Spaniard with the Spanish ambassador, and Sir Epicure Mammon
with a Polish lord.[66] Most of these attributions are erroneous
but they show how avid the search for personalities could be.
Sometimes spectators disapproved of a personal reference
which they believed that they had detected and hissed the
playwright. Jonson suffered in this way when *The New Inn*
was performed at Blackfriars; the spectators saw a special significance in the name "Cis" which he had given to the chambermaid, and they expressed their displeasure accordingly. In
a defensive epilogue written soon afterwards, Jonson hopes for
audiences "Such as will not hiss / Because the chambermaid
was named *Cis*," and disclaims any personal reference, protesting that Cis "only meant was, for a girle of wit." He subsequently changed the name "Cis" to "Pru."[67]

One result of the personal references in plays written for private theaters was that some members of the audience came
equipped with table-books in order to note down items for
scandalous gossip. In his prologue to a Blackfriars play, *The
Custom of the Country*, Fletcher asserts that there is nothing
in it for the man

> *that brings his Table-booke*
> *To write down, what againe he may repeate*
> *At some great Table, to deserve his meate,*[68]

and the same playwright in his prologue to a Paul's play, *The
Woman Hater*, issues a similar warning to those "lurking
amongst you in corners, with Table bookes, who haue some
hope to find fit matter to feede . . . mallice on."[69] Not all the
devotees of table-books were of this malicious breed, however.
Some playgoers brought them in order to note down jests and
witticisms from the plays. Sly, in Webster's Induction to *The
Malcontent*, represents one of these; he has seen the play often,
he remarks, and has "most of the ieasts heere in my table-
booke" (A3ᵛ). A playgoer of the same kind is mentioned by
Nabbes in the prologue to his Cockpit tragedy, *Hannibal and*

[66] *The Description of a New World* (London, 1668), p. 66.

[67] Herford and Simpson, 6:491, 391.

[68] Beaumont and Fletcher, *Comedies and Tragedies,* p. 25.

[69] London, 1607, A2ʳ.

Scipio, where he announces that "Ladies shall not blush" at his play

> *nor he in plush*
> *That from the Poets labours in the pit*
> *Informes himselfe for th' exercise of wit*
> *At Tavernes, gather notes.*

[A3ᵛ]

   Though there are few direct descriptions of the audiences of the Elizabethan private theaters, there is sufficient evidence to warrant the belief that they were mainly drawn from those parts of London adjacent to the theaters and that they consisted mainly of courtiers, gentlemen of the Inns of Court, wits, and women of fashion, together with such hangers-on as gamblers, soldiers, prostitutes, and would-be gallants. Citizens and artisans were in a minority, partly because of the relatively high prices of seats, partly because the plays were not entirely to their taste. The social constitution of the audience was therefore more like that of the Restoration theaters than that of the Elizabethan public playhouses. The arrogant manners and arbitrary judgements of some of the gallants, the presence of ladies in masks, the influence of cliques, and the general interest in personal applications also link this audience with that of the Restoration period. On the other hand, there is no evidence that the private theater audiences were ever guilty of the licentious and riotous behaviour which sometimes occurred in the Restoration theaters. This difference was, no doubt, partly due to the indefinable leaven of Jonson's "better-gather'd gallants" whose Jacobean or Caroline culture was more refined than that of their Restoration counterparts, though a comprehensive explanation of it would require an excursion into social and political history beyond the scope of this essay.

XV

J. W. SAUNDERS

Staging at the Globe, 1599–1613

How many entrances had the Globe stage? Was the curtained enclosure a recess, a booth, a mansion, or a property? Was the upper level a gallery, a tarras, a chamber, or a window? Fifty years ago we might have given confident answers to these fundamental questions; but the more we have learned about the Elizabethan playhouse, the less sure we seem to be. It is my purpose in this paper to explore a way out of the present position of scholarly stalemate by outlining certain principles, about which some general agreement may be achieved, and then applying them to a reexamination of the basic problems.

As a first principle, I would suggest that, as far as possible, *each investigation should be limited to the plays of one theater at a time.* Since other evidence is so scanty, we are forced to rely a great deal upon the internal evidence of the plays; but we ought not to assume that all plays, or even all the plays of one playwright, are of equal value. Many plays were produced in several different theaters, and there is no way of discovering which pieces of internal evidence apply to which playhouse. There were wide divergences between house and house. Some theaters were circular, some rectagonal, some octagonal; some had fixed stages, others had stages removable for animal shows; some were adapted from innyards, others from archery butts or tennis courts; some housed only a few hundred spectators, while others held nearly three thousand; and the private houses were artificially lit, while the public houses were open to the sun. Different physical environments created different staging conditions and practices.

For my own purposes I have selected the first Globe (1599–1613). We cannot have a complete list of the plays produced there, or in any theater. There are relatively few plays which

From *Shakespeare Quarterly*, 11 (1960):402–25. Reprinted by permission of the author and the editors of *Shakespeare Quarterly*.

we can certainly identify as Globe plays, and even these exist only in "corrupt" texts. I make use of terms like "corruption" in a different sense from the bibliographers: a "bad Quarto," in their sense, may be a good text for the historian of the stage, if it reflects accurately the staging practices of only one theater. Unfortunately, very few texts are really "good"; the best that we can do is to identify texts which embody the staging practices of only the one public playhouse, plays which, for instance, were played at the Globe but never at the Fortune or the Swan. Even these texts will be corrupted by directions deriving from performances in other theaters where the King's Men regularly appeared. Shakespeare's company, like the others, took their plays to Court or on tour in the provinces; after 1609 they occupied a private theater, the Blackfriars; in 1614 the Globe was rebuilt after the fire in the previous year. Even "good" texts, then, to an important extent are impure. But neither Shakespeare nor any other Globe dramatist is likely to have written for his company a text which required substantial modification when it was taken to the Blackfriars or, at short notice, to Court or on tour; acting texts were omnibus texts, suitable in the main for all occasions. Thus, if we can establish a list of plays confined to the one company, we shall be able to rely, taking a reasonable risk, on the internal evidence they provide about the staging practices of one public playhouse.

Sir Edmund Chambers has provided a list with which we can work.[1] Apart from Leslie Hotson's suggestion that the first performances of *Henry V* were given at the Curtain, rather than the Globe,[2] the list is still sound. In it 39 plays are divided into four groups, of differing value, which I shall call A, B, C, and D.

Group A

Plays produced at the first Globe between 1599 and 1609, that is, before the opening of the Blackfriars, which survive in printed texts dating from the same period (I give the date only of first publication, irrespective of the merit placed upon the edition by bibliographers):

[1] *The Elizabethan Stage* (1923), 3:105.

[2] *The Times* (London), March 26, 1954, p. 7.

Shakespeare's *Henry V* (Q 1600), *Much Ado about Nothing* (Q 1600), *Merry Wives of Windsor* (Q 1602), *Hamlet* (Q 1603), *King Lear* (Q 1608), *Troilus and Cressida* (Q 1609), and *Pericles* (Q 1609); Jonson's *Every Man out of his Humour* (Q 1600), *Sejanus* (Q 1605), and *Volpone* (Q 1605); Barnabe Barnes's *The Devil's Charter* (Q 1607); Cyril Tourneur's *The Revenger's Tragedy* (Q 1607); George Wilkins' *The Miseries of Enforced Marriage* (Q 1607); and the anonymous plays, *The London Prodigal* (Q 1605), *The Fair Maid of Bristow* (Q 1605), *A Yorkshire Tragedy* (Q 1608), and *The Merry Devil of Edmonton* (Q 1608).

Group B

Plays produced at the Globe between 1609 and 1613, while the first Globe and Blackfriars were both in use, and printed in texts of the same period or preserved in manuscripts from the period:

Chapman's *The Second Maiden's Tragedy* (MS 1611); Jonson's *Catiline* (Q 1611), and *The Alchemist* (Q 1612).

Group C

Plays produced at the Globe between 1599 and 1609 but surviving in texts published in 1622 or 1623, and liable therefore to incorporate modifications from productions at the Blackfriars or second Globe:

Shakespeare's *Julius Caesar* (F 1623), *Twelfth Night* (F 1623), *As You Like It* (F 1623), *All's Well that Ends Well* (F 1623), *Measure for Measure* (F 1623), *Othello* (Q 1622), *Macbeth* (F 1623), *Coriolanus* (F 1623), *Antony and Cleopatra* (F 1623), and *Timon of Athens* (F 1623).

Group D

Plays produced at the Globe, and probably the Blackfriars too, between 1609 and 1613, which survive in texts printed at various dates from 1619 to 1634:

Shakespeare's *Cymbeline* (F 1623), *The Winter's Tale* (F 1623), *The Tempest* (F 1623), and *Henry VIII* (F 1623); Beaumont and Fletcher's *The Maid's Tragedy* (Q 1619), *A King and no King* (Q 1619), and *Philaster* (Q 1620); Webster's *The Duchess of Malfi* (Q 1623) and the anonymous play, *Two Noble Kinsmen* (Q 1634).

In the following pages I record by each quotation the date of the text from which it is taken, and seek to give precedence to A plays over B, C and D, to B over C and D, and to C over D.

A second principle: *it is preferable to make deductions from the staging necessities inferred from the action of the play rather than from textual references to parts of the stage.* Stage-directions may be misleading, incomplete and irregular, not entirely to be trusted, but these are more reliable than casual references in the dialogue, which may be entirely metaphorical. Too many scholars have been led into error by their excite-ment over casual references. When Feste is ragging Malvolio (*Twelfth Night* IV, 2, C 1623 F), his reference to "the cleere stores toward the South north. . . . as lustrous as Ebony" makes better fun as nonsense than, *pace* Leslie Hotson, as an allusion to the windows of Whitehall; similarly, his "bay Windowes transparant as baricadoes" are hardly descriptive, *pace* John Cranford Adams, of the Globe Window-Stages. When Falstaff says (*Merry Wives of Windsor*, II, 2 A 1602 Q) "you might a looked thorow a grate like a geminy of babones," there is no need to conclude that he could not have made this remark without a grille on the stage to exemplify his allusion. Even when we are told (*The Second Maiden's Tragedy*, II, 2, B 1611 MS), that the "waye to chambringe" lay "vp yo'n staires," there need be no stairs or chamber visible: Elizabethan plays are full of local atmosphere, imaginative references to localities offstage. Too much respect for the letter of the text leads the investigator into absurdities, reducing him to looking for a lake on stage for Mariana's "moated-Grange" (*Measure for Measure*, IV, 1, C 1623 F), or for somewhere to tether a horse—"Enter Husband as being thrown off his horse, And falls" (*A York-shire Tragedy*, scene 8, A 1608 Q). In these pages, then, I shall try to apply common sense in answering these questions: What are the minimum requirements for this scene? How simplest may this scene be staged? What staging feature is inescapable here?

Sometimes it may not be quite fair to look for minima and simplicity. With Shakespeare we are on strong ground: he was sincerely reluctant to disgrace the name of Agincourt, or any-thing else, with too many ragged foils and other theatricals. No other dramatist exploited less the machinery and architecture of his theater, made less use, for instance, of the upper stage.[3] One of the first plays he wrote for the new Globe, *Much Ado about Nothing*, and one of the first he wrote after the opening of the Blackfriars, *The Winter's Tale*, are marked by a staging simplicity that would not tax the barest innyard stage. In contrast, Ben Jonson, while avoiding melodramatic spectacle, plays with the new theater like a child with a new toy, and fills *Every Man out of his Humour* with delighted references to the different parts of the "thronged round." And lesser dramatists, like Barnabe Barnes, seem to go out of their way to complicate the scene that they present. Some allowance must be made for these temperamental differences, but, in general, an argument based logically upon minimum necessities carries best conviction.

A third, and tolerant, principle: *different solutions for staging problems are not necessarily exclusive, and all scenes of a like kind need not be forced into the same setting.* I cannot see why, for instance, Elizabethan stages might not have employed two different kinds of enclosure, of different sizes, a tent and a room. Because the prison scenes in *Two Noble Kinsmen*, II, 1 and II, 2 (1634 Q, very much a D text), certainly take place on the upper stage, why must we assume that all prison scenes elsewhere were similarly staged, although Posthumus' prison in *Cymbeline* and Claudio's prison in *Measure for Measure*, were certainly staged on the Platform, and the direction "Enter . . . in prison" may imply nothing more than a player's entrance in chains? The Elizabethans were essentially pragmatic and empirical in their approach to staging problems, and our attempt to find uniform laws in *ad hoc* procedures has led to all kinds of fallacies, including Thorndike's "principle of alternation." Uniformity for its own sake was not a virtue which appealed to minds accustomed to adapt themselves, in all walks of life, to immediate exigencies rather than to long-term convenience.

Most of the stage historians have been prone to this error. Cranford Adams, for instance, persistently exaggerated the importance of acting areas at the rear of the Platform, leading him ultimately to the curious statement that "in the plays written between 1599 and 1610 Shakespeare mounts 43 per cent of all his scenes on the outer-stage alone. If one adds those other

[3] *Vide* Richard Hosley's paper in *Shakespeare Survey 10* (1957).

scenes in which the outer-stage is used in combination with another stage, the total mounts close to 55 per cent. These figures attest the importance of the Platform in the greatest period of English drama."[4] In other words, 45 per cent of the scenes did not use the Platform at all. It is incredible that any producer should set so much action at the rear of the stage, impossible that the great stage of the Globe, a thousand square feet of it, was left empty for nearly half the action. I estimate myself that, of 819 scenes in the 39 named plays, a minimum of 485 (very nearly 60 per cent) were played on the Platform alone, without bringing into the action the upper stage or an enclosure, that at least 746 were based upon Platform staging, with some ancillary use of other stages, and that at most some 73, less than 9 per cent, most of them quite short, had no use for the Platform. The Platform, situated centrally in the amphitheater, ought to have been by far the most important acting area, if natural laws of the theater apply, but it has been very tempting for stage-historians (Adams is merely the latest to be tempted) to conclude that if one scene in a play, or one scene of a certain setting, requires an "inner stage," then others, in the same play or of a like kind, must have been staged there also. And others have made different mistakes. Those who have advocated booth-stages for the curtained enclosures have rested their case too rigidly on the drawing of the Swan associated with De Witt, in which no recess is shown. But this drawing also depicts only two doors onto the stage, one of which must have been reserved, with a Booth erected, for the installation of properties to be "discovered" there, and the one remaining Stage-Door would have been inadequate for all the other purposes of the play. But if one assumes an error in the De Witt drawing, and permits a third means of access to the stage, why not accept a recess, with a third door in its rear? Similarly, it would seem that Leslie Hotson's case for "mansions," which has yet to be fully documented,[5] depends upon the fallacious assumption that the stages at Whitehall and Bankside were alike in most respects, whereas it is just as likely that the Globe had certain natural advantages, Window-Stages for instance,

[4] *SQ*, 2:3–11.

[5] *Shakespeare's Wooden O* appeared too late for consideration by the author.—Ed.

which had to be compensated for at Court. No one theory, then, need be entirely independent and exclusive, and a certain flexibility of approach is a major *desideratum* in a stage historian.

Above all, we ought to remember that *the design of an Elizabethan playhouse was determined less by rational choice than by the accumulation of traditions.* There was no architect to determine the best structure for the purpose. Every theater is a patchwork quilt, made up of bits and pieces from the Miracle arenas, the Mystery pageants, the mountebank scaffolds, the innyards, the animal rings, the Court halls, from any place in short which had been used for drama in the previous hundred years. It follows that if we propose any particular feature as part of the Globe stage, we ought to be able to explain how it got there. In other words, the feature was used because it was there, rather than there because it was useful. If we believe that the stage had a bay-window, we ought to explain how a window came to be built into a gallery, and if we believe that tents had workable doors, then we ought to demonstrate how structures so small and slight acquired such a sizable addition.

I propose now to reexamine, in the light of these basic principles, the fundamental staging problems, the questions of access, of the enclosure, and of the upper stage, together with one relatively minor problem, that of the "penthouses" and "hedge corners."

I. Access

How many doors were there? Within the same play one may find stage-directions which specify only two doors:

Henry V, V, 2 (A 1600 Q): Enter at one doore, the King of England. . . . And at the other doore, the King of France. . . .
Pericles, IV, 3 (A 1609 Q): Enter Pericles at one doore, with all his trayne, Cleon and Dioniza at the other.

and directions which suggest an indefinite number:

Henry V, V, 2 (at the same point as in the direction above, but in the 1623 F): Enter at one doore, King Henry. . . . At another, Queene Isabel, the King. . . .
Pericles, II, Prol. (in the same text as the direction above): Enter at one dore Pericles talking with Cleon, all the traine with them: Enter at an other dore, a Gentleman. . . .

This second form occurs rather more frequently than the first. But nowhere do we find a reference to three or more doors by specific number. The word *several* frequently occurs, but always in its Elizabethan sense of *separate*:

> *The Devil's Charter*, I, 1 (A 1607 Q): Enter marching after drummes & trumpets at two seuerall places. . . .
> *Measure for Measure*, V, 1 (C 1623 F): Enter Duke, Varrius, Lords, Angelo, Esculus, Lucio, Citizens at seuerall doores.
> *Timon of Athens*, I, 1 (C 1623 F): Enter Poet, Painter, Ieweller, Merchant, and Mercer, at seuerall doores.

It would seem that the Swan drawing was right for the Globe too: there were only two Stage-Doors.

But the action of other plays suggests that two means of access to the Platform would have been inadequate. In the fifth act of *The Merry Devil of Edmonton* (A 1608 Q), great care is taken by the dramatist to identify the two Stage-Doors with the doors of inns at Waltham, the George and its neighbour "ouerthwart"; in their "bay windows" are placed signs which, it is supposed, are changed overnight so that guests sleep in one rather than in the other. But if Stage-Door A represents inn A, and Stage-Door B inn B, what entrance to the Platform is used by players who come neither from A nor B, but from C or D (Friar Hildersham, for instance, or Benedic the Priest)? Where the doors are clearly marked, the use of them for other purposes confuses an audience which here must not be confused. In an earlier scene of the same play, IV, 2, one Stage-Door represents "Enfield Church porch," where Banks sits for some of the action; another entrance marks the road to the village, travelled for instance by the Sexton, and yet another is required for other players, Sir John, Blague and Smug, who are supposed to be "shifting for themselves" and returning to the village by different routes from a poaching expedition. The dramatist goes out of his way to make significant the geographical labelling of his two Stage-Doors, and then requires three. Much the same problem arises in *Pericles*, V, 1 (A 1609 Q). Pericles' ship here must be represented by the Platform; here all the action takes place, with twelve or fourteen players involved, and here is a trap for the use of Diana. Pericles' chamber, in which he lies in bed, may be represented by an enclosure or, more simply, by the curtained four-poster bed itself. Shakespeare here makes the geography important: we are to think of a ship with inner parts and of players coming aboard from a barge moored alongside. But if the Platform is the deck, with the Stage-Doors leading to the interior, how are the exterior entrances and exits made, by the Gentlemen and Sailors, by Lysimachus and his Lords, by Marina and her attendants? Or again, in *The Merry Wives of Windsor* (A 1602 Q), the play becomes difficult to follow unless one Stage-Door is clearly understood as the Garter Inn, and the other as Page's house; yet some players enter from a third, neutral direction. And in the fairy scene of this play, V, 5, three means of access are suggested in this direction:

> .... the Doctor comes one way & steales away a boy in red.
> And Slender another way he takes a boy in greene: And
> Fenton steales misteris Anne, being in white.

Battle scenes are particularly perplexed by precise geography. In *Coriolanus*, I, 4 (C 1623 F), we must understand a Volscian city with "Gates" (the Stage-Doors) and "Walles" (the Tiring-House gallery, or the top of a Booth backed against the Tiring-House). The Volscians emerge from their Gates, and the besieging Romans "are beat back to their Trenches." There is no "exeunt" given at this point, but immediately "Enter Martius Cursing," who proceeds to harangue the troops who have been given neither an exeunt nor a re-entry:

> .... Come on,
> If you'l stand fast, wee'l beate them to their Wiues,
> As they vs to our Trenches followes. ...

Later, there is "Another Alarum, and Martius followes them to gates, and is shut in" (by the enemy). Three lines later he enters the Gates, to emerge "bleeding," and "They fight, and all enter the City." Clearly, this is a siege of the Tiring-House, but if the Stage-Doors represent, so precisely, the Gates contested in the long action, where are the Roman "Trenches," which appear to be off stage and yet within sight of the audience (hence the uncertain directions covering the exit at this point)? Similarly, the English forces besieging Harfleur in *Henry V* (A 1600 Q) cannot enter the stage from a door in the besieged city itself. The 1623 Folio confirms, where the 1600 Quarto is deficient in directions, that the battle here was conducted with at least a minimum of "realism": "scaling ladders" are brought into place to scale the walls, and the City Gates are once more contested and finally entered in triumph. In a siege of the Tiring-House, how did besieging soldiers enter the Platform?

It is possible to argue that every scenic illusion on the Elizabethan stage may be broken when necessary, because this was no "picture stage." Even if a particular Stage-Door is virtually labelled as one geographic point, by convention it might change its identity even in the middle of a scene. I see the force of this argument, but am sure that a simpler explanation must be found for these scenes. Why go to the point of establishing a scenic illusion (the siege of a city, interplay between two neighboring houses, and so on) and then deliberately create business which breaks the illusion? It would seem that these playwrights relied upon some other means of access to the Platform, which is naturally brought into the action whenever the two Stage-Doors are blocked. After all, it is ridiculous for Adam, in *As You Like It*, II, 3 (C 1623 F), to look up at the Tiring-House and say to Orlando:

> Come not within these doores: within this roofe
> The enemie of all your graces liues. . . .

and then for the two players to exit through the very doors thus forbidden. In these scenes, it is not so much the words in the text which create the problem on a two-door stage, but the total necessity of the action described.

In many plays players are directed to cross the stage, from one entrance to another, without lingering long in view of the audience. Sometimes they seem to pause and survey the Tiring-House which they pass *en route*. Here is an instance from *A Yorkshire Tragedy* (A 1608 Q):

> Enter Husband with the officers . . . . as going by his house.
> *Husband:* I am right against my howse. . . .
> Enter his wife brought in a chaire. . . . Children laid out. . . .
> *Wife:* Oh, our two bleeding boyes laid forth vpon the
>   thresholde.

In another, *Two Noble Kinsmen*, I, 5 (D 1634 Q), three Queens enter "with the Hearses of their Knightes, in a Funerall

Solempnity," and they "Exeunt severally" in three different directions:

> *3 Qu.:* This funeral path, brings to your households grave:
> Ioy ceaze on you againe: peace sleepe with him.
> *2 Qu.:* And this to yours.
> *1 Qu.:* Yours this way: Heavens lend
> A thousand differing waies, to one sure end.
> *3 Qu.:* This world's a Citty full of straying Streetes,
> And Death's the market place, where each one meetes.

It would seem that there were means of bypassing the Tiring-House. If so, much more point is given to the processional parades of which Elizabethan dramatists were so fond. It is normally assumed that these were circuits of the stage between one Stage-Door and the other. Very seldom, however, is the word "door" used in these scenes, an exception occurring in *Cymbeline*, V, 2 (D 1623 F):

> Enter Lucius, Iachimo, and the Romane Army at one doore:
> and the Britaine Army at another. . . . They march ouer, and
> goe out.

The following instances are more usual:

> *The Revenger's Tragedy*, I, 1 (A 1607 Q):
> Enter Vendici, the Duke, Dutchesse, Lusurioso her sonne,
> Spurio the bastard, with a traine, passe ouer the Stage with
> Torch-light.
> *King Lear*, V, 2 (C 1623 F):
> Alarum within. Enter with Drumme and Colours, Lear,
> Cordelia, and Souldiers, ouer the Stage, and Exeunt.
> *Henry VIII*, I, 1 (D 1623 F):
> Enter Cardinall Wolsey, the Purse borne before him, certaine
> of the Guard, and two Secretaries with Papers: The Cardinall
> in his passage, fixeth his eye on Buckingham, and Bucking-
> ham on him, both full of disdaine. . . . Exeunt Cardinall, and
> his Traine.
> *Ibid.*, IV, 1:
> The Order of the Coronation. . . . Exeunt, first passing ouer
> the Stage in Order and State. . . .

Or, in other scenes requiring a crossing of the stage by one or two players:

> *Every Man out of his Humour*, IV, 2 (A 1600 Q):
> Enter Deliro, with Macilente, speaking as they passe ouer the
> Stage. . . .
> *Ibid.*, III, 1:
> Enter Shift: Walkes by. . . .

The average time taken to "pass over" the stage seems to be about twenty-five seconds, estimating from the accompanying dialogue at the rate of twenty lines a minute. This is a considerable interval of time, implying that players do not cross directly from one Stage-Door to another along the front of the Tiring-House.

Sometimes players crossing the stage are given a direction to enter but no exit. In *Troilus and Cressida*, I, 2 (A 1609 Q), Trojan heroes pass in this way, to the commentary of Pandarus and Cressida, watching from the Tiring-House. In *Pericles*, II, 2 (A 1609 Q), six knights similarly "pass by" Simonides and Thaisa. Then there is the "shew of eight Kings" before Macbeth in *Macbeth*, IV, 1 (C 1623 F). Cranford Adams suggests that these eight apparitions, followed by the Ghost of Banquo, were fleetingly seen through the aperture of a rear curtain or doorway, but it was not Elizabethan practice to secrete a spectacle in the rear stage, and in any case, the dialogue indicates that all nine figures are visible simultaneously (the Ghost points towards the others, and Macbeth comments on the regalia of the others while viewing the eighth king) as they cross in procession. Once again, there is no mention of doors in these processional spectacles.

I am suggesting that, while a circuit of the Platform between Stage-Doors is one possible answer to this problem, there is a strong alternative: that the Tiring-House was bypassed by players crossing the Platform where the audience can best see them, well downstage, and that the observers stand in, or in the vicinity of, the Tiring-House. How could this be done? Such a notion has always been ruled out by the evidence of the De Witt drawing of the Swan; but the question of access to the Swan Platform was governed by the necessity to have a Platform removable for animal shows, and, even so, it is quite possible that there were additional entrances at the wings of the Tiring-House, the whole of which in the drawing seems to protrude forwards. The Globe, on the other hand, had a fixed stage, of different characteristics; it may have had all kinds of assets to which the Swan could never aspire, wings adjoining the Twopenny Rooms, for instance, as well as a rear adjoining the Tiring-House. Moreover, I do not think proper weight has been given to R. C. Bald's suggestion, based on the sketch associated with the name of Hollar, that there were two external, or spectators', entrances to the Globe, lying to the North-East and the South-East.[6] Now in an open-air theater it is sound policy to set the stage to the North or the East, so that the afternoon sun lights up the stage. If the Globe Tiring-House were set in the easternmost bay of the octagonal structure, it follows that passages from the North-East and South-East spectators' entrances to the Yard must have passed between the Twopenny Rooms and the Tiring Rooms, thus dividing the Tiring-House from the auditorium. Such passages, opening into the Yard alleys on either side of the Platform, would have been much more convenient than the single passage in Cranford Adams' design which enters the Yard at a point directly opposite the Tiring-House where the "understanders" were most likely to congregate, blocking the way to the galleries. If these passages existed, it is certain that they would have been exploited by the players as a natural alternative means of access to the Platform. In Diagrams 2 and 3, I conjecture two alternative methods by which wing access could have been provided.

Most of us have been unhappy about a Globe Platform limited to two entrances. Sir Edmund Chambers, assuming three, still complained that, even so, the Elizabethan theater would have been "worse off than any of the early neoclassic theaters based upon Vitruvius, in which the *porta regia* and *portae minores* of the scenic wall were regularly supplemented by the *viae ad forum* in the *versurae* to right and left of the proscenium."[7] Our own medieval arenas, and even the Elizabethan innyard scaffolds, which players entered from the Yard, were not confined thus. Leslie Hotson attempts to meet the problem by having players lie about the perimeter of the Platform, "invisible," awaiting their cues; but he has yet to explain why players who take so much trouble to surprise their audiences with "discoveries" and "pat" entrances and spectacular visita-

[6] *Vide* his paper in *Shakespeare Quarterly*, 3:17–20.

[7] *Elizabethan Stage* (1923), 3:100.

tions through the traps, should dissipate the surprise in this manner. Wing access seems altogether more sound and unexceptionable.

II. THE UPPER STAGE

Most of the *certain* occasions when an upper stage was used at the Globe require a window. In *Every Man out of his Humour*, II, 1 (A 1600 Q), first the "waiting Gentlewoman appeares at the window," and then her mistress, to be wooed by Puntarvolo from the Platform beneath. In *Volpone*, II, 1 (A 1605 Q), the "mountebank" erects a scaffold under a "windore" from which Celia throws down her handkerchief. In *The Devil's Charter*, III, 2 (A 1607 Q), Alexander "out of a Casement" amorously invites Astor to "talke aboue" in his bedchamber. In *The Miseries of Enforced Marriage*, scene 9 (A 1607 Q), an Inn has a "Bay-window" decorated with the "signe of the Wolfe," and from this "upper chamber" Ilford "aboue" overhears the conversation of two players "beneath." Inn-signs are also placed in "bay windows" in *The Merry Devil of Edmonton* (A 1608 Q). In *Catiline*, III, 5 (B 1611 Q), Cicero and his party watch from a window above, while Cornelius and armed men hammer at a door below and a porter answers them from within. In *Othello*, I, 1 (C 1622 Q), Brabantio "at a window" has been aroused from sleep by the shouts of Iago. Other sleepers "above," Pharamond and Megra, are roused in *Philaster*, II, 4 (D 1620 Q). Then in *Henry VIII*, V, 2 (D 1623 F), "the King, and Buts, at a Windowe aboue" hide behind a "Curtaine close" to overhear business proceeding on the Platform. These windows, with bays and casements (if not with curtains, for which there is only D authority), cannot be simulated by the roof of a Booth or Mansion. They were certainly part of the Tiring-House Front. But it is an open question whether there was one Window-Stage or two; one large bay with two sides might well serve for scenes requiring "opposite" windows, like *The Merry Devil of Edmonton*, V, 1, or *The Miseries of Enforced Marriage*, scene 9.

Was there any other upper stage apart from the Windows? As far as the Globe was concerned, it appears that no other was really necessary. An upper stage is designated as the "walles" of a city in battle scenes: *Henry V*, III, 3 (A 1600 Q); *The Devil's Charter*, II, 1 and IV, 4 (A 1607 Q); *Coriolanus*, I, 4 (C 1623

F); *Timon of Athens*, V, 4 (C 1623 F); *The Maid's Tragedy*, V, 3 (D 1619 Q). With one exception, none of these scenes requires more than a few players at the upper level, and the exception, while lurid, is not impossible for a bay of modest proportions. In *The Devil's Charter*, IV, 4, Caesar's army gathers on the Platform, while "Enter vpon the walles Countesse Katherine, Iulio Sforza, Ensigne, souldiers, Drummes, Trumpets." After a parley, the battle begins:

> A charge with a peale of Ordinance: Caesar after two retreates entreth by scalado, her Ensigne-bearer slaine: Katherin recouereth the Ensigne, & fighteth with it in her hand. Heere she sheweth excellent magnanimity. Caesar the third time repulsed, at length entreth by scalado, surpriseth her, bringeth her downe with some prisoners. . . .

This scene could not be played on the tiny roof of a Mansion. The roof of a Booth, of handsome proportions, is a better proposition; and an enclosure of some kind is certainly required in this scene for the "discovery" of two boys "at Cardes" in a "Tent." But Katherine has to be able to see inside the Tent, which she could not do standing on top of it. A single bay window, spanning the entire Tiring-House Front, would be the best setting for this scene, but a smaller bay might well suffice. We need look no further than the windows for the setting of all these scenes.

Other upper-stage scenes, not described in terms of windows or walls, are also adequately staged in the windows. In *The Second Maiden's Tragedy*, V, 1 (B 1611 MS), Leonella enters "aboue in a Gallery with her loue Bellarius" and conceals him in a corner, so that he may overlook action on the Platform, with these words:

> thow knowst this gallerie well tis at thy vse now
> t'as bin at myne full often, thow mayst sitt
> like a most priuat gallant in y'on corner
> see all the plaie and nere be seene thy self. . . .

If the Globe had a spectators' gallery, or "Lords Room," like that shown in the De Witt drawing of the Swan, there would have been no vantage point in which a gallant might have sat unobserved from the auditorium, except possibly behind a pillar or something of that sort. Nor is there any such corner on top of a Booth or Mansion, which was open and conspicuous. Window-Stages, however, set at the sides rather than the rear of the stage, would have contained, in the angle nearest the twopenny rooms, just such a corner. In *The Duchess of Malfi*, V, 5 (D 1623 Q), there are no directions of "above," but Pescara and his companions, who overhear the shrieks of the dying Cardinal but cannot see him, indicate by remarks like "I'll see him hang'd, ere I'll goe downe to him," that they are standing on an upper stage. Later they exeunt from view and reappear on the Platform. Since it is difficult to exit in this way from the top of a Booth or Mansion, a part of the first-floor [i.e. the first floor above the street level] of the Tiring-House is the best setting here, the Window as well as anywhere. Prospero's appearance "on the top (inuisible)," in *The Tempest*, III, 3 (D 1623 F), might be staged on any upper level, even in the music gallery above the bay windows. Lastly, there is the prison setting in *Two Noble Kinsmen*, II, 1 and II, 2 (D 1634 Q). In the first of these scenes there is a direction "Palamon, and Arcite, above," and this reference in the text:

Jailer: . . . . . Looke yonder they are; that's Arcite lookes out.

Daughter: No Sir, no, that's Palamon: Arcite is the Lower of the twaine; you may perceive a part Of him.

In the second scene there is a direction "Enter Palamon, and Arcite in prison" and two references to "this window," through which the courtyard of the prison may be observed. "A part" of Arcite is all one would see of a player in a Window-Stage.

I cannot find any other scenes which may be assigned, at all reasonably, to the upper stage. There is no evidence that a four-poster bed, for bedchamber scenes, was ever installed in a window or gallery of the Tiring-House, or on the roof of a Booth or property. Indeed, in cold light, the notion is untenable. *Othello*, V, 2 (C 1622 Q) needs the Platform for the finale of the play, involving twelve players, three violent deaths, and a chair as well as the bed. "Enter Othello, and Desdemona in her bed" (C 1623 F) may imply a discovery with an enclosure or the bed pushed on from the rear; either way the Platform is the stage. Diagram 1 illustrates the relative merits, from lines of sight, of various positions of the bed, and effectively rules out Cranford Adams' "Chamber." Nothing is gained, theatrically, by staging climactic scenes, like *Hamlet*, III, 4, or *The Maid's Tragedy*, V, 2, on any kind of upper level; in fact, it is best to have the beds as far downstage as possible. Lastly, I see no reason why Imogen's bedchamber (*Cymbeline*, II, 2) has to be obscured in a rear stage: it does not matter if the surrounding furniture and decoration do not agree with Iachimo's description, which is clearly as fanciful as his note of the mole cinque-spotted on Imogen's left breast. There are no directions of "above" in any of these bedchamber scenes.

It is sometimes claimed that the monument scenes in *Antony and Cleopatra* were staged at an upper level in the Tiring-House. The text (C 1623 F) leaves no doubt that in *both* scenes the "Monument" is an elevated acting area accessible from below on two opposite sides. In IV, 15, stage-directions—"Enter Cleopatra, and her Maides aloft" and "They heaue Anthony aloft to Cleopatra"—imply that the hero is hoisted aloft, perhaps with the aid of block and pulley, and a two-sided structure is called for by the words:

> Looke out o'th other side your Monument,
> His guard haue brought him thither.

In V, 2, Cleopatra's attention is engaged on one side of the Monument while soldiers storm the citadel and take the women prisoner (a logical deduction from the action of the scene, although in the text the stage-direction describing the assault seems to be omitted between two consecutive speeches by Proculeius). But this last great scene of the play cannot be staged within the Tiring-House, leaving the Platform empty; nor will thirteen players bring "High Order, in this great Solmemnity," by crowding themselves, and three deaths, into a window or gallery, although the top of a Booth or property, if large enough, and well downstage, might just suffice. With the first scene, the protagonists cannot make much of themselves or their passion, precariously balanced on a windowsill or prone behind gallery balusters. Nor is the top of a Booth practicable here. The women "Exeunt, bearing of Anthonies body" without descending from the Monument into Roman hands below. From a Booth or property backed against the Tiring-House an exit might conceivably be made into the gallery (over the balusters, or through a gate we cannot prove existed?), but all the advantages of a downstage setting would be lost. It would seem that the two levels here can only be represented by the Platform and the Yard.

In *Julius Caesar* (C 1623 F), there is a need for a raised elevation described as a "pulpit" or "publike Chaire" in III, 2, and as a "hill" in V, 3. In the first scene there is a direction "Enter Brutus and goes into the pulpit" and references like "The Noble Brutus is ascended" and "Noble Antony go vp," but no exits or re-entrances marked, as we might expect if the players had had to leave the Platform to reach the higher level of the Tiring-House. In the second, Pindarus climbs "higher on that hill" and is given the directions "Pind. Aboue" and, after his descent, "Enter Pindarus." His assent occupies $2\frac{1}{2}$ lines of the play and his descent 2, insufficient time to leave the Platform for an upper level (in *The Second Maiden's Tragedy*, V, 1, Leonella takes nine lines to descend to the Platform from a Window). Indeed, Pindarus takes about the same time to reach his hilltop as Antony takes to reach the pulpit. Here we have the choice of a window reached by a visible *scalado*, or the top of a Booth or Mansion, or a property, and my preference is for the last. The reference to a "Chaire" suggests a Throne or "State," the one doubtless used for the meeting of the Senate in III, 1. Less certainly, the "hill" may have been the dais on which a throne is sometimes mounted:

> *Henry VIII* (D 1623 F):
> I, 2: ... the Cardinall places himselfe *vnder* the Kings feete on his right side.
> I, 2: King riseth from his State, takes her *vp*, kisses and placeth her by him.
> I, 4: A small Table *vnder* a State for the Cardinall. ...

(the words italicized support the notion of a dais).

What other possible uses for an upper stage are there? In *The Merry Wives of Windsor*, there is much talk of an upper chamber, and much running up and down stairs, but there are no directions of "above" and nothing visible at an upper level. Shakespeare doubtless made the wise decision not to confine so large a proportion of the action, in this play of closets and bed-chambers, to the rear of the stage. In *A Yorkshire Tragedy*, scene 5 (A 1608 Q), the husband tumbles the body of the maid down stairs:

> Ile
> breake your clamor with your neck down staires:
> Tumble, tumble, headlong. . . .
> Throws her down.

But she cannot be tumbled down a *scalado* from a window, and stairs off stage will not do. In any case, there is a likely "discovery" in this scene—"Enter a maide with a child in her armes, the mother by her a sleepe"—so that Platform staging before an enclosure seems called for. These stairs seem to lead down into the Yard. As for the suggestions that "presenters," as in *Every Man out of his Humour*, or "stage audiences," as in *The Maid's Tragedy*, were traditionally seated in the "Lords Room" aloft, I can find no supporting evidence in these Globe plays.

It would seem, then, that the use of an upper stage, at the Globe, may have been restricted entirely to the Window-Stages. There is nothing "above" which cannot be played there. There is nothing that suggests that the top of a Booth or Mansion would have been indispensable, nothing that even hints that Booths or Mansions had tops. On the other hand, the windows were certainly available. In Diagrams 2 and 3, I offer alternative versions of the disposition of the windows. In Diagram 2, I assume that the "twelvepenny rooms" aloft were shaped, at the Globe, like a wide bay, pilastered to give the effect of windows, a bay large enough to take comfortably the battle action of *The Devil's Charter*. In Diagram 3, I assume that the gallery in the Tiring-House was similar in design to that shown in the De Witt drawing of the Swan, and that the bay windows, therefore, were set at the sides of the Platform rather than the rear, providing opposite windows for *The Merry Devil of Edmonton* and a gallants' corner for *The Second Maiden's Tragedy*. Both versions depend upon one assumption: the Globe had bay windows, when the Swan had none, because some of the twelve-penny rooms at the Globe were shaped like bays, and it was these which were exploited as Window-Stages.

III. ENCLOSURES

In 29 of the 39 plays a stage-arras is necessary for the action: a prominent feature, then, of Globe productions, even if the De Witt drawing shows none at the Swan. In several plays a simple traverse across the rear of the Platform will suffice as concealment, for, say, an eavesdropper: for Falstaff (*Merry Wives of Windsor*, III, 3), Claudius and Polonius (*Hamlet*, III, 1), Polonius (*Hamlet* III, 4), Bonario (*Volpone*, III, 6), Hermione "like a Statue" (*Winter's Tale*, V, 3), Cariola (*Duchess of Malfi*, I, 1), and similar instances. There are many other places of concealment on the stage: the Window-Stages, as we have seen, "cabinets" and "penthouses," which I discuss below, places "behind the post," that is, behind the Stage-Posts supporting the Shadow, like that used by Frescobaldi in *The Devil's Charter*, III, 5. But wherever the place of concealment is not specified, it is safe to assume that the arras is intended; it may even be concealed by a complicated description, like that in *Sejanus*, IV, 3 (A 1605 Q), when Rufus and Opsius retire to their "holes":

> Here place your selues, betweene the roofe, and seeling,
> And when I bring him to his wordes of daunger,
> Reueale your selues, and take him.

No time at all elapses between the "wordes of daunger" and the arrest of Sabinus, so that we must assume that they are concealed about the Platform somewhere and not in an attic situated in the Shadow! It is difficult to see how there *can* be an acting area at the Globe "betweene the roofe, and seeling"; *faute de mieux*, the arras is convenient enough. This curtain seems to be only seven feet high or so, five feet lower than the floor of the first gallery, if Volpone's words are to be trusted (*Volpone*, V, 1, A 1605 Q):

> I'le get vp,
> Behind the curtine, on a stoole, and harken;
> Sometime, peepe ouer; see, how they doe looke. . . .

It cannot be very much higher than seven feet, if he is to be able to look over the top of it, even standing on a stool. And it is used so often that we may understand it as a permanent feature of the stage. The question now arises whether any other kind of curtain was required on the stage, or whether the traverse, screening off a part of the rear stage, provided the only enclosure. Are Booths, Studies, Mansions, Tents, Closets, any of them, necessary?

One kind of enclosure, used in forest and garden scenes, was certainly a property. This is the "tree," strong enough to support Sordido, who tries to hang himself on it, in *Every Man out of his Humour*, III, 7, large enough as a "brake of ferne" to conceal Millicent in *The Merry Devil of Edmonton*, IV, 1, as an "Iuy bush" to conceal Butler in *The Miseries of Enforced Marriage*, scene 8, or as a "bush" to conceal Philaster in *Philaster*, IV, 4 and Palamon in *Two Noble Kinsmen*, III, 1 and III, 7. Another property of the same kind but rather larger is described as an "arbor," a "wood-bine Couerture" and a "pleached bower" in *Much Ado about Nothing* (Benedick hides and Beatrice couches in it), as "Bushes" to conceal Thomas and John in *The Miseries of Enforced Marriage*, scene 8, as a "wood" or "bottome," for Clare and Ierningham in *The Merry Devil of Edmonton*, IV, 1, and as a "box tree," for Sir Toby, Sir Andrew and Fabian, in *Twelfth Night*, II, 5. This kind of enclosure is a special case.

In other scenes, a traverse conceals large properties which have been prepared for discovery, like Volpone's treasure in *Volpone*, I, 1 or Kent's stocks in *King Lear*, II, 4. Here the essential requirements are a front curtain, which a traverse would provide, a rear door, for the installation and removal of properties, and a trap door, shaped perhaps like a grave, for sepulchral visitations. The rear of the Platform has all these features, and is spacious where a Mansion, for instance, cannot be. Tombs are concealed in this enclosed area in *Pericles*, IV, 3, *Timon of Athens*, V, 3, *Much Ado about Nothing*, V, 3 and *The Second Maiden's Tragedy*, IV, 3 and IV, 4, where the directions specify a door and a trap (B 1611 MS):

Enter the Tirant agen at a farder dore, which opened, bringes hym to the Toombe wher the Lady lies buried; The Toombe here discouered ritchly set forthe.

On a sodayne in a kinde of Noyse like a Wynde, the dores clattering, the Toombstone flies open, and a great light appeares in the midst of the Toombe; His Lady as went owt, standing iust before hym all in white, Stuck with Iewells and a great crucifex on her brest.

The altar properties of chapels are "discovered" in *Sejanus*, V, 4, *The Duchess of Malfi*, III, 4, and in *Two Noble Kinsmen*, V, 1 (D 1634 Q), where, it would seem, three altars are required, dedicated, respectively, to Mars, Venus, and Diana, the third of which is situated over the trap to facilitate the manipulation of objects upon it:

> Doves are seene to flutter. . . . Here the Hynde vanishes under the Altar: and in the place ascends a Rose Tree. . . . the Rose fals from the Tree.

Ghostly voices are heard from this trap, in *The Second Maiden's Tragedy*, IV, 4 and in *The Duchess of Malfi*, V, 3 (D 1623 Q)—"Eccho, (from the Dutchesse Grave)." Doubtless, the same trap is used by the Ghost of Caesar, appearing to Brutus in his "Tent," in *Julius Caesar*, IV, 3, and by the Ghost of Banquo, appearing at the "Banquet," in *Macbeth*, III, 4. It may also be used by Timon, burying his gold in the "earth" (*Timon of Athens*, IV, 3) and by the Fishermen "drawing vp a Net" and finding "a rusty Armour" (*Pericles*, II, 1). Other gruesome objects, discovered in an enclosure, are corpses or dummy corpses:

> *The Revenger's Tragedy*, I, 4 (A 1607 Q):
> . . . . he Discouering the body of her dead to certaine Lords.
> *A Yorkshire Tragedy*, scene 10 (A 1608 Q):
> Children laid out.
> *The Duchess of Malfi*, IV, 1 (D 1623 Q):
> Here is discouer'd, (behind a Travers;) the artificiall figures of Antonio, and his children; appearing as if they were dead.
> *Ibid.*, IV, 2:
> Shewes the children strangled.

Beds were sometimes discovered in the same way. In the spectacular prologue of *The Merry Devil of Edmonton*, after the words "Draw the curtaines," Fabell is discovered "laide on his restlesse couch," with a clock and a "Necromantike chaire" (A 1608 Q). But elsewhere, although the use of an enclosure is likely, the directions may be read as the description of beds pushed out from a Stage-Door:

> *A Yorkshire Tragedy*, scene 5 (A 1608 Q):
> Enter a maide with a child in her armes, the mother by her a sleepe.

Othello, V, 2 (C 1623 F):
Enter Othello, and Desdemona in her bed.
Cymbeline, II, 2 (D 1623 F):
Enter Imogen, in her Bed, and a Lady.
The Maid's Tragedy, V, 2 (D 1619 Q):
King abed.

Banquets, as a general rule, were served in, rather than discovered:

The Devil's Charter, V, 4 (A 1607 Q):
. . . . a cuppord of plate brought in. . . . enter a table spread,
Viandes brought in.
The Revenger's Tragedy, V, 3 (A 1607 Q):
A furnished table is brought forth.
Timon of Athens, I, 2 (C 1623 F):
A great Banquet seru'd in.

Senates, settings which, like banquets, required the setting out of seats, were sometimes discovered, as in *Julius Caesar,* III, 1, where a special part of the Platform was designated "the Capitoll," or in *Othello,* I, 3 (C 1622 Q): "Enter Duke and Senators, set at a Table with lights and Attendants," and sometimes not:

Coriolanus, II, 2 (C 1623 F):
Enter two Officers, to lay Cushions, as it were, in the Capitoll.
Henry VIII, V, 2 (D 1623 F):
A Councell Table brought in with Chayres and Stooles, and placed vnder the State.

None of these scenes seems to require a four-sided enclosure; a traverse across the rear stage, with access from the Stage-Doors and the Grave Trap, satisfies the requirements, and with additional means of access to the Platform, from the wings, no problem need arise about entrances in front of the enclosed area.

On the other hand, something quite different is required for the scenes which specify a tent, hovel, cave, cell, prison, closet, cabinet or study. As far as tents are concerned, a key context occurs in the spectacular prologue of *The Devil's Charter* (A 1607 Q):

At one doore betwixt two other Cardinals, Roderigo in his purple habit close in conference with them, one of which hee guideth to a Tent, where a Table is furnished with diuers bagges of money, which that Cardinall beareth away: and to another

Tent the other Cardinall, where hee deliuereth him a great quantity of rich Plate. . . .

Two tents here are simultaneously visible, and while it might be possible to divide the rear stage behind the traverse by an additional transverse curtain, it is also clear that the Stage-Doors remain visible with the "tents" in position. The inescapable inference is that these tents were separate structures and situated away from the Stage-Doors. At least two tents are also required for *Troilus and Cressida*, III, 3, V, 1 and V, 2 (A 1609 Q), if Achilles and Calchas, and possibly others, had separate tents. Single tents suffice for the action of *Julius Caesar*, IV, 3, and *King Lear*, IV, 4 and IV, 7.

A "houell" occurs in *King Lear*, III, 4 and III, 6, significantly a play which also requires a tent (perhaps the same structure serves both purposes). A "Caue" "in the woods," at one point housing a tomb, is needed for *Timon of Athens*, IV, 3, V, 1 and V, 3, and another in *Cymbeline*, III, 3, III, 6, IV, 2 and IV, 4. There is a "Cell" in *The Tempest*, I, 2, III, 1, IV, 1 and V, 1, where "Prospero discouers Ferdinand and Miranda, playing at Chesse" (D 1623 F). All these terms imply a structure lowly and humble, to enter which players stoop, although we must not make too much of the words of Belarius in *Cymbeline* III, 3 (D 1623 F):

> A goodly day, not to keepe house with such,
> Whose Roofe's as lowe as ours: Sleepe Boyes, this gate
> Instructs you how t'adore the Heauens; and bowes you
> To a mornings holy office.

Some structure equally small and low is appropriate for the place in which Malvolio is imprisoned, completely obscured from view, in *Twelfth Night*, IV, 2. A similar structure, out on the Platform where it can be overhung by a "prodigious comet in deadly fire," simulates the "sad roome" in *The Revenger's Tragedy*, III, 5 (A 1607 Q).

In *The Merry Wives of Windsor*, I, 4, Simple hides, until he is found by Caius, in a confined space described in the 1602 Quarto as a "Counting-house" and in the 1623 Folio as a "Closset." This closet had a door, to judge from *The Second Maiden's Tragedy*, V, 1 (B 1611 MS), where Anselmus "locks him self in." A similar "Cabinet" is required for *The Duchess of Malfi*, V, 2. A "study" with a door and curtains is mentioned several times in *The Devil's Charter* (A 1607 Q):

I, 4:   Alexander in his study with bookes, coffers, his triple Crowne vpon a cushion before him.

IV, 1: Alexander commeth vpon the Stage out of his study with a booke in his hand.

V, 6:   Alexander vnbraced betwixt two Cardinalls in his study looking vpon a booke, whilst a groome draweth the Curtaine.

V, 6:   Alexander draweth the Curtaine of his studie where hee discouereth the diuill sitting in his pontificals. . . .

IV, 5: Bernardo knocketh at the study.

In this last scene, Alexander has exited "into his study," leaving instructions with his servant Bernardo to be informed at his "study doore" when Astor and Philippo have fallen asleep after the drugged wine. Bernardo obediently knocks and reports in nine lines of dialogue, at the end of which Alexander is seen "vpon the stage" "solus." Bernardo is given no exit, here nor in other parts of the scene, in which he is continually appearing and disappearing on errands; it is just possible, therefore, that the Study Door is in the rear of the enclosure, a Stage-Door perhaps, invisible to the audience. It is more likely that the stage would not be left empty, even for nine lines, and that this door, like the closet's, is fully visible. If so, we must conclude that we are faced here with a separate structure, not with merely a curtained area of the rear stage.

What kind of structure could represent these tents and hovels, caves and cells, closets and cabinets and studies? Cranford Adams' Study has no front door, although in Diagram 3, I suggest a disposition of the rear stage whereby the Stage-Doors may seem to open into the Study, as well as into the Tiring-House; in my Diagram, the enclosure is not strictly a recess, but the space underneath a large, single bay window in the Tiring-House Front. The disadvantage of this solution is that the enclosure is right at the rear of the Platform, as far from the audience as can be; that the height of the front curtain must somehow be adjustable to convey the impression of a lowly hovel or cave; and that transverse curtains would have to be used to divide the enclosure into two, where two tents are necessary. Leslie Hotson's "Mansions," or properties of similar size, will serve whenever the enclosure is not required to house large properties or more than a few players, but cannot cope, for instance, with the couch, chair, and clock in the prologue to *The Merry Devil of Edmonton;* and the size of the Mansion cannot be increased very much without defeating Hotson's object and obstructing the view of the audience in this arena theater. Walter Hodges' Booth will serve for all purposes, eliminating even the need for a rear traverse, provided that it has a visible door and is erected against the Tiring-House Front, at the rear of the stage, so that it does not block the view of the audience and has a Stage-Door at its rear for the installation and removal of large properties. With access to the Platform from the wings, there is no objection to surrendering a Stage-Door for this purpose. I cannot understand, however, why Booths or Mansions should have doors, as well as curtains: the historical factors which produced them are not clear. And, in any case, a Booth is much too large for cabinets and closets; there is no need to send a man on a boy's errand.

It would seem that the best solution is to use a Booth in one play, and Mansions in the next, but this suggests that enclosures were there because they were useful, rather than used because they were there. In Diagram 2, I suggest a method whereby enclosures of a respectable, all-purpose size, small enough for cabinets and large enough for sizable properties, may have been available on each side of the Platform and at points much nearer the audience than Adams' Study. If bay windows existed, one on each side of the stage, then the space underneath them must have been exploited, one way or another. The likeliest suggestion is that the Platform "bays" were additional twelvepenny rooms on the lower level. In my Diagram they have been adapted, with curtains, to provide enclosures, with a gate in their palings, by which gallants entered the "box" from the stage, to provide a visible Study Door. These "bays" would provide the smaller enclosures, while the traverse curtain provided a larger enclosed area for other kinds of scene, without calling in carpenters to erect any kind of structure on the Platform during a performance.

IV. THE PENTHOUSE

Platform bays would assist us to solve another problem, to which no satisfactory solution has yet been presented, the location of the "penthouse." This feature is mentioned in *Much Ado about Nothing*, III, 3 (A 1600 Q):

Stand thee close then vnder this penthouse, for it drissels raine. . . .

Here concealed, Borachio and Conrade cannot see the watchmen who listen to their words. Again, in *Troilus and Cressida*, V, 2 (A 1609 Q):

Stand, where the torch may not discouer vs. . . .

On this occasion Ulysses and Troilus conceal themselves, with Thersites, unknown to the other two, also hidden somewhere to their rear. There is also a "hedge corner" used for the ambush of Parolles in *All's Well that Ends Well*, IV, 1 (C 1623 F):

Enter one of the Frenchmen, with fiue or sixe other souldiers in ambush.

An ambush involving fewer players occurs in *Othello*, V, 1 (C 1622 Q), where Iago and Roderigo lie in wait for Cassio:

Here stand behind this Bulke, straite will he come,
Weare thy good Rapier bare, and put it home,
Quicke, quicke, feare nothing, I'le be at thy elboe. . . .

Such a "bulke" would be useful in other plays, for instance in *Every Man out of his Humour*, I, 2 and I, 3, where Macilente conceals himself, in one scene standing and in the other seated. If the Stage-Doors had pillars, then these might serve as a bulk to conceal Iago and Roderigo, who jump at Cassio as soon as he enters the stage. But the six or seven Frenchmen who ambush Parolles cannot possibly secrete themselves behind slender door-pillars, and in this instance Parolles must have advanced a fair distance on to the stage, speaking his soliloquy, before the trap is sprung. The interior of a Booth or Mansion, or some other enclosure, may have served as a shelter from the rain for Borachio and Conrade, or for Ulysses and Troilus, observing the action from its opening, but Thersites cannot be hidden from the view of the audience in the depths of an enclosure.

In *Every Man out of his Humour*, II, 1, *two* places of concealment are required. One is used by four players, Sogliardo, Carlo, Fastidius Brisk, and the page Cinedo (A 1600 Q):

. . . . stand by, close vnder this Tarras, & you shall see it done better than I can shew it.

In this position they are invisible to Puntarvolo, who stands at the rear of the Platform, and to the two ladies who talk with Puntarvolo from the Window-Stage, but visible to the audience and to the Presenters, who are probably sitting near the front of the stage. No position at the rear of the stage, along the Tiring-House Front, satisfies these requirements. Later, Puntarvolo observes Sordido and Fungoso approaching, perhaps by a Stage-Door; he waves to them, commands "retire your selues a space," and they then "withdraw at the other part of the stage," to a position whence they would be invisible to the lady at the window when she next reappears. Sordido and Fungoso apparently move to a place of concealment *opposite* that used by Sogliardo and his party, whom they do not meet. Finally, the Lady and her attendant enter the Platform, "and seeing them"—that is, Sogliardo and his friends—"turnes in againe." The game up, Sogliardo and two of his companions "step forth" to Puntarvolo.

The most important clue, I think, is the Lady's Platform entrance. She must enter by a wing access, because Sogliardo and his party are nowhere near the Stage-Doors and yet she observes them as soon as she appears. There is, as it happens, a "penthouse" on each side of the stage, in my Diagram 2, by the Platform bays, underneath the bay windows (whether these protrude forwards at the first story, like so many Elizabethan windows, or not). In this position, Sogliardo and his party are plainly visible to the audience and to the Presenters, but invisible to players standing on the rear of the Platform or in the windows (unless the latter leaned directly over the sill). In the other scenes, Cassio would have been ambushed from the bay as he entered by the wing access, Parolles would have had time to reach this position downstage before the Frenchmen spring out, and Thersites would have stood behind Ulysses and Troilus, deeper within the wing access. Those of my readers who are skeptical, about both this wing access, and platform bays, are asked to sketch in the movements in this scene of *Every Man out of his Humour* on any diagram of the Globe stage they care to draw. They will find it an intriguing problem; easy to solve in parts but not as a whole. In desperation, they may find that my suggestion is not entirely unacceptable.

In this survey, I have tried, without complete success, to

avoid downright commitment to any one theory, because it seems to me preferable to direct attention to the means of a *consensus gentium*. It would seem that our knowledge of the Globe stage would bring us within reach of an agreed final picture, if we could establish the exact contours of the stage at the head of the Yard alleys, where, I suggest, the passage from the spectators' entrances to the Yard converges with the wings of the Platform and the bays. Believing in access from the Platform to the Yard,[8] I should be glad to accept the notion that steps from this passage down to the Yard were also used, unexceptionably and quite naturally, by players. There would be no need to look further to discover how the Roman soldiers entered the Yard to raise Antony aloft to a Platform Monument (*Antony and Cleopatra,* IV, 15), or how Marina and others entered the Platform from a barge in the Yard (*Pericles,* V, 1), or how the soldiers besieging Corioli entered their "Trenches" (*Coriolanus,* I, 4), or how the Globe groundlings themselves obstructed royal processions (*Henry VIII,* V, 4), or how the maid's body was tumbled headlong down visible stairs (*A Yorkshire Tragedy,* scene 5), or how Caesar casts first Candy and then Frescobaldi into the River Tiber (*The Devil's Charter,* III, 5), or how players leaving the Platform could "go down" (*The Merry Devil of Edmonton,* I, 1, *Antony and Cleopatra,* II, 7, and elsewhere). And the references to ditches and stiles about the Platform stage need not be as fanciful as we may think. The "faire-fild Globe" is an elusive target for our eyes; just when we seem to have it, the picture dissolves and escapes us once more. But I am hopeful that my suggestions may lead the way to a reconstruction as clear and stable as we are ever likely to achieve.

[8] *Vide* my paper, "Vaulting the Rails," in *Shakespeare Survey* 7 (1954), pp. 69–81. See also Allardyce Nicoll's paper in *Shakespeare Survey* 12, pp. 47–55.

GLOBE PLAYHOUSE 1599–1613

DIAGRAM 1

This illustrates the relative advantages of the Adams Study and Hodges Booth over the Adams Chamber. Lines of sight in a cross-section demonstrate that a player lying on a bed in the "Chamber" would be invisible to the entire ground-floor audience.

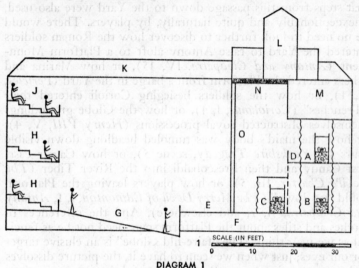

DIAGRAM 1

CROSS-SECTION

The figure in the enclosure represents a player in a bed.

A Adams "Chamber"	H Twopenny Rooms
B Adams "Study"	J Penny Gallery
C Hodges "Booth"	K Roof
D Adams "Tarras"	L Huts
E Platform	M Music Gallery
F Cellarage	N Shadow
G Yard	O Stage Posts

DIAGRAM 2

Note here

(i) The wing accesses formed by passages from the Spectators' Entrances to the Yard.

(ii) The enclosures, with front door and curtains, made possible by adaptation of bay twelvepenny rooms lying directly underneath bay windows on the first floor.

(iii) Rear traverse screening off the rear stage when necessary.

(iv) Penthouses or "hedge corners" made possible by the "bulks" of the bays.

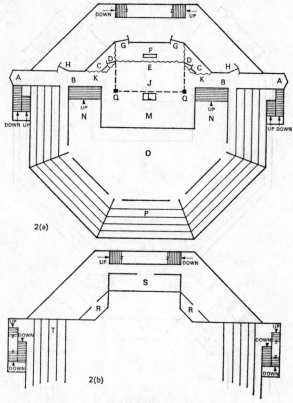

2(a)

2(b)

DIAGRAM 2

PLAN VIEW (FIRST ALTERNATIVE)

An impression not to scale

2(a) At Platform Level

2(b) At Window Level

A Spectators' Entrance	H Players Door	P Twopenny Rooms (Platform Level)
B Wing Access	J Area beneath Shadow	Q Stage Post
C Bay Enclosure	K Penthouse	R Bay Window
D Enclosure Gate	L Main Trap	S Twelvepenny Rooms (Platform Level)
E Traverse	M Platform	T Twopenny Rooms (Window Level)
F Grave Trap	N Yard Alley	
G Stage Door	O Yard	

DIAGRAM 3

Note here
  (i) Wing accesses set at a sharper angle than in Diagram 2.
 (ii) A single enclosure made possible by the adaptation of a single bay
       lying directly underneath the bay of twelvepenny rooms on the first
       floor.
(iii) Stage Doors angled so that they may seem to be doors into the en-
       closure as well as doors into the Tiring House.
 (iv) Penthouses or "hedge corners" made possible by the "bulks" of
       ground-floor twelvepenny rooms.

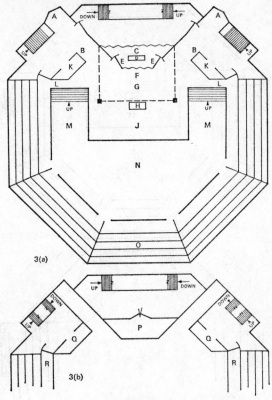

DIAGRAM 3

PLAN VIEW (SECOND ALTERNATIVE)

An impression not to scale

3(a) At Platform Level

3(b) At Window Level

A Spectators' Entrance   H Main Trap   O Twopenny Rooms
B Wing Access   J Platform   (Platform Level)
C Bay Enclosure   K Twelvepenny Room   P Single large Bay
D Grave Trap   (Platform Level)   Window
E Stage Door   L Penthouse   Q Twelvepenny Room
F Traverse   M Yard Alley   (Window Level)
G Area beneath Shadow   N Yard   R Twopenny Rooms
                                                         (Window Level)

BIBLIOGRAPHY

ADAMS, JOHN CRANFORD. *The Globe Playhouse.* 2d ed. New York: Barnes & Noble, 1961.

ADAMS, JOSEPH QUINCY. *Shakespearean Playhouses: A History of English Theatres from the Beginning to the Restoration.* Boston: Houghton Mifflin Co., 1917.

ARMSTRONG, WILLIAM A. "Actors and Theatres." *Shakespeare Survey 17* (1964): 191–204.

———. *Elizabethan Private Theatres: Facts and Problems.* Society for Theatre Research Pamphlet no. 6. London, 1958.

BALDWIN, THOMAS WHITFIELD. *The Organization and Personnel of the Shakespearean Company.* Princeton, N.J.: Princeton University Press, 1927.

BECKERMAN, BERNARD. *Shakespeare at the Globe, 1599–1609.* New York: Macmillan Co., 1962.

BENTLEY, GERALD EADES. *The Jacobean and Caroline Stage.* 7 vols. Oxford: Clarendon Press, 1941–68. Vol. 2, *Players.* Vol. 6, *Theaters.*

———. *Shakespeare and His Theatre.* Lincoln, Nebr.: University of Nebraska Press, 1964.

BETHELL, S. L. "Shakespeare's Actors." *Review of English Studies,* n.s., 1 (1950):193–205.

BRADBROOK, MURIEL. *The Rise of the Common Player.* Cambridge: Harvard University Press, 1962.

CHAMBERS, SIR EDMUND. *The Elizabethan Stage.* 4 vols. Oxford: Clarendon Press, 1923. Vol. 2.

DOWNER, ALAN S. "Prolegomenon to a Study of Elizabethan Acting." *Maske and Kothurn* 10 (1965):625–36.

FOAKES, R. A. "The Players Passion: Some Notes on Elizabethan Psychology and Acting." *Essays and Studies* 8 (1954):62–77.

FOAKES, R. A., and RICKERT, R. T., eds. *Henslowe's Diary.* Cambridge: Cambridge University Press, 1961.

GREG, W. W. *Dramatic Documents from the Elizabethan Playhouses.* 2 vols. Oxford: Clarendon Press, 1931.

HARBAGE, ALFRED. *Shakespeare's Audience.* New York: Columbia University Press, 1941.

———. *Shakespeare and the Rival Traditions.* New York: Macmillan Co., 1952.

BIBLIOGRAPHY

HILLEBRAND, HAROLD NEWCOMB. *The Child Actors: A Chapter in Elizabethan Stage History*. Urbana, Ill.: University of Illinois Press, 1926.

HODGES, C. WALTER. *Shakespeare and the Players*. London: E. Benn, 1948.

——. *The Globe Restored*. London: E. Benn, 1953.

HOTSON, LESLIE. *Shakespeare's Wooden O*. London: Hart-Davis, 1959.

ISAACS, J. *Production and Stage Management at the Blackfriars Theatre*. Shakespeare Association Pamphlet. London, 1933.

JOSEPH, B. L. *Elizabethan Acting*. 2d ed. London: Oxford University Press, 1964.

KING, T. J. "Staging of Plays at the Phoenix in Drury Lane, 1617–42." *Theatre Notebook* 19 (1965):146–66.

LAWRENCE, W. J. *The Physical Conditions of the Elizabethan Playhouses*. Cambridge: Harvard University Press, 1927.

——. *Pre-Restoration Stage Studies*. Cambridge: Harvard University Press, 1927.

——. *Old Theatre Days and Ways*. London: G. G. Harrap, 1935.

LINTHICUM, M. CHANNING. *Costume in the Drama of Shakespeare and His Contemporaries*. Oxford: Clarendon Press, 1936.

NAGLER, A. M. *Shakespeare's Stage*. New Haven: Yale University Press, 1958.

NICOLL, ALLARDYCE. *Stuart Masques and the Renaissance Stage*. New York: Harcourt, Brace, 1938.

PALME, PER. *Triumph of Peace: A Study of the Whitehall Banqueting House*. Stockholm: Almqvist & Wiksell, 1956.

REYNOLDS, GEORGE FULMER. "Staging Elizabethan Plays." *Shakespeare Association Bulletin* 24 (1949):258–63.

——. *The Staging of Elizabethan Plays at the Red Bull Theater, 1605–25*. New York: Kraus, 1940.

SHIRLEY, FRANCES A. *Shakespeare's Use of Off-Stage Sounds*. Lincoln, Nebr.: University of Nebraska Press, 1963.

SMITH, IRWIN. *Shakespeare's Blackfriars Playhouse: Its History and Its Design*. New York: New York University Press, 1964.

WICKHAM, GLYNNE. *Early English Stages, 1300 to 1660*. Vol. 2. London: Routledge, 1963.

WILSON, F. P. "The Elizabethan Theatre." *Neophilologus* 39 (1955): 40–58.

INDEX

"Actors' Names in Basic Shakespearean Texts" (Gaw), 112
Actors Remonstrance, or Complaint for the silencing of their profession, The, 80, 218, 222, 227, 230
Adam and Eve, 21
Adams, John Cranford, 238, 239–40, 246, 247, 251, 259, 260, 264
Adams, Joseph Quincy, 150; *Dramatic Records of Sir Henry Herbert*, 158
Admiral's Men. *See* Lord Admiral's Men
Adoration of the Shepherds, The (Chester mystery), 159
Alarum for London, 198
Alchemist, The (Jonson), 232–33
Alleyn, Edward, 15, 96
All Fooles (Chapman), 227
All's Well That Ends Well (Shakespeare), 198, 261
Almonry House, 215
Alphonsus King of Aragon (Greene), 197
Anatomie of Abuses (Stubbs), 66–67
Anatomy of Puck, The (Briggs), 133
Annales, or a Generall Chronicle of England . . . Continued . . . by Edmund Howes (Stow), 61, 69
Annals of the Stage (Collier). *See History of English Dramatic Poetry to the Time of Shakespeare and Annals of the Stage to the Restoration* (Collier)
Antiochus the Great, 182–83
Antipodes, The (Brome), 48, 169
Antonio and Mellida (Marston), 49
Antony and Cleopatra (Shakespeare), 71–73, 88–91, 93, 108, 110, 198, 200, 251–52, 263
Apology for Actors, An (Heywood), 104–6
Apology for the Life of Colley Cibber (Cibber), 97, 172
Arcadian Rhetoric, The (Fraunce), 47
Arden of Feversham, 206
Armin, Robert, 125
Art of English Poesie, The (Puttenham), 45
Ascham, Roger: *The Schoolmaster*, 50
Ashley, Anthony, 139, 142
Ashley, Francis, 142–43
As You Like It (Shakespeare), 71–73, 84–88, 93, 152–53, 162, 198, 244
Aubrey, John: *Brief Lives*, 232
Austin, William, 141–42; "Certaine deuine Hymnes, or Carrolls for Christmas-daie Togeather with diuers deuout and zealous Meditations vpon our Sauoiurs Passion," 141; "Meditations," 141

Baker, George Pierce: *The Development of Shakespeare as a Dramatist*, 73

Bald, R. C., 150–51, 247
Baldwin, T. W.: *The Organization and Personnel of the Shakespearean Company*, 74, 79, 97, 112–13
"Ballade in praise of London Prentices, and what they did at the Cock-pitt Play-house in Drury Lane, A" (Collier), xi
Balls, Francis, 193, 194, 195
Balls, Richard, 195
Baltimore, Lord. *See* Calvert, George
Bankhead, Tallulah, 91
Baring, Maurice: *Punch and Judy*, 71; *The Puppet Show of Memory*, 70–71
Barkham, Edward, 140
Barnavelt. See Sir John van Olden Barnavelt (Fletcher and Massinger)
Barnes, Barnabe, 239; *The Devil's Charter*, 210–11, 212, 213, 242, 248, 249, 253, 254, 257–58, 263
Bartholomew Fair (Jonson), 225
Baxter, Richard, 193, 194, 195
Beaumont, Francis, and John Fletcher, 184; *The Beggar's Bush*, 138; *The Bloody Brother*, 195; *Bonduca*, 137, 144, 152, 180; *The Chances*, 232; *The Custom of the Country*, 169, 233; *Demetrius and Enanthe*, 138, 141, 143–44, 146–49, 150, 153; *The Elder Brother*, 168; *The Faithful Shepherdess*, 68, 220–21, 222; *The Honest Man's Fortune*, 137, 152, 180; *The Island Princess*, 207; *The Knight of the Burning Pestle*, 43, 162–63; *The Little French Lawyer*, 166; *The Loyal Subject*, 77, 130; *The Maid in the Mill*, 207;

The Maid's Tragedy, 251, 253, 257; *Philaster*, 248, 255; *Rule a Wife and Have a Wife*, 220; *The Sea Voyage*, 199; *Sir John van Olden Barnavelt*, 138, 143–46, 153; *The Two Noble Kinsmen*, 166, 239, 244–45, 250, 255, 256; *Wit without Money*, 223; *The Woman Hater*, 233
Beeston, Christopher, 10, 97, 125
Beggar's Bush, The (Fletcher and Massinger), 138
Believe as You List (Massinger), 137–38, 152
Beltz, George, 173–74
Beltz, Samuel, 173–74, 189
Benfield, Robert, 194
Bentley, Gerald Eades: *The Jacobean and Caroline Stage*, viii, 28, 78, 126, 218–19; *Shakespeare: A Biographical Handbook*, 126; *Shakespeare and His Theatre*, 126; *The Swan of Avon and the Bricklayer of Westminster*, 71
Bethell, S. L.: *Shakespeare and the Popular Dramatic Tradition*, 42; "Shakespeare's Actors," 41, 44, 95
Bevington, David M.: *From Mankind to Marlowe*, 112
Biographical Chronicle of the English Drama, 1559–1642, A (Fleay), xi
Blacke Booke, The (Middleton), 151
Blackfriars Theater, 215–34
Blasts of Retrait. See Second and Third Blast of Retrait from Plays and Theatres (Munday)
Bloody Brother, The (Fletcher and Jonson), 195
Boas, Guy, 74; *Shakespeare and the Young Actor*, 74
Bond, R. Warwick, 148

Bonduca (Beaumont and Fletcher), 137, 144, 152, 180
Bonetti, Rocco, 157
Book of Airs, A (Campion), 48
Borgman, Albert S.: *Thomas Shadwell: His Life and Comedies*, 78
Boswell, James (1778–1882), x
Bradbrook, Muriel C.: *Elizabethan Stage Conditions*, 73, 94; *The Rise of the Common Player*, 55; *Themes and Conventions of Elizabethan Tragedy*, 42, 99–100, 101
Brennoralt (Suckling), 169
Bretnor, Thomas, 232
Bride, The (Nabbes), 219, 232
Brideoak, Ralph, 224
Bridgewater, Earl of. *See* Egerton, John
Brief Lives (Aubrey), 232
Briggs, Katherine M.: *The Anatomy of Puck*, 133
British Theatre, The (Chetwood), 171–72
Bromberg, Murray: "Theatrical Wagers," 10
Brome, Richard, 23, 28; *The Antipodes*, 48, 169, 218
Bryan, George, 125
Bryan, Joseph. *See* "Certaine selected Psalmes of Dauid (in Verse)"
Buc, George, 143, 145–46; "Discourse or Treatise of the Third University," 69
Bullen, Arthur Henry, 150, 152
Bulwer, John, 48; *Chirologia*, 46–47, 102–3; *Chironomia*, 46–47, 102–3
Burbage, James, 63, 64, 215–16
Burbage, Richard, 43, 46, 48–49, 74–75, 81, 90, 92, 96, 98, 100–101, 102, 103, 107, 109, 111, 125

Burt, Nicholas, 193, 194, 195
Bussy D'Ambois (Chapman), 163

Caesar and Pompey (Chapman), 53–54
Calisto and Melebea (Rastell), 137
Calvert, George, 1st Baron Baltimore, 142
Cambridge, 58
Campion, Thomas: *A Book of Airs*, 48
Captives, The (Heywood), 137
Cardinal, The (Shirley), 168
Careless Shepherdess, The (Goffe), 218, 219, 220, 221, 223, 230
Carew, Thomas, 229
Carey, Thomas. *See* "Certaine selected Psalmes of Dauid (in Verse)"
Case Is Altered, The (Jonson), 163–64
Catiline (Jonson), 248
Cavendish, Margaret, Duchess of Newcastle: *The Descriptions of a New World*, 232–33
Cayet, P. V. P.: *Chronologie Septenaire*, 181–82
"Certaine deuine Hymnes, or Carrolls for Christmas-daie Togeather with diuers deuout and zealous Meditations vpon our Sauiours Passion" (Austin), 141
"Certaine selected Psalmes of Dauid (in Verse)" (Davison, Bryan, Gipps, and Carey), 141
Chamberlain, John, 207–8
Chambers, Edmund, 94; *The Elizabethan Stage*, 43, 62, 113, 156, 236, 247; *William Shakespeare: A Study of the Facts and Problems*, 81, 126
Chances, The (Fletcher), 232

Chapman, George: *All Fooles,* 227; *Bussy D'Ambois,* 163; *Caesar and Pompey,* 53–54; *Charlemagne,* 100; *The Revenge of Bussy D'Ambois,* 165

Chapman, George, Ben Jonson, and John Marston: *Eastward Ho,* 207

Character of a Common Player, The (Cocke), 68–69, 96

Characters (Overbury), 102, 103

Charlemagne (Chapman), 100

Charles I, King of England, 182

Chester, Charles, 232

Chettle, Henry: *Kind Harts Dreame,* 67

Chettle, Henry, and Thomas Dekker: *King Sebastian of Portugal,* 181, 183

Chetwood, W. R., 174; *The British Theatre,* 171–72

Child Actors, The (Hildebrand), 74

Children of the Chapel (Wallace), 224–25

Children of the Chapel Royal, 62, 64–65, 71

Chirologia (Bulwer), 46–47, 102–3

Chironomia (Bulwer), 46–47, 102–3

Chronicle History of the London Stage, A (Fleay), 150

Chronologie Septenaire (Cayet), 181–82

Cibber, Colley: *Apology for the Life of Colley Cibber,* 70, 97, 172, 173

City Madam, The (Massinger), 223, 229

City Match, The (Mayne), 223–24

Cleveland, John, 229

Clode, C. M.: *Memorials,* 139

Cocke, J.: *The Character of a Common Player,* 68–69, 96

Cockpit (Phoenix) Theater, 216–34

Cole, William, 140

Collectanea Anglo-Poetica (Corser), 141

Collier, John Payne, xi, 177, 189–92; "Ballade in praise of London Prentices, and what they did at the Cock-pitt Playhouse in Drury Lane, A," xi; *History of English Dramatic Poetry to the Time of Shakespeare and Annals of the Stage to the Restoration,* xi

Comedy of Errors, The (Shakespeare), 123

Condell, Henry, 125, 145, 225–26, 227

Continuation of the lamentable Aduentures of Dom Sebastian, A, 181

Cooper, Anne, 142

Cooper, John, 142

Coriolanus (Shakespeare), 49, 163, 198, 200, 201, 243, 248–49, 257, 263

Corrections to the Text of 'Believe as You List' (Tannenbaum), 192

Corser, T., 174; *Collectanea Anglo-Poetica,* 141

Coryat, Thimas: *Coryat's Crudities,* 76–77, 80

Cotgrave, Randle, 187

Covent Garden (Nabbes), 229

Cowley, Richard, 111, 125

Craig, Edith, and Christopher St. John: *Ellen Terry's Memoirs,* 75

Crane, John, 139

Crane, Ralph: "The Most Auntient Historie of God and Man" (?), 141; "A Summarie and true Distinction, betweene the Lawe, & yᵉ Ghospel," 141; *The Workes Of Mercy* (later republished as *The Pilgrimes New-yeares-Gift*), 138–40, 142–43, 146, 155

Croker, T. Crofton, 173–74, 175, 176, 177, 179, 189–92; *Remarks on an article inserted in the Papers of the Shakespeare Society*, 189–90

Crowley, Robert: "The Last Trumpet," 56

Cruickshank, A. H.: *Philip Massinger*, 177, 192

Cunningham, Francis, 174, 177, 190–92

Curtain Theater, 56, 64, 68

Custom of the Country, The (Fletcher and Massinger), 169, 233

Cymbeline (Shakespeare), 152, 239, 245, 251, 257, 258

Cynthia's Revels (Jonson), 224, 227–28, 230

Cyprian Conqueror, The, 102

Darstellerpahl und Rollenvertheilung bei Shakespeare (Sack), 112–13

Davenant, William, 172; *The Unfortunate Lovers*, 159, 168

David, Richard, 129; *Shakespeare's Love's Labour's Lost*, 128, 129

Davies, John: *In Rufum*, 223

Davies, W. Robertson: *Shakespeare's Boy Actors*, 77, 79

Davis, Francis. *See* "Certaine selected Psalmes of Dauid (in Verse)"

Davis, Henry Newnham, 175

Davis, Lockyer, 149

Davison, Christopher. *See* "Certaine selected Psalmes of Dauid (in Verse)"

Dee, John, 232–33

Defence of Poesie (Sidney), 10

Dekker, Thomas, xv, 28, 64, 137; *The Gull's Hornbook*, 224, 227; *A Knights Coniuring*, 158; *Lanthorne and Candle-light*, 140; *Satiromastix*, 209, 212; *The Shoemaker's Holiday*, 206; *The Wonder of a Kingdome*, 157. *See also* Chettle, Henry, and Thomas Dekker; Middleton, Thomas, and Thomas Dekker

De la Casa, John: *Rich Cabinet Furnished with Varietie of Descriptions*, 157

Demetrius and Enanthe (Fletcher), 138, 141, 143–44, 146–49, 150, 153

Descriptions of a New World, The (Cavendish), 232–33

Development of Shakespeare as a Dramatist, The (Baker), 73

Devil is an Ass, The (Jonson), 77, 226–27, 232

Devil's Charter, The (Barnes), 210–11, 212, 213, 242, 248, 249, 253, 254, 257–58, 259, 263

Devil's Law Case, The (Webster), 166

De Witt, John, 240, 246, 249–50, 253–54

"Diary of John Greene, The," 219

Dicke of Devonshire, 166–67

Digby, Kenelm, 141, 148

"Discourse or Treatise of the Third University" (Buc), 69

Disguise Plots in Elizabethan Drama (Freeburg), 85–86

"Diuine Pastorall Eglogue, A" (Randolph), 142

Doctor Faustus (Marlowe), 199

Donne, John, 82

Doubtful Heir, The (Shirley), 231

Douce, Francis, 150

Dowle, Rowland, 195

Downes, John: *Roscius Anglicanus*, 78, 98

Downfall of Robert Earl of Huntingdon, The (Munday), 164

Dramatic Records (Herbert), 150

Drayton, Michael, 216

Drury Lane Theater, 172, 173

Dryden, John: *Of Dramatick Poesie*, 10

Duchess of Malfi, The (Webster), 52, 250, 254, 256, 258–59

Duke, John, 125

Duke of Millan, The (Massinger), 176–77

Dumb Knight, The (Markham), 165

Duvivier, Julien, 74

Dyce, Alexander, 146–47, 150, 176

Early London Theatres (Ordish), 157–58

Eastward Ho (Chapman, Jonson, and Marston), 207

Edwards, Richard: *Palamon and Arcite*, 59

Egerton, John, Earl of Bridgewater, 140, 142

Elder Brother, The (Fletcher), 168

Eliot, T. S.: *Elizabethan Essays*, 108

Elizabeth, Queen of England, 62

"Elizabethan Acting" (Harbage), 43, 49, 80, 94, 96

Elizabethan Acting (Joseph), 45, 47, 49, 101–3, 104–5

Elizabethan Essays (Eliot), 108

Elizabethan Stage, The (Chambers), 156, 236, 247

"Elizabethan Stage and Shakespeare's Entrance Announcements, The" (Smith), 201

Elizabethan Stage Conditions (Bradbrook), 73, 94

Ellen Terry's Memoirs (Craig and St. John), 75

Elyot, Thomas: *The Governor*, 50

Engelen, J.: "Die Schauspieler-Ökonomie in Shakespeares Dramen," 112–13

England's Joy, 207

English Drama and Stage under the Tudor and Stuart Princes, 1543–1664, The (Hazlitt), 80–81, 157, 218

English Dramatic Companies (Murray), 189, 195

English Literary Autographs 1550–1650 (Greg), 143

Epicoene (Jonson), 218, 220, 221, 222

Every Man in His Humour (Jonson), 124–25, 157, 230–31

Every Man out of His Humour (Jonson), 201, 202–3, 214, 232, 239, 248, 253, 255, 261–62

Evolution of the English Drama up to Shakespeare, The (Wallace), 157

"Excellent Actor, An" (Webster), 43, 46, 102

Faire Quarrel, A (Middleton), 157, 166

Fairholt, F. W., 189, 190

Fair Maid of Bristow, The, 198

Fair Maid of the West, The (Heywood), 187

Faithful Shepherdess, The (Fletcher), 220–21, 222

Fallen Idol, The (film), 74

"False Faces on Shakespeare's Stage" (Hotson), 209
Farmer, J. S., 191–92
Farrant, Richard, 215
Father Hubburds Tales (Middleton), 151
"Faultie Fauorite, The," 142
Field, Nathan, 23; *Woman Is a Weathercock,* 165
Film Star in Belgravia, A (Henrey), 74
Fisher, Jasper: *Fuimus Troes: The True Trojans,* 166
Fiske, Nicholas, 232
Fitzgeoffrey, Henry: *Satyres and Satyricall Epigrams: With Certaine Observations at Blackfryers,* 219, 221, 222–23, 226, 231
Fleay, Frederick Gard: *A Biographical Chronicle of the English Drama, 1559–1642,* xi, 151: *The Life and Work of William Shakespeare,* 134; *A Chronicle History of the London Stage,* 150
Flecknoe, Richard, 102; *Love's Kingdom,* ix, 103; *A Short Discourse of the English Stage,* viii–ix, 46, 48–49
Fletcher, John. *See* Beaumont, Francis, and John Fletcher
Florio, John, 208
Foakes, R. A.: "Player's Passion, The," 80
Foreman, Simon, 232
Fortune by Land and Sea (Heywood), 169
Fortune Theater, 35, 68, 158, 216
Four Prentices of London, The, 162–63
Fraunce, Abraham: *The Arcadian Rhetoric,* 47
Freeburg, Victor Oscar: *Disguise Plots in Elizabethan Drama,* 85–86
Friar Bacon and Friar Bungay (Greene), 161
Friar Francis, 19
Frijlinck, W. P., 143, 153
Froissart, Jean, 60–61
From Mankind to Marlowe (Bevington), 112
Fuimus Troes: The True Trojans (Fisher), 166
Fuller, Nicholas, 175

Gager, William, 58–59
Game at Chess, A (Middleton), 138, 143–44, 148, 149–51, 153
Gardiner, S. R.: *The Political Element in Massinger,* 191
Garrick, Carrington, 173
Garrick, David, 96, 173–74, 225
Gaw, Allison: "Actors' Names in Basic Shakespearean Texts," 112
Gayton, Edmund: *Pleasant Notes upon Don Quixote,* 103–4, 230
Gentili, Alberico, 59
George a Greene, the Pinner of Wakefield (Greene[?]), 162
Gifford, William, 173, 176–77, 190
Gildersleeve, Virginia C.: *Government Regulation of the Elizabethan Drama,* 63
Gippe, Richard. *See* "Certaine selected Psalmes of Dauid (in Verse)"
Glapthorne, Henry: *The Ladies' Privilege,* 220, 226, 231
Globe Restored, The (Hodges), 208
Globe Theater, xii–xiii, 68, 101, 125, 149, 174, 196–214, 235–66
Goblins, The (Suckling), 168–69
Goethe, Johann Wolfgang von, 75–76

Goethe's Travels in Italy (Nisbeth), 76
Goffe, Alexander, 195
Goffe, Thomas: *The Careless Shepherdess*, 218, 219, 220, 221, 223, 230
Goldoni, Carlo: *La Locandiera*, 75–76
Gondomar, Count of, Diego Sarmiento de Acuña, 150
Gosson, Stephen, xiv, 67
Government Regulation of the Elizabethan Drama (Gildersleeve), 63
Governor, The (Elyot), 50
Granville-Barker, Harley: *Prefaces to Shakespeare*, 70, 71, 85, 89, 90, 97
Graves, Thornton S., 155; "A Note on the Swan Theatre," 207; "The Stage Sword and Dagger," 156
"Great Companies," 56–57
Greene, John, 219
Greene, Robert, 72; *Alphonsus King of Aragon*, 197; *Friar Bacon and Friar Bungay*, 161; *George a Greene, the Pinner of Wakefield*(?), 162; *Menaphon*, 54; *Orlando Furioso*, 161–62; *Pandosto. The Triumphe of Time*, 81
Greenwich Strollers, The, 187
Greg, W. W., 137–38, 158, 172; *English Literary Autographs 1550–1650*, 143; "The Handwritings of the Manuscript," 65; *Henslowe Papers*, 154; *Henslowe's Diary*, 158; "Prompt Copies, Private Transcripts, and 'The Playhouse Scrivener,'" 138, 148; *Two Elizabethan Stage Abridgements: The Battle of Alcazar and Orlando Furioso*, 161

Gresham, Edward, 232
Greville, Curtis, 193
Griffin, Benjamin, 149
Guardian, The (Massinger), 207
Gull's Hornbook, The (Dekker), 224, 227

H., J.: *The House of Correction*, 217
Hairy Ape, The (O'Neill), 100
Halliwell, J. O. *See* Halliwell-Phillipps, James Orchard
Halliwell-Phillipps, James Orchard, 173–74, 175, 176, 177, 191
Hamlet (Shakespeare), 49, 52, 80, 92, 104, 127, 163, 198, 214, 251, 254
Hammond, William, 151, 155
"Handwritings of the Manuscript, The" (Greg), 65
Hannibal and Scipio (Nabbes), 158, 220, 233–34
Harbage, Alfred, 94–95, 106–7; "Elizabethan Acting," 43, 49, 77, 80, 94, 96, 104; *Shakespeare and the Rival Traditions*, 215, 224, 225; *Shakespeare's Audience*, 61
Harlech, Lord. *See* Ormsby-Gore, William George Arthur
Haselden, R. B., 142
Hazlitt, W. C.: *The English Drama and Stage under the Tudor and Stuart Princes, 1543–1664*, 80–81, 157, 218
Heming, John, 125, 145, 225–26, 227
Henrey, Bobby, 74
Henrey, Madelaine: *A Film Star in Belgravia*, 74
I Henry IV (Shakespeare), 123, 153, 163
II Henry IV (Shakespeare), 123, 125

Henry V (Shakespeare), ix–x, 123, 152, 200, 236, 241, 243–44

Henry VI (Shakespeare), 123, 152

III Henry VI (Shakespeare), 44, 123

Henry VIII (Shakespeare and Fletcher), 126, 159, 245, 252, 257, 263

Henslowe, Philip, 65, 67, 123, 158, 177, 181

Henslowe Papers (Greg), 154

Henslowe's Diary (Greg), 158

Hepburn, Katharine, 91

Herbert, Henry, x, 147, 149–50, 170–72, 176, 180–81, 183–84, 189, 191; *Dramatic Records,* 150

Heywood, Thomas, xv, 28, 42–43, 48, 50, 137; *An Apology for Actors,* 42, 48, 104–6; *The Captives,* 137; *The Fair Maid of the West,* 187; *Fortune by Land and Sea,* 168–69; *The Four Prentices of London,* 162–63; *The Iron Age,* 168; *The Rape of Lucrece,* 164

Hieronimo. See *Spanish Tragedy, The* (Kyd)

Hillebrand, Harold Newcomb: *The Child Actors,* 74

Historia Histrionica, An Historical Account of the English-Stage, Shewing the Ancient use, Improvement, and Perfection, of Dramatick Representations, in This Nation. In a Dialogue of Plays and Players . . . (Wright[?]), viii–ix

"Historical Account of the Rise and Progress of the English Stage, and of the Economy and Usages of our Ancient Theatres, An" (Malone), x

Historical Memoires on the Reigns of Queen Elizabeth and King James (Osborne), 216

History of Britain, The (Wilson), 217

History of English Dramatic Poetry to the Time of Shakespeare and Annals of the Stage to the Restoration (Collier), xi

History of English Law, A (Holdsworth), 60

History of the Restoration Drama, A (Nicoll), 172

History of the World (Raleigh), 182

Histriomastix (Prynne), xiv

Hobbes, Thomas, 193, 195

Hodges, C. Walter, 260, 264; *The Globe Restored,* 208

Holdsworth, William S.: *A History of English Law,* 60

Holinshed, Raphael, 92

Hollar, Wenceslaus, 247

Holmes, Thomas, 149, 151

Honest Man's Fortune, The (Beaumont and Fletcher), 137, 152, 180

Honyman, John, 193

Hope Theater, xv, 23, 25, 225

Horestes (Pickering), 159–60

Horne, James, 195

Hotson, Leslie, 236, 238, 240–41, 247–48, 259–60; "False Faces on Shakespeare's Stage," 209; *Shakespeare's Wooden O,* 240

House of Correction, The (J. H.), 217

Howard, C., *The Poems of Sir John Davies,* 223

Humorous Lieutenant, The. See *Demetrius and Enanthe* (Fletcher)

Huntington Library, 142, 150, 155

Ieronimo (fencing master), 157

Imposture, The (Shirley), 167–68

In Rufum (Davies), 223

Iron Age, The (Heywood), 168

Island Princess, The (Fletcher), 207

Jack Drum's Entertainment (Marston), 221

Jacob (Towneley mystery), 159

Jacobean and Caroline Stage, The (Bentley), viii, 218–19

Jaggards (printers), 155

James, Edward Woolford, 175

James I, King of England, 182

Jeronimo, 160

Jew of Malta, The (Marlowe), 160–61

Jigs, 35

Johnson, Samuel, 47

Johnson, William, 63

Jones, Inigo, 232

Jones, Thomas, 175

Jonson, Ben, xv, 28, 50, 68, 107; *The Alchemist*, 232–33; *Bartholomew Fair*, 225; *The Case Is Altered*, 163–64; *Catiline*, 248; *Cynthia's Revels*, 224, 227–28, 230; *The Devil is an Ass*, 77, 226–27, 232; *Epicoene*, 77, 218, 220, 221, 222; *Every Man in His Humour*, 124–25, 157, 230–31; *Every Man out of His Humour*, 198, 201, 202–3, 214, 232, 239, 246, 248, 253, 255, 261–62; *The Magnetic Lady*, 222, 224, 228–29; *The New Inn*, 228–29, 233; *Sejanus*, 198, 254, 256; *The Staple of News*, 220, 221, 229–30, 232; *Timber*, 45; "To the worthy Author," in *The Faithful Shepherdess* (Fletcher), 220–21; *Volpone*, 210, 212, 232, 248, 254, 255. See also Chapman, George, Ben Jonson, and John Marston

Jonsonus Virbius, 224

Joseph, B. L.: *Elizabethan Acting*, 41, 44, 45, 47, 49, 80, 95, 101–3, 104–5; *The Tragic Actor*, 94

Judge, The (Massinger), 171

Julius Caesar (Shakespeare), 113–22, 198, 252, 256, 257, 258

Kelly, Edward, 232–33

Kemp, William, 15, 48, 111, 125

Kett's Rebellion, 61

Killigrew, Thomas (1612–83), 172, 174

Kind Harts Dreame (Chettle), 67

King John (Shakespeare), 123

King Lear (Shakespeare), 152, 198, 245, 255, 258

King Sebastian of Portugal (Chettle and Dekker), 181, 183

King's Men, 68, 71, 74, 81, 98, 125, 216

King's Office of the Revels 1610–22, The (Marcham), 138

Klein, David, 94

Knight, G. Wilson: *The Wheel of Fire*, 52–53

Knight of the Burning Pestle, The (Beaumont and Fletcher), 43, 162–63

Knights Coniuring, A (Dekker), 158

Kyd, Thomas: *The Spanish Tragedy* (*Hieronimo*), 26, 230–31

Kynaston, Edward, 77–78, 98, 130

Ladies' Privilege, The (Glapthorne), 220, 226, 231

Lady Elizabeth's Company, 23

Laneham, John, 63
Langbaine, Gerard, 148
Lanthorne and Candle-light (Dekker), 140
"Last Trumpet, The" (Crowley), 56
Lawrence, William J., xiii; *Pre-Restoration Stage Studies*, 112
Lee, Sidney, 75; *Shakespeare and the Modern Stage*, 73, 89
Legge, Thomas: *Richardus Tertius*, 58
Leicester's Men, 56, 61–62, 63–64
Leigh, Vivien, 91
Life and Work of William Shakespeare, The (Fleay), 134
List of Dramatic Authors and their Works, A (in fourth edition of Cibber's *Apology*), 172
Little French Lawyer, The (Fletcher), 166
Locandiera, La (Goldoni), 75–76
Lodge, Thomas, 50, 72; *Rosalynde. Euphues golden legacie*, 84–85; *Scillaes Metamorphosis*, 139
London Prodigal, The, 198
"Londons Lamentable Estate, in any great Visitation" (Massinger[?]), 141
Look About You, 164
Lord Admiral's Men, 56–57, 67, 68, 123–24
Lord Chamberlain's-King's Company, 56–57, 67, 68, 71, 110–36, 143, 145, 146, 148, 152, 171, 193–95, 198
Love's Cruelty (Shirley), 167
Love's Kingdom (Flecknoe), ix
Love's Labour's Lost (Shakespeare), 123, 127–31
Lowin, John, 193
Loyal Subject, The (Beaumont and Fletcher), 77, 130
Lyly, John, 157

McAfee, Helen: *Pepys on the Restoration Stage*, 77–78
Macbeth (Shakespeare), 92, 146, 152–53, 203–4, 246, 256
McNeir, Waldo, 94, 103–4
Magnetic Lady, The (Jonson), 222, 224, 228–29
Mago, William, 193, 194, 195
Maid in the Mill, The (Fletcher and Rowley), 207
Maid's Tragedy, The (Beaumont and Fletcher), 251, 253, 257
Malcontent, The (Marston), 96, 220, 232, 233; Induction to (Webster), 220, 232, 233
Malone, Edmond, x–xi, 149–50; "An Historical Account of the Rise and Progress of the English Stage, and of the Economy and Usages of Our Ancient Theatres," x; *Plays and Poems of William Shakespeare*, x
Manly, J. M.: *Specimens of Pre-Shakespearean Drama*, 159
Marcham, Frank: *The King's Office of the Revels 1610–22*, 138
Markham, Gervase: *The Dumb Knight*, 165
Marlowe, Christopher, 45; *Doctor Faustus*, 199; *The Jew of Malta*, 160–61; *Tamburlaine*, 45
Marston, John: *Antonio and Mellida*, 49; *Jack Drum's Entertainment*, 221; *The Malcontent*, 96, 220, 232, 233; *Sophonisba*, 53, 165. See also Chapman, George, Ben Jonson, and John Marston
Massinger, Philip: *Believe as you List*, 137–38, 152, 170–95; *The City Madam*, 223, 229; *The Duke of Millan*, 176–77; *The Guardian*, 207; *The Judge*,

171; "Londons Lamentable Estate, in any great Visitation"(?), 141; *The Parliament of Love*, 177; *The Renegado*, 207; *The Unnatural Combat*, 166

Mayne, Jasper: *The City Match*, 223–24

Measure for Measure (Shakespeare), 152, 198, 238, 239, 242

"Meditations" (Austin), 141

Mei Lan-fang, 76

Memoirs of the Life of Charles Macklin, 96

Memorials (Clode), 139

Menaphon (Greene), 54

Merchant of Venice, The (Shakespeare), 51, 115, 120–21, 123

Merchant Taylors' Company, 58

Merry Devil of Edmonton, The, 210, 242, 248, 253, 255, 256, 260, 263

Merry Wives of Windsor, The (Shakespeare), 152, 154, 209, 212, 238, 243, 252–53, 254, 258

Messalina vignette (1640), 208

Middleton, Thomas: *The Blacke Booke*, 151; *A Faire Quarrel*, 157, 166; *Father Hubburds Tales*, 151; *A Game at Chess*, 138, 143–44, 148, 149–51, 153; "A Song in seuerall Parts," 140; *The Witch*, 138, 143–44, 148, 149, 150, 151–52, 153

Middleton, Thomas, and Thomas Dekker: *The Roaring Girl*, 165, 213, 224

Midsummer Night's Dream, A (Reinhardt film), 130–33

Midsummer Night's Dream, A (Shakespeare), 110–11, 123, 130–34, 187

Mildmay, Humphrey, 218–19, 223, 224, 226

Mirrour of Monsters, The (Rankins), 64, 67

Miseries of Enforced Marriage, The (Wilkins), 198, 205, 248, 255

Montague, C. E.: *A Writer's Notes on His Trade*, 72

Morgan, Bridget, 140

Moseley, Humphrey, 147, 150, 171

"Most Auntient Historie of God and Man, The" (Crane[?]), 141

Much Ado about Nothing (Shakespeare), 120, 123, 125, 195, 239, 255, 261

Munck, Lewin, 139, 140

Munday, Anthony, 137, 145; *The Downfall of Robert Earl of Huntington*, 164; *A Second and Third Blast of Retrait from Plays and Theatres*, 66; *The Strangest Adventure containing a discourse concerning the success of the King of Portugal, Dom Sebastian*, 181–82

Murray, J. T.: *English Dramatic Companies*, 189, 195

Nabbes, Thomas: *The Bride*, 219, 232; *Covent Garden*, 229; *Hannibal and Scipio*, 158, 220, 233–34

Nagler, A. M.: *Shakespeare's Stage*, 80; *Sources of Theatrical History*, 75

Nashe, Thomas, 54; *The Unfortunate Traveller*, 51

Nathan, George Jean: *Theatre Book of the Year*, 99

Newcastle, Duchess of. *See* Cavendish, Margaret

Newington Butts Theater, 67

New Inn, The (Jonson), 228–29, 233

Nicoll, A., 263; *A History of the Restoration Drama*, 172

Nispeth, Charles: *Goethe's Travels in Italy*, 76

Nobody and Somebody, 162

North, Thomas, 72; *Plutarch's Lives, translated out of French into English by Thomas North*, 89, 90–91

Northbrooke, John, 66

"Note on the Swan Theatre, A" (Graves), 207

Of Dramatick Poesie (Dryden), 10

Olivier, Laurence, 75, 109, 112

O'Neill, Eugene: *The Hairy Ape*, 100

On Producing Shakespeare (Watkins), 73–74

Open Stage, The (Southern), 197

Ordish, T. F.: *Early London Theatres*, 157–58

Organization and Personnel of the Shakespearean Company, The (Baldwin), 97, 112–13

Orlando Furioso (Greene), 161–62

Ormsby-Gore, W. (grandfather of William George Arthur), 146

Ormsby-Gore, William George Arthur, 4th Baron Harlech, 138, 143

Orson, S. W., 191, 192

Osborne, Dorothy, 139, 140

Osborne, Francis: *Historical Memoires on the Reigns of Queen Elizabeth and King James*, 216

Othello (Shakespeare), 96, 97, 98, 100, 101, 152, 195, 201, 248, 250–51, 257, 261

"*Othello* and *The Alchemist* at Oxford" (Tillotson), 98

Overbury, Thomas: *Characters*, 102, 103

Overthrow of Stage-Playes, Th' (Rainolds), 59

Oxford, 58

Palamon and Arcite (Edwards), 59

Pallant, Robert, 10

Pandosto. The Triumphe of Time (Greene), 81

Parliament of Love, The (Massinger), 177

Passions of the Mind, The (Wright), 47

Patrick, William, 193, 194, 195

Paul's Theater, 215–34

Pavy, Solomon, 71

Peirs, John, 141

Penn, William, 193, 194

Pepys, John, 151

Pepys, Richard, 151

Pepys, Samuel, 77–78, 130, 148, 195

Pepys on the Restoration Stage (McAfee), 77–78

Pericles (Shakespeare), 211, 212, 241, 242–43, 255, 256, 263

Perkins, Richard, 10

Perkyn, John, 63

Philaster (Beaumont and Fletcher), 248, 255

Philip II, King of Spain, 181

Philip III, King of Spain, 181

Philip Massinger (Cruickshank), 177, 192

Phillips, Augustine, 125

Phoenix Theater. *See* Cockpit Theater

Pickering, John: *Horestes*, 159–60

Pilgrimes New-yeares-Gift, The

(Crane). See *Workes of Mercy, The* (Crane)

Platter, Thomas, 113, 121

"Player's Passion, The" (Foakes), 80

Play of Plays, 67

Plays and Poems of William Shakespeare (Malone), x

Pleasant and Stately Morall, of Three Lords and Three Ladies of London, The (Wilson), 57

Pleasant Notes upon Don Quixote (Gayton), 103–4

Plutarch, 182; *Plutarch's Lives, translated out of French into English by Thomas North*, 89, 90–91

Poems of Sir John Davies, The (Howard), 223

Political Element in Massinger, The (Gardiner), 191

Pollard, A. W., 145; *Shakespeare Folios and Quartos*, 152

Pollard, Thomas, 193

Pope, Alexander, ix–x

Pope, Thomas, 125

Porter's Hall Theater, 216–34

Prefaces to Shakespeare (Granville-Barker), 71, 85, 89

Pre-Restoration Stage Studies (Lawrence), 112

"Prompt Copies, Private Transcripts, and 'The Playhouse Scrivener'" (Greg), 138, 148

Prynne, William: *Histriomastix*, xiv, 97–98

Punch and Judy (Baring), 71

Puppet Show of Memory, The (Baring), 70–71

Puttenham, Richard: *The Art of English Poesie*, 45

Queen's (Anne) Men, 10, 51

Queen's (Elizabeth) Men, 56, 67, 125

Quin, James, 96

Rainolds, John: *Th' Overthrow of Stage-Plays*, 59

Raleigh, Walter: *History of the World*, 182

Randolph, Thomas, 229; "A diuine Pastorall Eglogue," 142

Rankins, William, 66; *The Mirrour of Monsters*, 64, 67

Rape of Lucrece, The (Heywood), 164

Rastell, John: *Calisto and Melebea*, 137

Reade, Timothy, 32

Red Bull Theater, xv, 35, 51, 158, 164, 168, 195, 216

Reed, Carol, 74

Reed, Isaac, 149

Reinhardt, Max, 130–33

Remarks on an article inserted in the Papers of the Shakespeare Society (Croker), 189–90

Renegado, The (Massinger), 207

Return from Parnassus, The, 48

Revenge of Bussy D'Ambois, The, 165

Revenger's Tragedy, The (Tourneur), 210, 212, 245, 256, 257, 258

Reynolds, George Fulmer: *The Staging of Elizabethan Plays at the Red Bull Theater, 1605–1625*, xiii–xiv, 208

Rhodes, R. Crompton, 154

Richard II (Shakespeare), 116, 123, 153

Richard III (Shakespeare), 99, 123

Richardus Tertius (Legge), 58

Rich Cabinet Furnished with Varietie of Descriptions (de la Casa), 157

Index

Rise of the Common Player, The (Bradbrook), 55

Roaring Girl, The (Middleton and Dekker), 165, 213, 224

Robin Hood and the Knight, 159

Robinson, Richard, 77, 193

Romeo and Juliet (Shakespeare), 44–45, 120, 123, 157, 163

Rosalynde. Euphues golden legacie (Lodge), 84–85

Roscius Anglicanus (Downes), 78, 98

Rose Theater, 65, 67, 68

Rowe, Nicholas, ix

Rowley, William, 52, 177

Roxana vignette (1632), 197, 208, 214

Rule a Wife and Have a Wife (Fletcher), 220

Sack, M.: *Darstellerpahl und Rollenvertheilung bei Shakespeare,* 112–13

Salisbury Court Theater, xv, 28–37, 216–34

Satiromastix (Dekker), 209, 212

Satyres and Satyricall Epigrams: With Certaine Observations at Blackfryers (Fitzgeoffrey), 219, 221, 222–23, 226, 231

Saunders, J. W.: "Vaulting the Rails," 263

Savory, Abraham, 232

Saxo Grammaticus, 92

"Schauspieler - Ökonomie in Shakespeares Dramen, Die" (Engelen), 112–13

Schelling, F. E., 192

Schoolmaster, The (Ascham), 50

Scillaes Metamorphosis (Lodge), 139

Sea Voyage, The (Fletcher), 199

Sebastian, King of Portugal, 181

Second Maiden's Tragedy, The, 51, 146, 154, 207, 238, 249–50, 252, 253, 255, 256, 258

Second and Third Blast of Retrait from Plays and Theatres, A (Munday), 66

Sejanus (Jonson), 254, 256

Sermon Preached at Paules Crosse, A (Stockwood), 64

Shadwell, Thomas: *The Virtuoso,* 78

Shakespeare, William, ix–xiii, 68, 125, 137, 145, 151, 157; *All's Well That Ends Well,* 198, 261; *Antony and Cleopatra,* 71–73, 88–91, 93, 108, 110, 198, 200, 251–52, 263; *As You Like It,* 71–73, 84–88, 93, 152–53, 162, 198, 244; *The Comedy of Errors,* 123; *Coriolanus,* 49, 163, 198, 200, 201, 243, 248–49, 257, 263; *Cymbeline,* 152, 239, 245, 251, 257, 258; *Hamlet,* 49, 52, 80, 92, 104, 127, 163, 198, 214, 251, 254; *I Henry IV,* 123, 153, 163; *II Henry IV,* 123, 125; *Henry V,* ix–x, 123, 152, 200, 236, 241, 243–44; *Henry VI,* 123, 152; *III Henry VI,* 44, 123; *Henry VIII,* 126, 159, 245, 252, 257, 263; *Julius Caesar,* 113–22, 198, 252, 256, 257, 258; *King John,* 123; *King Lear,* 152, 198, 245, 255, 258; *Love's Labour's Lost,* 123, 127–31; *Macbeth,* 92, 146, 152–53, 198, 203–4, 246, 256; *Measure for Measure,* 152, 198, 238, 239, 242; *The Merchant of Venice,* 51, 115, 120–21, 123; *The Merry Wives of Windsor,* 152, 154, 209, 212, 238, 243, 252–53, 254, 258; *A Midsummer Night's Dream,* 110–11, 123, 130–34, 187; *Much Ado about Nothing,* 120, 123, 125, 195,

239, 255, 261; *Othello*, 96, 97, 98, 100, 101, 152, 195, 198, 201, 248, 250–51, 257, 261; *Pericles*, 211, 212, 241, 242–43, 246, 255, 256, 263; *Richard II*, 116, 123, 153; *Richard III*, 99, 123; *Romeo and Juliet*, 44–45, 120, 123, 157, 163; *The Taming of the Shrew*, 50–51, 75, 99–100, 123; *The Tempest*, 114, 152, 153, 154, 250, 258; *Timon of Athens*, 52–53, 198, 200, 201, 242, 248–49, 255, 256, 257, 258; *Titus Andronicus*, 26, 115, 123; *Troilus and Cressida*, 163, 210, 246, 258, 261; *Twelfth Night*, 152, 198, 238, 255, 258; *The Two Gentlemen of Verona*, 52, 123, 124, 152, 154; *The Winter's Tale*, 51, 71–73, 81–84, 93, 114–15, 152, 154, 239, 254

Shakespeare: A Biographical Handbook (Bentley), 126

Shakespeare and His Theatre (Bentley), 126

Shakespeare and the Modern Stage (Lee), 73, 89

Shakespeare and the Popular Dramatic Tradition (Bethell), 42

Shakespeare and the Rival Traditions (Harbage), 215, 224, 225

Shakespeare and the Young Actor (Boas), 74

Shakespeare Folios and Quartos (Pollard), 152

Shakespeare Jahrbuch, xii, 112

"Shakespeare's Actors" (Bethell), 95

Shakespeare's Audience (Harbage), 61

Shakespeare's Boy Actors (Robertson), 77, 79

Shakespeare's Love's Labour's Lost (David), 128, 129

Shakespeare's Stage (Nagler), 80

Shakespeare's Wooden O (Hotson), 240

Shakespeare's Young Lovers (Stoll), 93

Shakespeare Without Tears (Webster), 92–93

Shakespere Allusion Book, 97, 111

Shanks, John, 195

Sharpe, Richard, 195

Sharpman, Edward, 111

Sherman, R. A., 192

Shirley, James: *The Cardinal*, 168; *The Doubtful Heir*, 231; *The Imposture*, 167–68; *Love's Cruelty*, 167

Shoemaker's Holiday, The (Dekker), 206

Short Discourse of the English Stage, A (Flecknoe), viii–ix, 46, 48–49

Sica, Vittorio de, 74

Sidney, Philip, 50; *Defence of Poesie*, 10, 53

Simpson, Percy, 225

Sinklo (Sincler), John, 111–12, 125

Sir John van Olden Barnavelt (Fletcher and Massinger), 138, 143–46, 153

Sir Thomas More, 65, 137, 145, 170

Sisson, C. J., 137–38

Skinners' Company, 21

Sly, William, 125

Smith, Anthony, 195

Smith, Warren D.: "The Elizabethan Stage and Shakespeare's Entrance Announcements," 201

Smock Alley Theater (Dublin), 172

"Song in seuerall parts, A" (Middleton), 140

Sophonisba (Marston), 53, 165

Sources of Theatrical History (Nagler), 75

Southern, Richard: *The Open Stage*, 197

Spanish Tragedy, The (Hieronimo) (Kyd), 230–31

Spanish Viceroy, The, 150

Specimens of Pre-Shakespearean Drama (Manly), 159

"Stage Sword and Dagger, The" (Graves), 156

Staging of Elizabethan Plays at the Red Bull Theater, 1605–1625, The (Reynolds), xiii–xiv, 208

Staple of News, The (Jonson), 220, 221, 229–30, 232

Steevens, George, 149

Stewart, C. J., 150, 151

Stockwood, John: *A Sermon Preached at Paules Crosse*, 64

Stoll, E. E.: *Shakespeare's Young Lovers*, 93

Stow, John: *Annales, or a Generall Chronicle of England . . . Continued . . . by Edmund Howes*, 61, 69

Strangest Adventure containing a discourse concerning the success of the King of Portugal, Dom Sebastian, The (Munday), 181–82

Stubbs, Philip: *Anatomie of Abuses*, 66–67

Suckling, John: *Brennoralt*, 169; *The Goblins*, 168–69

"Sumarie; and true Distinction, betweene the Lawe, & ye Ghospel, A" (Crane), 141

Sutton, Thomas, 232

Swan of Avon and the Bricklayer of Westminster, The (Bentley), 71

Swanston, Elyard, 193

Swan Theater, 156, 207–9, 212, 240, 242, 246, 249–50, 253–54

Symonds, E. M.: "The Diary of John Greene," 219

Symons, Arthur, 191–92

Tamburlaine (Marlowe), 45

Tamer Cham, 45

Taming of the Shrew, The (Shakespeare), 50–51, 75, 99–100, 123

Tannenbaum, S. A.: *Corrections to the Text of 'Believe as You List,'* 192

Tarleton, Richard, 15, 24, 67

Tawyer (actor), 112

Taylor, Joseph, 193

Tempest, The (Shakespeare), 114, 152, 153, 154, 250, 258

Terry, Ellen, 75

Theatre, 56, 64

Theatre Book of the Year (Nathan), 99

"Theatrical Wagers" (Bromberg), 10

Themes and Conventions of Elizabethan Tragedy (Bradbrook), 99–100, 101

Theobald, Lewis, ix

Thomas Lord Cromwell, 209–10, 212

Thomas Shadwell: His Life and Comedies (Borgman), 78

Thompson, Edward Maunde, 174–75

Tillotson, Geoffrey: "*Othello* and *The Alchemist* at Oxford," 98

Tilney, Edmund, 65, 67–68

Timber (Jonson), 45

Timon of Athens (Shakespeare),

52–53, 198, 200, 201, 242, 248–
49, 255, 256, 257, 258
Titus Andronicus (Shakespeare),
26, 115, 123
Tomson, George, 195
Tourneur, Cyril: *The Revenger's
Tragedy*, 210, 212, 245, 256,
257, 258
Tragic Actor, The (Joseph), 94
Trial of Treasure, The (moral-
ity), 159
Triggs, William, 195
Troilus and Cressida (Shake-
speare), 163, 210, 246, 258, 261
*True History of Dom Sebastian,
The* (pamphlet), 181
Tryall of Chevalry, The, 164–65
Tullio, Marco, 181
Twelfth Night (Shakespeare),
152, 198, 238, 255, 258
*Two Elizabethan Stage Abridge-
ments: The Battle of Alcazar
and Orlando Furioso* (Greg),
161
Two Gentlemen of Verona, The
(Shakespeare), 52, 123, 124,
152, 154
Two Noble Kinsmen, The
(Shakespeare and Fletcher),
166, 239, 244–45, 250, 255, 256
Tyler, Wat, 61

Unfortunate Lovers, The (Dave-
nant), 159, 168
Unfortunate Traveller, The
(Nashe), 51
Unnatural Combat, The (Mas-
singer), 166

"Vaulting the Rails" (Saunders),
263
Vennar, Richard, 207–8
Vernon, George, 195
Vincenzio (fencing master), 157

Virtuoso, The (Shadwell), 78
Vitruvius Pollio, Marcus, 247
Volpone (Jonson), 210, 212, 232,
248, 254, 255

Wallace, C. W.: *Children of the
Chapel*, 217, 224–25; *Evolution
of the English Drama up to
Shakespeare*, 157
Walworth, William, 61
Warburton, John, 172–73
Warner, George, 175, 176, 180,
189, 191
Warning for Fair Women, A,
124, 198, 200, 201, 204–5, 214
Watkins, Ronald: *On Producing
Shakespeare*, 73–74
Webster, John, 10; *The Devil's
Law Case*, 166; *The Duchess
of Malfi*, 52, 250, 254, 256, 258;
"An Excellent Actor," 43, 46,
102; Induction to *The Mal-
content* (Marston), 220, 232,
233; *The White Devil*, 10, 51,
163, 165–66
Webster, Margaret: *Shakespeare
Without Tears*, 92–93
Westcott, Sebastian, 215
Wheel of Fire, The (Knight),
52–53
White Devil, The (Webster),
10, 51, 163, 165–66
Whitefriars Theater, 216–34
Wilkins, George: *The Miseries
of Enforced Marriage*, 98, 205,
248, 255
*William Shakespeare: A Study
of the Facts and Problems*
(Chambers), 81, 126
Wilson, Arthur: *The History of
Britain*, 217
Wilson, Harry (lute player), 195
Wilson, Iacke, 195
Wilson, J. Dover, 114, 154

Wilson, Nicholas, 195

Wilson, Robert, 63; *The Pleasant and Stately Morall, of Three Lords and Three Ladies of London*, 57

Winter's Tale, The (Shakespeare), 51, 71–73, 81–84, 93, 114–15, 152, 154, 239, 254

Witch, The (Middleton), 138, 143–44, 148, 149, 150, 151–52, 153

Wits frontispiece (1632), 208, 214

Wit without Money (Fletcher), 223

Woman Hater, The (Fletcher), 233

Woman Is a Weathercock, A (Field), 165

Wonder of a Kingdome, The (Dekker), 157

Woodford, Thomas, 216

Workes Of Mercy, The (later republished as *The Pilgrimes New-yeares-Gift*) (Crane), 138–40, 142–43, 146, 155

Wright, James [?]: *Historia Histrionica, An Historical Account of the English-Stage, Shewing the Ancient Use, Improvement, and Perfection, of Dramatick Representations, in This Nation. In a Dialogue of Plays and Players . . .* , viii–ix, 79

Wright, Thomas: *The Passions of the Mind*, 47

Writer's Notes on His Trade, A (Montague), 72

Wynne, William W. E., 146

Yorkshire Tragedy, A, 198, 238, 244, 253, 256, 263